PERSONS, PLACES, AND THINGS <u>AROUND</u> THE FINGER LAKES REGION

The Heart of New York State

by

Emerson Klees

Friends of the Finger Lakes Publishing, Rochester, New York

Library of Congress Catalog Card Number 94-94335

ISBN 0-9635990-4-6

Printed in the United States of America
9 8 7 6 5 4 3 2 1

PREFACE

PERSONS, PLACES, AND THINGS <u>AROUND</u> THE FINGER LAKES REGION, The Heart of New York State provides an overview of the area surrounding the six major lakes of the Finger Lakes Region, an area of friendly people and scenic lake country beauty. The region provides outstanding vacation opportunities spread over an area comprised of fourteen counties, 264 municipalities, and 6,125 square miles. The area has a rich history and many famous sons and daughters. Numerous historic sites and museums chronicle their accomplishments.

This book is an introduction to the Finger Lakes Region for those who are not familiar with it and a collective reference for those who already know the area. This book provides an overview of the five minor lakes: Conesus, Hemlock, Canadice, and Honeoye, in the West, and Otisco in the East. It also provides an overview of Rochester, the western gateway to the region; Syracuse, the eastern gateway; and Corning and Elmira, the southern gateways. In addition, it provides information on the four compass directions surrounding the six major lakes: west of the lakes including hunt country and Letchworth State Park, north of the lakes with the Erie Canal and Lake Ontario, east of the lakes with the beautiful country surrounding Cortland and Homer, and south of the lakes with its soaring sites and the scenic Chemung and Susquehanna River valleys.

This is the second in a series of books about the region. It has three sections:
1. A prologue with some of the early history--HOW THE REGION EVOLVED
2. The body of the book about things to do and places to see in the region, including biographical sketches of Finger Lakes people--WHAT THE AREA HAS NOW
3. An epilogue with brief comments on conservation--WHAT IS BEING DONE TO PRESERVE THE REGION FOR THE FUTURE

The first book in the series, *PERSONS, PLACES, AND THINGS <u>IN</u> THE FINGER LAKES REGION, The Heart of New York State*, provides an overview of the six major Finger Lakes: Canandaigua, Keuka, Seneca, Cayuga, Owasco, and Skaneateles. This heart-shaped area is bounded by the I-390 Expressway in the West, the New York State Thruway in the North, the I-81 Expressway and Route 13 in the East, and the Southern Tier Expressway in the South.

This series of books is not intended to provide detailed information about the timing of scheduled events in the region. The authors of the regional newspapers' summer supplements do an excellent job of providing that information. Also, a number of books are available about specific areas of interest in the region, including:

1. *20 Bicycle Tours in the Finger Lakes* by Mark Roth and Sally Walters
2. *25 Walks in the Finger Lakes Region* by Bill Ehling
3. *The Finger Lakes Region: Its Origin and Nature* by O. D. von Engeln
4. *Restaurant Guide to the Finger Lakes Region* by C. DeMotte and K. W. Sundgren
5. *Finger Lakes Wineries* by Susan Weiner

The Finger Lakes Association in Penn Yan publishes an annual *I Love New York Finger Lakes Travel Guide* with a wealth of information about the region, including an extensive calendar of events. The New York State Office of Parks, Recreation and Historic Preservation publishes many informative brochures. The local Chambers of Commerce also provide many helpful pamphlets, and are prepared to answer questions about the area. In addition, Friends of the Finger Lakes offers informative, narrated audio tour tapes of the region.

LIST OF PHOTOGRAPHS

Front cover:

1. Glen Iris Inn, Letchworth State Park

2. Eastern shoreline of Otisco Lake

3. Southern end of Honeoye Lake

4. Sodus Point Lighthouse, Sodus Bay

5. "Sainte Marie Among the Iroquois" (The French Fort), Syracuse

6. Eastman House International Museum of Photography, Rochester

7. Genesee Valley Hunt, Geneseo

8. Balloon Rallye, Dansville

9. Corning Museum of Glass, Corning

Back cover:

Middle Falls and Portage Bridge, Letchworth State Park

Inside of the book:

1. Erie Canal lock, Lyons

2. Wild Water Derby, Manchester

3. Genesee Valley Hunt, Geneseo

4. High Falls and downtown Rochester

5. Chimney Bluffs, east of Sodus Bay on Lake Ontario

6. Syracuse University crew, Onondaga outlet

7. 1890 House Museum, Cortland

8. Gliders at Harris Hill, near Elmira Heights

9. Genesee Country Museum, near Mumford

10. Mark Twain's Octagonal Study, Elmira College

11. Tioga Gardens and Conservatory, Owego

Reverse side of map

Table of Contents

Photographs were provided by the Finger Lakes Association of Penn Yan, NY, C. S. Kenyon of Rochester, NY, Caroline Ringland of Geneseo, NY, and Dr. Bruce Stewart of Pittsford, NY.

Cover design is by Dunn and Rice Design, Inc., Rochester, NY.

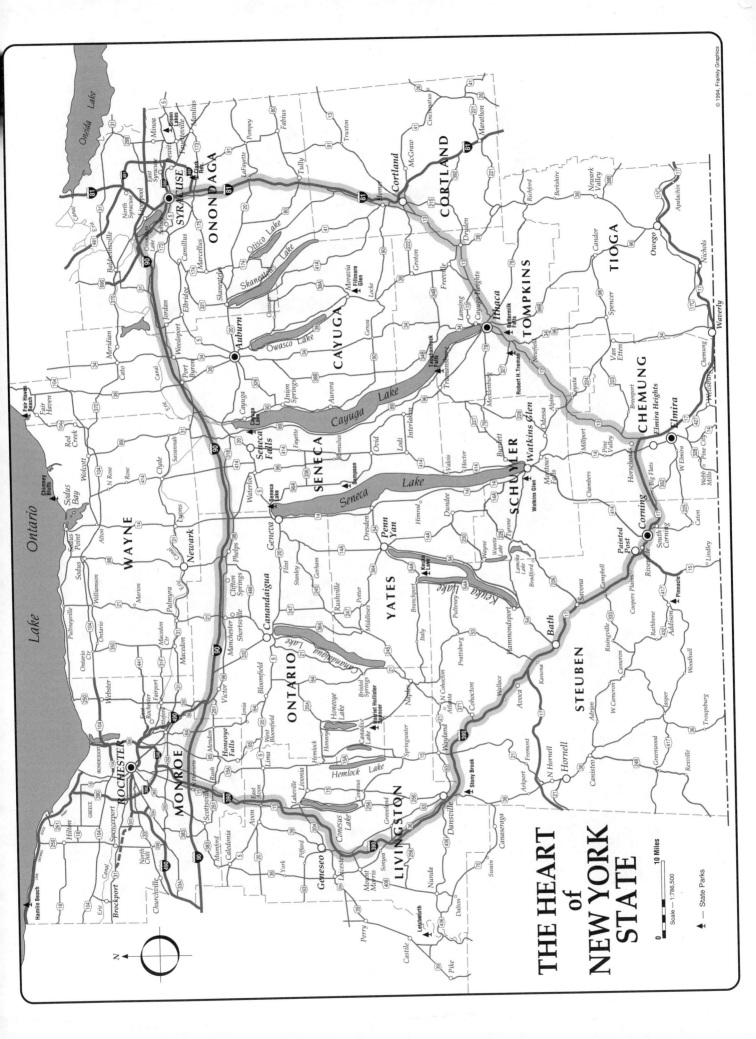

THE HEART
of
NEW YORK STATE

10 Miles

Scale — 1:786,500

▲ — State Parks

N

© 1994, Frankly Graphics

Table of Contents

Erie Canal Lock, Lyons

Table of Contents

TABLE OF CONTENTS

PERSON, PLACES, AND THINGS <u>AROUND</u> THE FINGER LAKES REGION

The Heart of New York State

Table of Contents

Table of Contents

Wild Water Derby, Manchester

PROLOGUE

[Eleven] long slim lakes of larkspur blue,
No gems have such entrancing hue.
Like storm clouds in an azure sky,
They've charmed me when their waves were high.
They've charmed me when they were serene,
These precious jewels inlaid in green.
When viewed, at night, from points afar,
How beautiful their lit towns are!
Health-giving sport their fishing makes,
These world-famous Finger Lakes.
Here tourists flock, for Nature brings
The loveliest of outdoor things.

The Finger Lakes by Edwin Becker

EARLY HISTORY OF THE FINGER LAKES REGION

The prologue of the first book in this series, *Persons, Places, and Things In The Finger Lakes Region*, provides an overview of the formation of the Finger Lakes by glacial activity. It also contains a brief discussion of the Indian migration into the region, the Sullivan Campaign, the Phelps-Gorham Purchase, and the early settlement of the area in the late 1700s and early 1800s. This prologue provides a few of the regional history highlights of the 1800s.

THE BURNED-OVER DISTRICT

The Burned-over District is the name applied to western New York State from the Adirondacks and the Catskills to Lake Erie during the first half of the nineteenth century. The name refers to an area that experienced a large number of religious revivals. The term "Burned-over District" was given to the region between Lake Ontario and the Adirondacks by Charles Grandison Finney, the most dynamic evangelist of his day. In his opinion, early Methodist circuit riders had diverted people from the proper religious instruction that he was attempting to provide.

In his book, *Listen for a Lonesome Drum*, Carl Carmer viewed it as a "Spirit Way:"

Across the entire breadth of York State, undeviatingly, a hilly strip scarcely twenty-five miles wide invites the world's wonder. It is a broad psychic highway, a thoroughfare of the occult whose great stations number the mystic seven. For where, in its rolling course from east of Albany to west of Buffalo, it has reached one of seven isolated and lonely heights, voices out of other worlds have spoken with spiritual authority to men and women, and the invisible mantles of the prophets have been laid on consecrated shoulders. In no other area of the Western Hemisphere have so many evidences of an existence transcending mortal living been manifest. It is impossible to reckon the number of listeners who on the plateaus of this strange midstate adventure have knelt before seen or unseen supernatural visitants to hear counsel. And the sum of those whose lives have been affected by that counsel, save for the fact that it is in the millions, is incalculable.

Three of the seven instances referred to by Mr. Carmer occurred in the Finger Lakes Region: Jemima Wilkinson, the Publick Universal Friend, and her community at Jerusalem in Yates County; the Fox sisters and their experiences with spiritualism at Hydeville, near Newark; and the founding of the Mormon religion at Palmyra by Joseph Smith. The other four of the "mystic seven" are: Mother Ann Lee and the Shakers; William Miller, who made predictions of the end of the world, and the Millerites; John Humphrey Noyes and the Oneida Community; and Thomas Harris and the Harrisites at Brocton on the shores of Lake Erie.

In addition to these instances, the Finger Lakes Region was a center of the Anti-Masonic movement between 1826 and 1850. It was a hotbed of both the abolitionist and temperance movements, and, most notably, it was the core of the Women's Rights Movement in the United States. In order to understand why this agricultural lake country encountered such restlessness, it is necessary to look at the settlers of the region, where they came from, and the religious background they brought with them.

Settlement in the Finger Lakes Region began in the late 1780s, and was dominated by Yankees from New England. Also, many settlers came up the Susquehanna River from Pennsylvania. Many of the New Englanders had settled first in the eastern New York counties, and then pulled up stakes and resettled in the lake country. Not many of the pioneers came from Boston or the fertile Connecticut River Valley; many came from the hill country of New Hampshire and Vermont and from other areas of Connecticut.

Many of the settlers from New England were Baptists, Congregationalists, or Methodists. Presbyterians and one branch of the Congregationialists merged in 1801 in the Plan of Union. All of the major denominations, except the Episcopalians, were revivalistic. The Baptists and the Methodists were more emotional and easier for common people to understand than the Presbyterians. From 1815-18, there were six revivals in Rhode Island, fifteen in Connecticut, twenty-one each in New Jersey, eastern New York, and Pennsylvania, forty-five in Vermont, sixty-four in Massachusetts, and eighty in the Burned-over District.

An increase in religious revivals in 1826 is credited to the influence of Charles Finney, a truly motivational speaker. This increase in activity continued from 1826 through 1837. Work on the Erie Canal began in 1817, and its completion in 1825 brought significant economic changes to the region. Population growth was phenomenal in the 1820s: Albany grew by 96 percent, Buffalo by 314 percent, Utica by 183 percent, Rochester by 512 percent, and Syracuse by 282 percent. Growth in church congregations came with the growth in population.

In 1831, Charles Finney came to Rochester for a revivalist meeting that was one of the largest up until that time. The three Presbyterian churches did not get along with one another, but they pulled together to bring Finney to Rochester. His sermons included "The Carnal Mind is Emnity Against God" and "The Wages of Sin Is Death." Church membership boomed. The next peak in revivalism came in 1837, a year of recession. Interest in the church always increased in bad times.

The Fox sisters were the most notable examples of spiritualists in the Burned-over District, but there were other examples. In fact, the region had more mediums in 1859 than any other region of the United States. There were twenty-seven in Ohio, fifty-five in Massachusetts, and seventy-one in New York.

The religious fervor of the region burned itself out over the last half of the nineteenth century. However, some of the legacies of the Burned-over District survived into the twentieth century: the Mormon Church; several Adventist denominations, including the Seventh-Day Adventists; two species of Methodism, including the Free Methodists; and some spiritualist groups. The American tradition was enriched by these legacies, which formed a pathway to modern versions of religion.

THE ERIE CANAL

One of the first people to suggest the construction of a canal connecting Lake Erie with the Hudson River was Gouverneur Morris in 1803. In 1810, he was appointed to a commission to plan the canal. James Geddes, a lawyer and surveyor from Syracuse, was appointed to survey the prospective route of the canal. Construction of the 83-lock Erie Canal along a 363-mile route from Albany to Buffalo began at Rome on July 4, 1817. The ninety-four mile section of the canal from Rome west to the Seneca River was chosen to be constructed first, because it had a long, flat stretch of favorable terrain requiring only six locks. It was easier digging than other sections, and the landowners were more receptive.

Governor DeWitt Clinton sent Canvass White to England to study canal-building techniques. White came home, and experimented with various types of cements. He discovered a hydraulic cement that would set under water. It was made from limestone that he burned and mixed with sand. This breakthrough saved considerable time and money in constructing the canal. The canal, built with sloping sides, was forty feet wide at the top and twenty feet wide at the bottom, with a towpath along one side. The water was only four feet deep.

The canal builders constructed eighteen aqueducts to carry the canal over rivers and streams, and contended with a difference in elevation between Lake Erie and the Hudson River of 568 feet. Two of the most difficult projects during the construction were digging through rock in the eastern section of the canal near Albany, and accommodating a sixty-foot drop in elevation at Lockport. Nathan Roberts solved the problem at Lockport with a double set of five-step locks, one set of locks each for eastbound and westbound traffic.

The canal from Rochester to Albany was opened in 1823; the cost of shipping a barrel of flour between those two cities dropped from $3.00 to $.75. The full length of the Erie Canal was opened in 1825, with the ceremony-filled Buffalo to Albany cruise of Governor DeWitt Clinton on the *Seneca Chief*. Two barrels of Lake Erie water were transported by the governor to dump into New York harbor, symbolizing the joining of the two bodies of water. The $7,000,000 spent to build the canal ($2,000,000 over the original estimate) was not considered a good expenditure by the populace. They were proved wrong. The canal was economically successful beyond even Clinton's dreams.

The increase in the use of the canal outstripped its capacity; traffic jams became commonplace. Between 1835 and 1862, many changes were made in the canal to facilitate the increased traffic: width at the top of the canal was increased from 40 feet to 70 feet, width at the bottom was expanded from 28 to 56 feet, and the depth was increased from four feet to seven feet. In addition, the waterway was straightened, the number of locks was reduced from 83 to 72, and at most lock locations a double lock was built to allow two-way traffic.

By the beginning of the twentieth century, railroads were providing stiff competition for the Erie Canal. Canal managers wanted to take advantage of advanced engineering skills and steam tugboats. Construction began in 1905 to: increase lock sizes to 45 feet wide by 328 feet long, reduce the number of locks from 72 to 35, and increase the depth of the canal from 7 feet to 12 feet.

Many of the rivers along the route of the canal that were not utilized during earlier construction were incorporated now, including the Clyde, Oneida, Oswego, Mohawk, and Seneca. The canal system was comprised of the new Erie Canal, the Cayuga-Seneca Canal between Cayuga and Seneca Lakes, the Oswego Canal from Syracuse to Oswego, and the Champlain Canal from Albany to Lake Champlain. It was called the New York State Barge Canal System when it opened in 1918.

The new canal system carried increasing amounts of traffic, but, eventually, efficient railroad freight traffic and truck traffic caused the demise of commercial use of the canal. The finishing touches were applied by the completion in the late 1950s of the New York

State Thruway and the St. Lawrence Seaway, which linked the Great Lakes with Atlantic Ocean.

RAILROADS

Beginning in the 1830s, railroad tracks began to spread across New York State. Many of the early railroads were short lines used as feeders to the Erie Canal. In fact, the law said that if a railroad diverted business from the canal system, it was obligated to compensate the canal by giving up part of its profit. By the 1850s, railroads were in use in all parts of the state, and were no longer principally used as feeders for the canal. Railroads were going where the canals could not go; they were beginning to replace the canals as the dominant method of transportation.

The Erie Railroad was completed in 1851. The Erie's track was laid along the Delaware River valley, through the Catskill Mountains, and across the Southern Tier of New York State. It joined Piermont on the Hudson River with Dunkirk on Lake Erie. Daniel Webster rode the initial train across southern New York State, and waved to crowds from a rocking chair fastened to an open flatcar. The Erie Railroad was a financial nightmare for investors in its early days. It was mismanaged, overcapitalized, and wasteful, but it eventually paid dividends and became financially successful.

The Delaware, Lackawanna and Western Railroad, which went from Hoboken, New Jersey, to Buffalo, New York, was one of the smaller but important railroads. The railroad, which was organized April 14, 1851, included branches from Binghamton to Oswego on Lake Ontario and from Owego in the Southern Tier to Ithaca. In organizing, the Erie Railroad absorbed the Owego-Ithaca Railroad, which was established in 1834, and the Oswego-Syracuse line that had been in operation since 1848.

Eventually, the cost of maintaining two sets of tracks forced the two old rivals, the Erie Railroad and the Lackawanna Railroad, to merge. In November 1955, the two railroads combined their Binghamton and Elmira freight houses; they also agreed to use only one set of the two parallel sets of track between Binghamton and Corning. The official merger of the two railroads into the Erie-Lackawanna Railroad occurred on October 17, 1960.

Although railroad tracks crossed the northern part of New York State, they were independent lines requiring passengers to change trains seven times between New York City and Buffalo. Finally, Cornelius Vanderbilt, financier and steamboat operator, combined the independent lines into one continuous railroad in 1870, and called it the New York Central. Vanderbilt also obtained the exclusive right-of-way into New York City, and built Grand Central Station in 1871.

Genesee Valley Hunt, Geneseo

TABLE OF CONTENTS

CHAPTER 1

WEST OF THE LAKES

PAGE NO.

CHAPTER 1

WEST OF THE LAKES

"Aim for the Genesee Country;"
Her folk of its wonders will tell,
There are legends and lore which make famous
The hamlets and towns where they dwell;
....
Twixt the park in the south ...
And the Flower City--near the Great Lake
There lies our good Genesee Country,
The Glory and Pride of the State.

From *Our Genesee Country* by Adah Lyle Kidder

WEST OF THE LAKES--INTRODUCTION

WEST OF THE LAKES--DESCRIPTION

The area west of the six major Finger Lakes contains one principal river, the Genesee River, and four minor Finger Lakes: Conesus, Hemlock, Canadice, and Honeoye. It is an area of varied terrain with mountains, valleys, gorges, forests, and open farm land.

Canadice Lake has the highest elevation of the eleven Finger Lakes, and Hemlock Lake has the second highest elevation. Only Skaneateles Lake is higher than Conesus and Honeoye Lakes. Hemlock and Canadice Lakes supply water to Rochester, which also is provided water by Lake Ontario. The outlets for all four lakes are north-flowing streams. The outlet for Conesus Lake is Conesus Creek, which drains into the Genesee River at Avon. The outflow from Hemlock, Canadice, and Honeoye Lakes is carried by Honeoye Creek through Honeoye Falls, entering the Genesee River near West Rush.

The Genesee River is at the western edge of the Finger Lakes Region as it flows through the gorges of Letchworth State Park. The 190-mile-long river becomes a meandering waterway as it flows northward through Mt. Morris and Avon on the way to its outlet into Lake Ontario at Rochester. The Mt. Morris Dam provides flood control along the river between Mt. Morris and Rochester.

The area west of the major Finger Lakes has many beautiful parks. These include 17-mile-long Letchworth State Park, which has three major waterfalls, and Stony Brook State Park in Dansville, a glen formed by post-glacial streams. The "horse country" around Geneseo and the events of the Genesee Valley Hunt provide a distinctive character to the area west of Conesus Lake.

WEST OF THE LAKES--BRIEF HISTORY

The first white man to explore the Genesee Valley was Etienne Brule, courier and interpreter for Samuel de Champlain, father of New France and founder of Quebec. Brule crossed the Genesee River in 1615, and was followed into the region by French trappers. The earliest white residents of the region were French Jesuit priests. Father Rene Fremin and Father Julien Garnier, who lived at the Seneca Indian village of Totiakton on Honeoye Creek, were two of the earliest. The French maintained a presence in the valley until they were defeated in the French and Indian War.

The General John Sullivan Expedition in 1779, commissioned by General Washington to prevent the Iroquois from joining with the British to attack the Continental Army from the west, entered the area from the northern end of Canandaigua Lake. Sullivan's Army proceeded west to the northern end of Honeoye Lake, where they built a small fort, Fort Cummings. They continued westward across the northern ends of Canadice and Hemlock Lakes to their next encampment, at the southern end of Conesus Lake.

From this encampment, a twenty-eight man scouting party, led by Lieutenant Boyd and Sargeant Parker, was sent to reconnoiter the Seneca Indian village at Chenussio, which was located just west of the Genesee River. Their party was ambushed by 300 Indians led by Chief Joseph Bryant. The Ambuscade Monument in Groveland is a memorial to the members of the scouting party who died near the site in 1779. Boyd and Parker were captured alive and taken to the Indian village of Chenussio, near Cuylerville, where they were tortured, mutilated, and killed.

Honeoye--After the Revolutionary War, many of the men who had served in Sullivan's Army returned to settle in the area. In 1789, the first two white settlers, Gideon and William Pitts, arrived in the Village of Honeoye from Dighton, Massachussetts. They represented the Genesee Company, later the Dighton Land Company, and came to purchase land for settlement. Their father was Captain Peter Pitts, who surveyed the land for the company. He drew 3,000 acres near the foot of Honeoye Lake in a lottery, and moved there from Massachusetts in 1790.

The Pitt family built a log cabin, which was later replaced with a long house. Their nearest neighbors were James and William Wadsworth in Geneseo. The Pitts provided a stopping place for travelers passing through the region. They were visited by the Duke de Liancourt in 1795 and by Louis Phillippe, the future French King, and Talleyrand in 1805. The first name for the Village of Honeoye was Pittstown.

In 1843, fifteen-year-old Mary Jane Hawes, who was to become one of the most popular novelists of her time, moved from Massachusetts to Honeoye to teach school. She married Daniel Holmes, a young lawyer from Honeoye, and moved to Brockport, where she wrote thirty-eight sentimental novels over a fifty-year period.

In 1884, Helen Pitts, a descendent of the Pitts family, made the national news by marrying Frederick Douglass, the African-American editor and leader from Rochester. Douglass was the recorder of deeds for the District of Columbia; Helen was his secretary. Their interracial marriage caused a stir. Douglass, who was undisturbed by the so-called controversy, said, "My first wife was the color of my mother. My second wife is the color of my father."

Canadice--The Town of Canadice was formed from the Town of Richmond on April 15th, 1829. The first settlers of Canadice were Aaron Hunt, a Revolutionary War veteran from New Jersey, and his son-in-law, Jacob Holdren, who arrived in the spring of 1796. Holdren was a carpenter and millwright; he built many of the first mills in the area.

Hemlock--The first settler near the hamlet of Hemlock was Philip Short, who moved onto land near the foot of Hemlock Lake in 1795. John Hanna and John Emmonds were other early settlers of the area. The Town of Livonia at the foot of Hemlock Lake is named for a Russian Province; the Town of Springwater at the head of Hemlock Lake was originally called Hemlock Valley.

Conesus--The first permanent settler in the Conesus Lake area was John Boseley. He built a flour mill in 1793-94 just north of the present Village of Lakeville, at the foot of the lake. The Town of Conesus was formed from Livonia and Groveland on April 12, 1819, and founded as Freeport. It was renamed Conesus on April 15, 1825. The first settler at the head of the lake was James Henderson, who moved to the area from Pennsylvania in 1793.

Conesus and Hemlock Lakes were the only two of the four minor Finger Lakes in the area west of the major Finger Lakes that participated in the steamboat era. The area surrounding Canadice Lake has never been heavily built up with cottages, and the introduction of summer homes on Honeoye Lake came well after the popularity of steamboats had waned. When Canadice and Hemlock Lakes began supplying water to the City of Rochester, the cottages and summer homes on Hemlock Lake were torn down.

Jerry Bolles operated the first steamboat on Conesus Lake, the 50-foot-long *Jessie* that had a capacity of 100 passengers. Colonel James McPherson, builder of the first cottage on the east side of Conesus Lake, owned the second steamboat, the steam yacht *Musette*.

The Colonel had the three-decker steamboat *McPherson* built at Lakeville in 1883. Later steamboats were the *H. T. Jaeger*, the *White Swan*, the *Cyclone*, and the *Livingston*.

One of the early hotels on Conesus Lake was Jerry Bolles' Lake Crest, which is now part of Stella Maris, the Catholic camp. The Excelsior Springs Hotel, on the east side of the lake, had mineral springs nearby. The largest hotel was the 70-room Livingston Inn at McPherson's Point. It had a covered dancing pavillion, large ice houses, two sailing yachts, and thirty St. Lawrence and Whitehall fishing boats. In the late 1890s, two twenty-coach trains made the round trip on summer Sundays between the Erie Railroad station in Rochester and Lakeville, at the northern end of Conesus Lake.

The first steamboat on Hemlock Lake was the *Seth Green;* it had a length of thirty-nine feet and a nine-foot beam. The next steamboat was the *Corabelle*, which was forty-five feet long with a beam of ten and a half feet. Later steamboats on Hemlock Lake were called the *Mollie Tefft*, the *Nellie*, and the *Wave*.

Before they were torn down in the late 1800s when Hemlock Lake began to supply water to Rochester, the lake had one hundred cottages and five hotels. The hotels were the Half Way House, the three-story Jacques with its expansive piazzas in the northwestern part of the lake, the Lake Shore Hotel and dance hall, the Port House at the head of the lake, and the St. James Hotel from which all boat cruises originated.

Construction of the first water conduit to Rochester in 1873-76, the second conduit in 1893-94, and the third one in 1914-18, ended the steamboat era on Hemlock Lake. The time of the steamboats on Conesus was over by World War I also, but for a different reason. The railroads and the automobile became the favored means of transportation.

Genesee Valley--The family that has had the greatest impact on the area west of the lakes is the Wadsworth family of Geneseo. James and William Wadsworth left their home in Durham, Connecticut, and moved to the Genesee Valley in the spring of 1790. They purchased 2,000 acres at eight cents an acre from their uncle, Jeremiah Wadsworth, who kept another 2,000 acres for himself.

James, who was twenty-two in 1790, was a polished Yale graduate who had taught in Montreal. William was twenty-nine, rougher around the edges than James, and an outdoor type. William traveled to Genesee country by oxcart; James went by way of New York to purchase supplies, then via sloop to Albany, and westward by waterway and by horseback. They built a rough log cabin at Geneseo, and acquired another 4,000 acres of land. James became a land agent; William was a farmer, town official, and captain of the militia.

The Wadsworths established a farm tenancy system on their lands that was one of the earliest in the United States. Their first crops were corn, flax, and hemp. Later, wheat became the dominant crop in the Genesee Valley. They raised cattle, but shifted to Merino sheep and developed the largest sheep farm in the country. By 1800, the Wadsworths owned 35,000 acres of land.

In 1800, James Wadsworth built the Homestead at the southern edge of the Village of Geneseo. He married Naomi Wolcott of Connecticut in 1804. They had three daughters and two sons, James S. and William W. Wadsworth. The elder William Wadsworth never married. He served as a Major General of militia in the War of 1812. When General Van Rensselaer was wounded at the Battle of Queenstown Heights, William assumed command of the American forces. William died in 1833, leaving his share of the estate to the children of James.

The second generation of Wadsworths in the Genesee Valley added to the family's holdings. James S. Wadsworth built Hartford House at the northern edge of the Village of Geneseo, across town from the Homestead. He named it for the English Lord Hertford (pronounced "Hartford"). James S. lived in style, maintained an expensive stable in Geneseo, and a townhouse in New York. He attained the rank of general in the Civil War, fought at Bull Run and Gettysburg, and served as the military governor of Washington, D. C. He died from wounds suffered at the Battle of the Wilderness.

The Genesee Valley Hunt was founded in 1876 by Major W. Austin Wadsworth, the son of William W. Wadsworth (James S. Wadworth's brother). The hunt tradition was carried on by Austin's son, William P. Wadsworth.

James S. Wadsworth's son, James W. Wadsworth, was called "the boss." He was known for his Victorian authoritarian manner . The boss' son, James W. Wadsworth, Jr., was a distinguished member of the House of Representatives and Senate for thirty-five years. His son, James J. Wadsworth, was Ambassador to the United Nations in President Eisenhower's administration.

WEST OF THE LAKES--THINGS

ITEMS OF INTEREST

In distant hills the streamlets have their source,
And, rippling, race along their pebbly course.
They wend their way through woods and flowery meads,
Their shores in shade of alders and of reeds.
Their waters teem with nimble speckled trout,
Tempting the angler's hook to draw them out.
Thus, from the hills flow down upon the lea,
The rills, when meeting, form the Genesee.
....

From *Valley of the Genesee* by C. E. Furman

GENESEE RIVER

The Genesee River is the only river to cross the entire width of New York State, and is one of the few major rivers that flows north. It meanders for approximately 190 miles from its origins in spring-fed ponds in Gold, Pennsylvania. The source of the Genesee River in Potter County, Pennsylvania, is near the headwaters of the Allegheny River and the Susquehanna River. The Iroquois Indians considered the river and its valley together when they named the river Genesee, meaning "beautiful valley."

The sea covered the Genesee Valley, as it covered the adjacent Finger Lakes Region, until 350 to 400 million years ago during the Devonian Period. When the sea receded from the valley, it left layers of mud, sand, and silt, which can be seen as compressed layers in the Letchworth State Park gorge. An extended period of erosion and weathering followed the Devonian Era. It created broad escarpments in the hard rock layers, such as those south of Dansville, and formed lowlands and stream valleys in the softer layers.

The character of the Genesee Valley and the Finger Lakes was created by cyclical glacial erosion and glacial deposits, a process which deepened the north-south valleys and filled the east-west valleys. The major changes to the Genesee River were in the areas of Letchworth State Park and Rochester. Glacial residue filled an older channel from Portageville to Sonyea, and a similar channel was filled in between Avon and Irondequoit Bay, the original mouth of the Genesee River.

The Genesee-Canaseraga Valley from Geneseo to Dansville was a large lake similar to the Finger Lakes. The rich, fertile farmland in that area today was obviously underwater for much of its history. After the glacier in the region retreated about 13,000 years ago, it readvanced to within five miles north of Geneseo, and filled in the valley near Ashantee with glacial debris that partially blocked the original outlet of the Genesee River.

With the withdrawal of the glacier in the Wisconsin Ice Age, the new Genesee River followed its original course from Pennsylvania to Portageville, where the old, northeast pathway to Sonyea was now blocked by glacial deposits of the Portageville moraine. From here, the new Genesee River proceeded north across the Letchworth plateau, eventually eroding the plateau into the gorge that exists today. Similar erosion occurred at Rochester, when the new channel of the Genesee River to Lake Ontario was carved in rock older than that in Letchworth State Park.

The main geological features between Avon and Dansville are linked with the Genesee River, which meanders across a flat sediment-filled floor with "ox-bows," where the river doubles back on itself. The Dansville trough between Mt. Morris and Dansville now contains Caneseraga Creek. It was formed by the much larger "Dansville River," the east branch of the original Genesee River with headwaters near the present Canandaigua Lake.

GENESEE VALLEY HUNT

The Genesee Valley Hunt, the second oldest fox hunt in the United States, was founded in 1876 as the Livingston County Hunt by Major William Austin Wadsworth. The oldest hunt club is the Rose Tree Foxhunting Club of Media, Pennsylvania, which is located outside of Philadelphia. Major Wadsworth was the Master of Foxhounds (M.F.H.), and Charles Carroll of Groveland served as Huntsman.

Major Wadsworth formed his own pack of foxhounds by cross-breeding English, Irish, and Welsh hounds with American hounds. He bred the foxhounds for cry (quality and volume of voice), drive, nose (ability to detect the scent of the fox), speed, and stamina. He hired kennelmen and "whippers-in," who control the hounds in the field.

The name Livingston Valley Hunt was changed to Genesee Valley Hunt in 1881. The hunt selected a navy blue and buff riding coat modeled on the Continental Army uniform, rather than the scarlet riding coat copied from the British Redcoat uniform. However, the hunt's full-dress coats for evening are scarlet with chartreuse lapels. Major Wadsworth wrote a set of instructions, referred to as the "Hunt Bible," for participants in the hunt. It contained wry words of wisdom, such as:

> The Master of Foxhounds is a great and mystic personage to be lowly, meekly, and reverently looked up to, helped, considered, and given the right of way at all times. His ways are not other men's ways, and his language and actions are not to be judged by their standard. All that can be asked of him is that he furnish good sport as a rule, and so long as he does that, he is amenable to no criticism, subject to no law and fettered by no

> conventionality while in the field.... As a general rule he can enjoy your
> conversation and society more when not in the field with hounds, riders,
> foxes and damages on his mind.

By the mid-1880s, the Genesee Valley Hunt was considered to be the hunting center of the United States. Enthusiasts came from as far away as Buffalo, Cleveland, New York City, and Washington, D. C. In 1885, the hunt sponsored a point to point steeplechase that became the oldest hunt race in the United States. Major Wadsworth began a tradition of Independence Day games based on cavalry exercises on the grounds of the Homestead. They included knocking the plumes off opponents' helmets, picking up rings with lances, and slicing lemons in two with sabers. A few years before he became President, Theodore Roosevelt was praised for "the vigor of his blows in the cavalry fight." He replied: "One of the pleasantest days I ever spent in the saddle was after Mr. Wadsworth's hounds."

Major Wadsworth served in the Spanish-American War in 1898, turning over his responsibilities as M.F.H. to his cousin, James S. Wadsworth. After the war, he resumed his role of M.F.H. until 1917, when he gave up hunting due to poor health. He died in 1918 and his son, William P. Wadsworth, took on the responsibility of exercising the pack. Like his father, he wrote a book about foxhunting; his book is entitled *Riding to Hounds in America: An Introduction for Foxhunters.* It includes advice such as:

> A hound has a stern (pronounced "starn" by the British) instead of a tail.
> A hound may wag his stern only in greeting. If he moves it as a signal of
> excitement when striking a line, or while working a old line, he "feathers."
> When hunting, a hound never "barks"--he "opens," "gives tongue,"
> "throws his tongue," or "speaks."

> ... I am convinced that he [the fox] also is a sportsman and has a sense of
> humor, as I can see no other reason for a fox to stay above ground and
> permit himself to be hunted in a country so full of holes as my own....

> Good manners may be defined as habitual consideration for the rights and
> feelings of other people with whom we come in contact. Hunting etiquette
> may be defined as the rules by which good manners may be best expressed
> under conditions prevailing in the hunting field.... These rules are of
> course merely common sense and common politeness....

The hunt season is formally opened on the Saturday closest to October 1st by a parade of hounds and mounted riders on Geneseo's Main Street from the Wadsworth Homestead at the southern end of the village to another Wadsworth home, Hartford House, at the northern end. The riders wear their formal dress: navy blue hunt coat, buff waistcoat and stock, breeches, black boots, and a reinforced top hat. William P. Wadsworth noted that, "Some of the pleasure derived by those who hunt ... comes from the feeling of tradition and from the spectacle of people properly and conventionally dressed for the event."

The area around Geneseo is "horse country." The spring, summer, and fall events of the Genesee Valley Hunt provide a distinctive flavor to the Genesee Valley.

MT. MORRIS DAM

The Mt. Morris Dam and Reservoir is located in a deep gorge of the Genesee River at the northern end of Letchworth State Park. It is located near the Village of Mt. Morris and forty miles upstream from Rochester. The dam was authorized by congress in the Flood Control Act of 1944, and completed in 1952 by the U. S. Army Corps of Engineers. The concrete gravity dam is 1,028 feet long, 20 feet wide at the top, and 221 feet wide at its base. The top of the dam is 790 feet above sea level, and is 215 feet above the streambed.

The spillway is 550 feet long, and has a crest elevation of 760 feet. Water is released through nine five-foot by seven-foot conduits in the base of the spillway sections. The capacity of the reservoir is 301,600 acre-feet (one acre of water one foot deep). The Flood Control Pool is seventeen river-miles long and 3,300 acres in area.

The dam and reservoir provide flood protection to farms, industrial sites, and residential areas for sixty-seven miles to Rochester and the mouth of the Genesee River in Lake Ontario. The facility was built to reduce the threat of floods in the region. A severe flood in 1865 developed water flows in excess of twenty-four million gallons per minute, which is over half the flow of Niagara Falls. A major flood ravaged the Genesee River Valley an average of every seven years from 1865 to 1950.

In the first 32 years of operation, the dam and reservoir prevented an estimated $344 million of damage, $210 million of which was estimated to have been prevented during tropical storm "Agnes" in June, 1972. From June 15th to November 1st, a conservation pool elevation of 600 feet is maintained to enhance the scenic beauty of Letchworth State Park. Arrangements can be made for group tours of the dam by writing or phoning the U. S. Army Corps of Engineers at Mt. Morris.

NEW YORK STATE INTERNATIONAL RACEWAY PARK

New York International Raceway Park is one and a half miles north of Leicester on New Road, off Route 36. International Hot Rod Association races are held on a paved quarter-mile dragstrip from mid-April until mid-November. Races include Super Pro, Pro, Super Stock, Bikes, Stock (street legal cars only), Competition, and Junior Dragster.

PORTAGE RAILROAD BRIDGE

A wooden railroad bridge was constructed in 1851-52 at a narrow point across the Genesee River gorge, near the Upper Falls. The bridge was built on thirteen 30-foot-high stone pillars, and used 246 acres of timber. It was over 800 feet long with 190-foot-high trestles and 14-foot-high trusses, or 234 feet above the river bed, including the height of the stone pillars. It was constructed so that any part could be removed and repaired or replaced without weakening the structure.

The dedication ceremony, attended by Governor Washington Hunt and President Loder and other officials of the Erie Railroad, was held on August 25, 1852. Guards were posted on the bridge around the clock to protect it from arsonists and vandals.

Early in the morning of May 6, 1875, one of the guards discovered a fire at the western end of the bridge, and endeavored to use a fire hose to put it out. He was unable to turn on the valve. The spectacular fire lit up the entire area, and, at 4:15 AM, the superstructure of the western end of the bridge sank into the gorge with a loud roar.

The Erie Railroad replaced the wooden bridge with one made of 1,300,000 pounds of iron. Alternate stone piers were removed, and the new bridge was built on the remaining piers topped by four square feet of additional stone and capped with cast iron plates. The new bridge, 817 feet long and 255 feet high, was built on independent spans; the collapse of one span would not affect the other spans. Allowance for expansion and contraction was provided by steel rollers placed upon a bedplate at the western end of the bridge. The first train crossed the new bridge on July 31, 1875.

In 1903, 260 tons of iron were replaced by an equal weight of steel. The Portage Bridge, billed as a "wonder of the world," is still an impressive sight today.

LAKES

CONESUS LAKE

Yon aged group of maples mark
Flying shadows long and dark
While round their leaning stems entwine,
The folding arm of the heavy vine.
Long, long ago Conesus made
His dwelling in their grateful shade
About them curls as in time of yore
The smoke of his corn like lodge no more
With its rude walls hung with trophies torn
From the heads of fallen foes.
But his name by a lake and stream is borne
That in its channel deeply worn
Near Avon foames and flowes.

A Poem by W. H. C. Hosmer

The Indian name for Conesus is Ga-ne-a-sos, which means "always beautiful." Conesus Lake is 7.8 miles long, and is four-fifths of a mile wide at its widest point. The narrowest point on the lake is at its midpoint, at Long Point on the west side and McPherson point on the east side. It is 59 feet deep, and has a shoreline 18.5 miles long. The lake has a watershed of 89 square miles, and contains 42.6 billion gallons of water. It is 818 feet above sea level.

One third of the area around the lake is forested with hardwoods, such as oak and sugar maples; another half is farmed. The villages of Avon, Geneseo, and York use the lake as a public water supply. It was the first lake in New York State to have sewers installed completely around its circumference.

HEMLOCK LAKE

Beautiful, lovely Hemlock Lake
Grant me the liberty I take--
Once more I come, here to abide
Awhile by thee, and at thy side
Will wait the coming of the morn,--
The rising sun and hills adorn--
To pass the day in sober thought,
And view the works by nature wrought.

Hemlock Lake by "W. N."

Hemlock Lake is 6.7 miles long, half a mile wide at its widest point, and has an average width of four-tenths of a mile. It is 90 feet deep, and has a shoreline 17.1 miles long. The lake has a watershed of 43 square miles, and contains 28.7 billion gallons of water. It is 905 feet above sea level.

The watershed, which is owned by the City of Rochester, consists mainly of forests of northern hardwood. Hemlock Lake is joined to neighboring Canadice Lake by a spillway. Henrietta, Rochester, Rush, and Livonia use the lake as public water supply. Access to the lake is allowed by permit only; outboard motors are limited to under ten horsepower.

CANADICE LAKE

A beautiful lake is the Canadice,
    And tribesman dwelt on its banks of yore,
But a hundred years have vanished thrice
    Since hearth-stones smoked upon the shore:
The Munsee dreamed not of a foe;
Unstrung were the warrior's arm and bow;
And, couched on skins, he little thought
    The fall of his nation was at hand:

His ear no rattle of serpent caught,
No gliding ghost a warning brought
While came the Mengwe band.

A Legend of the Canadice by W. H. C. Hosmer

The Indian word Canadice means "long lake." Canadice Lake is 3.2 miles long, four-tenths of a mile wide at its widest point, and has an average width of one-third of a mile. It is 83 feet deep, and has a shoreline 7.2 miles long. The lake has a watershed of 12 square miles, and a volume of 11.6 billion gallons. Canadice Lake is 1,099 feet above sea level; it is the highest in elevation, and the smallest, of the eleven Finger Lakes.

The watershed, like the watershed of Hemlock Lake, is owned by the City of Rochester. Canadice Lake is joined to neighboring Hemlock Lake by a spillway. The area surrounding the lake is heavily forested with northern hardwoods. Henrietta, Livonia, Rochester, and Rush use the lake as public water supply. Access to the lake is by permit only; outboard motors under ten horsepower are allowed.

HONEOYE LAKE

The morning awakes with an azurine sky,
Quiescent the lake with the greenish-blue dye,
The sun is ascending behind the wet pines,
His flauntings careering in tremulous lines.

He peers through the forest with visage ablaze,
His fiery streams rousing the indolent haze,
The dreamy pall staggers when pierced by his lance,
And passes from sight with the morning's advance.

Now, Sol walks the blue with no joy in his eye,
While watching the cloud-drift ascend in the sky,
It tumbles and rolls as it purples the West,
Enshrouding the orb with its billowy crest.

Upon the horizon a dark shadow falls,
Then over the lake town and harborage walls,
The water exhibits a glimmering sheen,
Then gradually changes to myrtle-leaf green.

The Lake at Sunrise by Edwin Becker

The Indian name for Honeoye Lake is Ha-ne-a-yeh, which means "finger, lying." The lake is 4.1 miles long, seven-eighths of a mile wide at its widest point, and has an average width of two-thirds of a mile. It is 30 feet deep, the shallowest of the Finger Lakes, and has a shoreline 10.8 miles long. The lake has a volume of 9.5 billion gallons, and has a watershed of 36.7 square miles. It is 818 feet above sea level.

Honeoye Lake is one of the least agricultural of the Finger Lakes, and it is one of the least steeply sloped. No municipalities use the lake for public water supply. The lake, like Conesus Lake, has sewers completely around its circumference.

LEGENDS AND STORIES

THE GENESEE VALLEY CANAL

Canal construction was a popular activity in the United States during the first half of the nineteenth century. With the completion of the Erie Canal in 1825, residents of the Genesee Valley petitioned for the construction of a canal to connect the Erie Canal with the Allegheny River. The proposed canal would open up markets in Pittsburgh and the Ohio River Valley to western New York merchants. Charles Carroll of Groveland and Micah Brooks of Nunda proposed legislation to authorize the building of the new waterway.

In 1827, Governor DeWitt Clinton proposed "the survey of a route for a canal, to unite the Erie Canal at Rochester with the Allegheny River." James Geddes, the engineer who surveyed and built the Erie Canal, surveyed a potential route for the canal. The New York State Legislature authorized the construction of the Genesee Valley Canal on May 6, 1836. The proposed canal would extend from Rochester to Olean, with a branch to Dansville. The bed of the canal from Rochester to Sonyea, with the side-cut to Dansville, was relatively flat and few locks were required; this section of the canal opened in 1841.

The canal's route from Nunda south was through rocky, rugged country, particularly in the "Deep Cut" near Oakland. An attempt was made to dig a tunnel over 1,000 feet long through the palisade below the Middle Falls at Portage. Elisha Johnson, who was to become Rochester's fifth mayor, directed the effort until it was stopped by landslides. The canal went through Fillmore, Houghton, Caneadea, Belfast, and Cuba.

The Genesee Valley Canal was joined with the Allegheny River in 1862. The canal was 125 miles long. It contributed to the success of the Erie Canal by feeding traffic to it, but it was not financially successful itself. With the high cost of canal maintenance and the widespread building of railroads in the last half of the 1800s, the Canal was no longer competitive. It was closed in 1878; the right of way was sold in 1880 to the Genesee Valley Canal Railroad Company, who built a railroad along the towpath of the canal.

The Genesee Valley benefited from the canal. The lumber industry cleared the land, and shipped the lumber via the canal. Wheat was cultivated on many of the cleared acres.

The lumber was used to build new homes and businesses. The canal was a significant contributing factor to the increase of prosperity in the region.

THE LEGEND OF RED WING

Red Wing, the daughter of an Seneca Indian chief, frequently accompanied her parents on fishing and hunting trips to a place with rolling hills along the "Trail of the Seneca." Her favorite spot on the trail was a cool, moist glen with moss-covered rocks, wild grape vines, and towering trees that provided a heavy, green canopy.

Red Wing was courted, in Indian fashion, by two Seneca warriors, Lone Pine and Sun Fish. Lone Pine was the suitor chosen by Red Wing, and soon after their marriage they walked along a trail through Red Wing's favorite glen with a party of Indians from their tribe. They arrived at a high, dangerous part of the trail, and Sun Fish pushed the unsuspecting Lone Pine over the precipice. Just before Lone Pine went over the edge, he grabbed Sun Fish by the ankle, and pulled him to death with him.

Before the party realized what was happening, Red Wing uttered a piercing cry, plunged over the cliff, and was united with her husband in death. The glen where Lone Pine, Red Wing, and Sun Fish joined the Great Spirit is in Stony Brook State Park.

THE HORSEWOMAN WITH ENDURANCE

Mrs. Herbert Wadsworth, formerly Martha Blow of St. Louis, was a small, red-haired woman known as a great horsewoman. Herbert and Martha lived in their stone mansion Ashantee (a shanty) south of Avon, near the confluence of Conesus Creek and the Genesee River. One day in 1910, Martha read in the newspaper that Theodore Roosevelt had ridden a horse 100 miles in a single day. Martha, who knew Teddy from his visits to the Wadsworth Homestead in Geneseo, was unimpressed with his feat.

She rode 212 miles in nineteen hours and twenty minutes in a circular route around the Genesee Valley; her route encompassed Conesus Lake. U. S. Army Cavalry officers were required to ride ninety miles in three consecutive days on one horse. Martha used three horses in her endurance test. Upon her return home, she was heard muttering, "I guess I showed that old Rough Rider up."

Her most notable equestrian feat was a thirty-day ride from Washington, D. C., to Ashantee via West Virginia. She arrived at home in the valley just in time to perform hostess functions for a formal dinner that she had scheduled for the evening of her return. She appeared draped with diamonds in one of her trademark clinging gowns, similar to her single-piece silk wedding gown that could be drawn through her wedding ring.

THE MASTODON

In January, 1991, construction workers dug up the skull of a mastodon in a peat bog near Avon. The skull belonged to a mastodon that had roamed western New York 10,000 to 12,000 years ago. Mastodons, ancestors of the elephant, were indigenous to the southern Great Lakes region until after the second Ice Age. Scientists uncovered the entire skeleton, which survived intact in the spot where the animal died while lying on its side.

The skeleton was found about five feet below the surface in layers of peat and marl (earth, sand, and shells). Scientists estimate that the mastodon was about eight to nine feet tall at the shoulder. Mastodon bones have been found at other "digs," but finding a complete skeleton is rare. Scientists at the State University of New York--College at Geneseo guided the effort to preserve the skeleton intact.

THE PLEDGE OF ALLEGIANCE

Francis Bellamy, a native of Mt. Morris, wrote the Pledge of Allegiance in August, 1892. The Pledge of Allegiance, as he originally wrote it is:

> I pledge allegiance to my flag
> and to the Republic
> for which it stands--
> one Nation indivisible--
> with liberty and justice for all.

Bellamy worked for *The Youth's Companion,* a children's adventure story magazine. In 1888, the magazine asked their readers to help buy United States flags for their schools. The children contributed enough pennies, nickels, and dimes to buy 30,000 flags.

In 1892, the magazine had another project for their readers--celebrating the 400th anniversary of Columbus' arrival in the new world. Bellamy and one of his co-workers, James Upham, proposed a school celebration called Columbus Day. They planned for the children to raise their American flags, and to say something together to honor the flag. Bellamy traveled to Washington, D. C., to discuss the celebration with President Benjamin Harrison, who made Columbus Day a national holiday.

The next edition of *The Youth's Companion* included Bellamy's twenty-three word flag pledge. On Columbus Day in 1892, twelve million schoolchildren recited the Pledge of Allegiance. Bellamy was in Boston that day, where he heard 6,000 children say the words. In 1923, a group of American war veterans proposed a slight change in the wording of the pledge. They changed the first line from "I pledge allegiance to my flag" to "I pledge allegiance to the flag of the United States of America." They also suggested that the right hand should be placed over the heart while reciting the pledge.

James Upham, Bellamy's co-worker, also claimed to be the author of the Pledge of Allegiance. In 1939, the United States Flag Association investigated his claims, and declared Bellamy to be the author. Congress made the pledge official on the fiftieth anniversary of the pledge, in October, 1942, by making it law. One year later, the United States Supreme Court ruled that no one could be forced to say the Pledge of Allegiance. In 1954, Congressmen Louis Rabaut suggested adding the phrase "under God" to the line "one nation indivisible," because President Abraham Lincoln had called the United States "this nation, under God" in his Gettysburg Address.

The Pledge of Allegiance used today, with minor changes to Bellamy's original version, is:

> I pledge allegiance to the flag
> of the United States of America
> and to the republic
> for which it stands,
> one nation under God, indivisible,
> with liberty and justice for all.

THE STORY OF THE SHORT BENCH

During the negotiation of the Big Tree Treaty at Geneseo in 1797, the Seneca chief Red Jacket asked Thomas Morris if he could talk with him. Thomas Morris, who was representing his father, Robert Morris, in purchasing the land from the Indians, sat down on a bench with Red Jacket. As they talked, Red Jacket moved closer and closer to Morris, which forced him to slide along the length of the bench upon which they were sitting.

Finally, Morris ran out of bench. He broke off the discussion, and told Red Jacket that if he moved any farther, he, Morris, would be sitting on the floor. Red Jacket said that he was pleased to see that Morris finally understood the plight of the Indian. The Indians had been displaced farther and farther to the west, and now they were selling their land west of the Genesee River to the white man. In Red Jacket's opinion, the Indians had no more bench upon which to sit, and would, symbolically, be sitting on the floor.

PARKS, FORESTS AND TRAILS

CONESUS INLET FISH AND WILDLIFE MANAGEMENT AREA

The Conesus Inlet Fish and Wildlife Management Area, located at the southern end of Conesus Lake in the Town of Conesus, contains over 1,120 acres of flat floodplain with steep hills to the east and west. It is bounded in the north by Conesus Lake, in the east by East Swamp Road, in the south by Guiltner Road, and in the west by West Swamp Road

(Route 256). The management area consists mainly of marsh vegetation, with a border of brush, open land, and swamp hardwoods.

The New York State Department of Environmental Conservation purchased this land in the late 1960s to conserve and protect an important wetland resource. They purchased an additional 83 acres in 1979 to provide access to Conesus Lake, and to preserve a major northern pike spawning habitat. Management area objectives are to maintain a pike spawning and rearing habitat in the inlet and adjoining wetlands, a site for the use of waterfowl in the marsh, and an upland habitat along the edges of the area.

Public recreational use is encouraged, including bird watching, environmental education, fishing, hiking, hunting, and photography. Several parking lots provide access, and two scenic overlooks offer opportunities to observe wildlife. Car-top boat launch access to the lake is provided via a fishermen's parking area on Conesus Lake, at the northern end of the area. Upland and wetland habitats, where wildlife species can be viewed, are accessed by a nature trail along the western edge of the management area.

Game indigenous to the Conesus Inlet Fish and Wildlife Management Area includes: rabbits, deer, pheasants, ruffed grouse, squirrels, and waterfowl. Grey and red foxes, mink, muskrats, and raccoons provide trapping opportunities. Other species that may be observed in the area are: amphibians, marshbirds, shorebirds, songbirds, raptors, and reptiles. The area is open to the public all year.

HARRIET HOLLISTER SPENCER PARK

Harriet Hollister Spencer Park is off Canadice Hill Road, six miles south of the Village of Honeoye. The park provides a beautiful view of Honeoye Lake to the east and of Rochester to the north. It has picnic tables, hiking trails, and slopes for sledding, as well as cross-country skiing and snowmobiling trails.

HONEOYE LAKE STATE MARINE PARK

Honeoye Lake State Marine Park is off Route 20A, four miles south of the Village of Honeoye on East Lake Road. The park has a boat launching area and parking for over thirty vehicles with trailers.

LETCHWORTH STATE PARK

Letchworth State Park, thirty-five miles south of Rochester, is one of the most beautiful natural settings in the eastern United States. The Genesee River flows through seventeen miles of canyons and valleys in the park. The up to 600-foot high walls of the Genesee River gorge, three major waterfalls (the highest of which is 107 feet), and the surrounding forests provide a spectacular example of gorge and waterfall scenery. The 14,350 acre park can be entered at Mt. Morris, Perry, Castile, and Portageville. The Castile entrance is open all year; the other three entrances are closed during the winter.

The park has over seventy camping cabins, fishing areas, eight picnic grounds, two swimming pools (one at the northern end and one at the southern end), and a diving pool. It also has tent and trailer sites, and winter sport facilities for cross-country skiing, ice skating, and sledding. The cabins are available for rental from early April through early November. Cabin reservations, which are strongly advised, are accepted beginning January 1st. Letchworth Park has twenty-five trails, of which fourteen are rated easy and eleven rated moderate. They include some steep slopes that range in length from one-eighth mile to four and a half miles. There are two restaurants, the Glen Iris Inn and the Lower Falls Restaurant; snack bars are located throughout the park.

The sandstone and shale in the walls of the gorge were formed during the Devonian period, when the region was submerged in shallow interior seas. The river valley was formed by tens of millions of years of erosion that wore away the rock. Glaciers deposited large quantities of glacial residue, including rocks that blocked the original river valley. The seventeen miles of canyons and valleys of the Genesee River gorge through Letchworth Park are the result of the glacial blocking of an early riverbed.

The grave of Mary Jemison, "white woman of the Genesee," and a restored Seneca Indian Council House are located on a ridge behind the Glen Iris Inn. Nearby is the Museum of Pioneer and Indian History, which features displays depicting early regional settlement. A 800-foot-long railroad bridge, the Portage Bridge, spans the gorge 234 feet above the river at the Upper Falls.

Letchworth State Park is named for William Pryor Letchworth, a Buffalo manufacturer of saddlery and carriage hardware, philanthropist, and student of nature. His impression of the area upon seeing it for the first time in the spring of 1858 was: "I was so charmed with the infinite variety of the delicate beauties nature had brought so close together--which seemed to invite me to a study of her yet uncomprehended attractions...." He retired from business in 1871 at the age of forty-seven, and moved to Glen Iris. Letchworth and his friends named the unusual features and scenic outlooks, including Devil's Oven, Inspiration Point, Sugar Loaf Rock, and Tea Table Rock. He gave his 1,000 acre estate to the State of New York in 1907.

RATTLESNAKE HILL WILDLIFE MANAGEMENT AREA

The Rattlesnake Hill Wildlife Management Area, located eight miles west of Dansville in the Town of Nunda, is 5,100 acres of upland terrain. The tract, purchased in 1930s by the Federal Resettlement Administration, is named for the timber rattlesnake found in some of the remote sections. The area provides many habitats for wildlife; it contains apple orchards, conifer plantations, mature woodlands, open meadows, and overgrown fields.

The wildlife management area is inhabited by many game species, including rabbits, squirrels, ruffed grouse, deer, turkeys, and woodcock. The area is open to public hunting. The Department of Environmental Conservation, which maintains the area, has developed marsh units to provide hunting for waterfowl. These marshes also provide a habitat for beavers, mink, and raccoons. Parts of Canaseraga Creek, Hovey Brook, and Sugar Creek, which are in or adjacent to the management area, are known as trout waters. In addition, each year several of the deeper water impoundments are stocked with trout.

Access roads through the area, which are closed to unauthorized vehicles, are available for use as foot trails. Several small campsites are available to be used by organized educational groups by special permit. Other uses of the area, in addition to hunting and fishing, include bird-watching, cross-country skiing, horseback riding, nature study, picnicking, and trapping.

STONY BROOK STATE PARK

Stony Brook State Park, which is located three miles south of Dansville off Route 36, was established in 1928, when 250 acres was acquired by the Finger Lakes State Parks Commission. The park has been expanded to 577 acres of hilly woodland. It has a deep gorge and three waterfalls. The gorge contains notable rock formations and steep cliff walls. The park terrain ranges from 750 feet to 1,250 feet above sea level.

Stony Brook State Park has 130 campsites (no utilities, RVs allowed), swimming in two stream-fed gorge pools that have adjoining bathhouses, playing fields, tennis courts, and horse-shoe pits. The park also has hiking trails in the gorge and the woods, a picnic shelter, and picnic areas with fireplaces and 400 picnic tables. Within the park are concession stands, hot showers, flush toilets, pay telephones, and a trailer dumping station near the upper park entrance.

The park is open all year; camping is permitted from mid-May to mid-October; all gorge trails are closed during the winter. Winter sports include cross-country skiing, sledding, and snowmobiling.

SHOWS AND FESTIVALS

1941 HISTORICAL AIRCRAFT GROUP AIR SHOW

The 1941 Wings of Eagles Air Show is an annual event sponsored by the National Warplane Museum in Geneseo. Over 20,000 visitors attend the show each year. Aerial dogfights are recreated overhead, and low-level "strafing" runs delight the audience. It is held the third weekend in August; over 100 World War II vintage aircraft take part in the show. Participating aircraft arrive on Friday, and air show performances are scheduled for Saturday and Sunday. The 1941 Wings of Eagles Air Show moved to Batavia in 1994. An airshow sponsored by the 1941 Historical Aircraft Group will continue to be held at Geneseo on the third weekend in August.

GENESEE VALLEY HORSE HUNT TRIALS

The Genesee Valley Horse Hunt Trials are held in mid-September at Nations Farm on Nations Road in Geneseo, off Route 39. The trials feature dressage, and cross-country and stadium jumping trials. Spectators are admitted free to the horse hunt trials.

Dressage events test the horses' physical development, mastery of basic paces, and obedience to unspoken commands. The cross-country jumping events judge a horse's jumping ability, and its endurance as the competition continues over an extended period.

GENESEE VALLEY HUNT RACE MEET

The Genesee Valley Hunt Race Meet, which has been held since 1929, is held in early October. The highlights of the race meet are the eight steeplechase races, but the meet also includes a carriage parade, horse-drawn hayrides, and intercollegiate competitions. Other activities are the hunter pace, a parade of hounds, pony rides for children, and terrier races. Tailgate picnics and visiting the boutiques are popular at noon. In past years, a fly-by of World War II aircraft from the National Warplane Museum at Geneseo was scheduled.

The Genesee Valley Hunt Race Meet is held at Nations Farm on Nations Farm Road, off Route 39 in Geneseo. Proceeds from the event benefit the Genesee Valley Conservancy and the Genesee Rotary Club.

GENESEE VALLEY RIDING CLUB SPRING HORSE TRIALS

Several hundred horses and riders compete for trophies and prize money in the Spring Horse Trials of the Genesee Valley Riding Club held in early June. The spring horse trials, a benefit for the Association of the Visually Impaired of Greater Rochester, attract the best combined training event riders in the Northeast. The trials, considered to be "the complete test of horse and rider," are modeled on the Olympic Three Day Event. The Three Day Event was developed from the cavalry tradition of testing the ability of military couriers to carry messages rapidly while traversing difficult natural obstacles.

The horses and riders are evaluated on their ability to display controlled grace in dressage on Saturday. The same horses and riders jump large obstacles in a natural setting of meadows, streams, and woods. On Sunday afternoon, the horse and rider pairs negotiate a twisting, turning series of jumps marked by brightly colored poles. Accuracy and time determine the champions. Competitors are from New York State, about twelve neighboring states, and several Canadian provinces. They ride a wide variety of horses, including German stallions, Irish Connemaras, and thoroughbreds.

The public is invited to attend. A nominal fee is charged for the Sunday events. Food and beverages are available on the grounds both days. In previous years, the dressage events on Saturday were held at White Devon Farm, on Route 39 north of Geneseo; Sunday events were conducted at nearby Nations Farm, on Nations Road, west of its intersection with Route 39.

OKTOBERFEST AND BALLOON RALLYE

The Ocktoberfest and Balloon Rallye, held Friday evening through Sunday of Labor Day Weekend in Dansville, has antique and flea markets, arts and crafts, a balloon rally with approximately 100 hot-air balloons, German food, and old world music. Hot-air balloon ascensions are offered.

The Oktoberfest is held in Babcock Park off Morey Avenue, which intersects Main Street (Route 63). All other events are held at Pickard Field, Dansville Municipal Airport. Oktoberfest celebrates the heritage of the settlers of the valley and its current residents.

WATERFALLS

Many of these waterfalls are on private property; owner's rights should be respected, particularly if the property is posted.

FALL BROOK GORGE

Fall Brook Gorge, a registered national landmark, has a 100-foot waterfall in a 200-foot chasm. It is located on Cuylerville Road between Geneseo and Mt. Morris.

JAYCOCK CREEK FALLS

Jaycock Creek Falls is a 40-foot waterfall in Wheeler Gully, off Nations Road north of Geneseo.

LITTLE MILL CREEK FALLS

Little Mill Creek Falls is a 50-foot waterfall on Whiteman Gulf off Route 63 in Dansville.

LOWER FALLS--LETCHWORTH STATE PARK

Lower Falls, one of three major falls within two miles of one another along the Genesee River, is a 70-foot waterfall in the southern end of Letchworth State Park. Access to the Lower Falls is provided by a path that leads down to the canyon and crosses a footbridge over a flume (a narrow channel in the gorge). Table Rock is a large, flat surface of sandstone at the flume. Cathedral Rock, a good example of erosion, is a pinnacle on the east side of the falls.

MIDDLE FALLS--LETCHWORTH STATE PARK

Middle Falls, the most scenic of the three major falls at the southern end of Letchworth State Park, is a 107-foot waterfall on the Genesee River. It is located a half mile downstream from Upper Falls.

PAPERMILL FALLS

Papermill Falls is a 20-foot cascade on Conesus Creek, off Papermill Road south of Avon.

REYNOLDS GULLY

There are two waterfalls in Reynolds Gully at the southern end of Hemlock Lake, off Route 15A.

STONE FALLS

Stone Falls is a 40-foot waterfall on Mill Creek, off Stone Falls Road in Dansville.

UPPER FALLS--LETCHWORTH STATE PARK

Upper Falls is a 71-foot waterfall on the Genesee River at the southern end of Letchworth State Park, near the Portageville entrance. The Dehgewanus Creek flows into the Genesee River near the Upper Falls. The Upper Falls can viewed from the Portage railroad bridge.

WEST OF THE LAKES--PLACES

COLLEGES AND UNIVERSITIES

STATE UNIVERSITY OF NEW YORK--COLLEGE AT GENESEO

The State University of New York--College at Geneseo opened in 1871 as the Geneseo Normal and Training School. It became part of the State University of New York system in 1948, and has offered programs in the arts and sciences, as well as teacher education, since 1962. The campus is located at the western edge of the historic village of Geneseo on Route 20A, several miles west of Exit 8 of the I-390 Expressway.

The principal mission of the college is "to provide such opportunities for those who seek a sound education in a liberal arts discipline and have the talent, motivation, and prior education to profit from such opportunities." The college's motto is "Let each become all he is capable of being." The college has an enrollment of approximately 5,000 students.

SUNY--College at Geneseo has a national reputation as a high-quality public institution that has become increasingly selective. The college places high each year in the *U. S. News and World Report* fall issue, which provides ratings of regional colleges. Since the 1980s, Geneseo has been at or near the top of *Money Magazine's* ratings of best values in higher education in the United States.

LIVINGSTON CAMPUS CENTER-GENESEE COMMUNITY COLLEGE

The Livingston Campus Center, located off Route 20A at 5999 Big Tree Road in Lakeville, is a unit of the Genesee Community College at Batavia. The community college serves a student body of over 3,500 students in a 2,300 square-mile service area. It offers degree and certificate programs in thirty-five academic fields, as well as a wide variety of continuing education courses and business and professional training programs.

The Livingston Campus Center contains five classrooms, two modern computer laboratories, and a telecourse / study area. The center offers courses leading to certificates and Associate Degrees in Applied Science, Science, and Arts.

MUNICIPALITIES

AVON

The Village of Avon is located near one of the historic crossroads of western New York, the intersection of Routes 5 and 20 and Route 15. Routes 5 and 20 provided the main east-west route between Albany and Buffalo prior to the building of the New York

State Thruway in the 1950s. Routes 5 and 20 were constructed by virtually paving the principal Indian trail (and stage coach road) in the northern part of the state. Avon is just west of Route 15, which was one of the major north-south routes prior to the construction of the I-390 Expressway in the 1970s. Among Avon's attractions are the Avon Inn, the Annual Corn Festival in August, and the Annual Farm Harvest Festival in September.

The Village of Avon has provided a stopping place for travelers since late 1789, when Gilbert Barry built a home and tavern out of logs. It was the only public house on the Indian trail between the Genesee River and Fort Niagara. The visiting Duc de la Rochefoucauld noted in his diary in the late 18th century: "The inhabitants here are few, but among them is one of the best inns we have seen for some time. Mr. Berry keeps it, a good civil man."

Another early inn called the Hosmer Stand, built by James Wadsworth of Geneseo in 1806, was run by the Hosmer family for many years. Among the famous visitors to the Hosmer Stand were Commodore Matthew Perry, negotiator of the treaty that opened Japan to the West, and several exiles from the Napoleanic Wars: Joseph Bonaparte, Marechal Grouchy, General Jean Moreau, and Louis Philippe (who became the King of France).

The Seneca Indians considered the sulphur springs in the southwest part of town that they called Canawaugus, "place-of-bad-smelling-water," to have healing powers. After the War of 1812, the springs attracted many visitors, including fashionable southerners. The water was pungent and tinted blue; a physician compared it with the water of Saratoga Springs, and considered it to be "cathartic, diuretic, diaphoric (perspiration-producing), and tonic." The construction of a bath house and "showering box" near the springs was followed by the construction of the American Hotel (later renamed Congress Hall), Knickerbocker Hall, the United States Hotel, the Argyle Hotel, and the Livingston Hotel.

Dr. Orren Phelps built a racetrack nearby called Congress Park. Mrs. Herbert Wadsworth revived the use of the track for racing and showing horses, which continued until the 1920s. Later, it became a quiet park called Avon Springs Downs.

DANSVILLE

The Village of Dansville is located at the intersection of routes 36, 63, and 245; it is also on the I-390 Expressway. Dansville is known for beautiful Stony Brook State Park, the home of the American Red Cross (Clara Barton Chapter No. 1), the Annual Dogwood Festival in May, and the Oktoberfest & Balloon Rallye on Labor Day weekend. The Dansville airport is the headquarters for the Rochester Soaring Club and its many gliders.

The first settlers in Dansville were Mr. and Mrs. Cornelius McCoy and their children, David, James, and Mary. The McCoys emigrated from northern Ireland in 1788, and settled in Northumberland County, Pennsylvania. They moved to the area in June, 1795, and lived in a surveyer's hut while building a log cabin. Amariah Hammond built the second log cabin in Dansville, and moved his family from Bath in 1796.

In 1796, a spring erupted from the side of a hill in Dansville, pushing dirt, rocks, and trees down the hillside. Local residents referred to it as the "all healing spring." Nathaniel Bingham and Lyman Granger built a four-story building in 1853 to house people in need of a water-cure. The building passed through several owners, and was purchased in 1858 by Dr. James C. Jackson, who named it "Our Home on the Hillside."

Many of Dr. Jackson's patients were women suffering from nervous disorders. They were administered cold-water baths, half-baths, plunges, sitz baths, and wet-sheet wrappings. The patients also benefited from exercise, loose clothing, "positive mental and moral influences," and a vegetarian diet. Such hydropathic institutes were popular through the end of the nineteenth century.

Dr. Jackson invented a graham-flour cereal called Granula that he served to a group of visiting Seventh-Day Adventists; they eventually moved to Grand Rapids, Michigan, and founded the Western Health Reform Institute. Dr. John Kellogg, the manager of the institute, and his brother originated a similar cereal called Granose. Their patient, C. W. Post, created a cereal of his own; he called it Grape Nuts.

Clara Barton moved to Dansville in 1876, after a year's debilitating illness, to take the cure at "Our Home on the Hillside." She began to improve immediately, and was fully recovered within a year. She made friends in Dansville, bought a home in the village, and lived there for ten years. With her cure came energy, which she turned to the establishment of the Red Cross in the United States.

Clara traveled to Washington, D. C., to convince President Garfield's cabinet of the importance of establishing an American Red Cross. She convinced them, but President Garfield's assassination in the summer 1881 meant that she would have to convince President Chester Arthur's new cabinet. She returned home to Dansville discouraged, but found that the citizens of Dansville supported her effort. They formed the first local chapter of the Red Cross on August 22, 1881. On March 16, 1882, Congress signed the Treaty of Geneva, which made the U. S. a member of the International Red Cross.

In 1882, the management of the Home on the Hillside passed to Dr. Jackson's son and daughter-in-law, Dr. James H. and Dr. Kate Jackson. The main building burned that year and was replaced by the five-story brick structure that still stands. The building again passed through many hands. One of the twentieth-century owners was Bernarr McFadden, who purchased it in 1929; he operated it as the Physical Culture Hotel.

In the 1800s, Dansville was a center for the logging industry, which benefited from the construction of the Genesee Valley Canal. The section of the canal from Rochester to Dansville, a distance of fifty-two miles, was finished in 1840.

GENESEO

The Village of Geneseo is located four miles west of Conesus Lake, at the intersection of routes 20A and 63. Geneseo, the county seat of Livingston County, is listed in the National Historic Registry. It is the home of the State University of New York--College at Geneseo, the Genesee Valley Hunt, the National Warplane Museum, and the Big Tree Inn.

An important treaty with the Iroquois Indians was signed at Geneseo in 1797 at the Big Tree, a white oak tree with a 36-foot circumference that served as a Seneca meeting place. Robert Morris, financier of the Revolutionary War, secured from Massachusetts in 1791 the right to buy the land from the Genesee River west to Lake Erie from the Indians. He sold the land to the Holland Land Company, a group of Dutch land speculators.

Thomas Morris represented his father in the negotiations; he was assisted by Charles Williamson, land agent for Lord Pulteney. President Washington appointed Jeremiah Wadsworth to represent the United States as commissioner. William Bayard and Joseph Ellicott represented Holland Land Company's interests. The Indians sold their land to Morris, except for 200,000 acres for nine Indian reservations, for $100,000. Since the total sale involved 14,000,000 acres, the Indians received less than one cent per acre.

Two of the early settlers in the area were James and William Wadsworth from Connecticut. They purchased 2,000 acres of land from Jeremiah Wadsworth, a distant relative, and brought their fortunes with them. The Wadsworth family, shrewd in business and public-service oriented, established a healthy farm economy in the region, and a thriving community at Geneseo. James Wadsworth's son, James S., became a general in the Civil War, fought at Bull Run and Gettysburg, and was military governor of Washington, D. C.

James S. Wadsworth's son, James W., was a State Assemblyman, State Controller, and Congressmen; he was known as "The Boss." The boss' son, James W. Jr., was a State Assemblyman, Congressman, and U. S. Senator. In the late 1950s, James J. Wadsworth, the son of James W. Wadsworth, Jr., served as the United States Ambassador to the United Nations in President Eisenhower's administration.

LIMA

Lima, which bills itself as the crossroads of western New York, is located at the crossroads of Routes 5 and 20 and Route 15A. The Village of Lima was founded in 1788 near the intersection of two principal Iroquois Indian trails. When Routes 5 and 20 were the main east-west thoroughfare between Albany and Buffalo, and Route 15A was a principal north-south route, Lima was one of the "crossroads of western New York." It was founded as the hamlet of Charleston, but was renamed Lima, a modification of Old Lyme. Many of the early settlers were from Old Lyme, Connecticut.

In 1830, the Methodist Church established the Genesee Wesleyan Seminary in Lima. It became Genesee College, which moved to Syracuse in 1871. It became the nucleus of Syracuse University. Faculty and graduates of the early Lima educational institution include Henry J. Raymond, founder of the New York Times, and Frances Willard, a leader in the temperance movement. The Greek Revival buildings of the Genesee Wesleyan Seminary, now the Elim Bible Institute, are listed in the National Historic Register.

MT. MORRIS

Mt. Morris is located on the Genesee River at the intersection of routes 36 and 408, forty miles south of Rochester. The northern entrance to Letchworth State Park is at Mt. Morris. The Mt. Morris flood control dam is nearby, in the northern end of Letchworth State Park. Because of the dam, Mt. Morris calls itself "the best town by a dam site."

Albert Lorenz Park, a Livingston County Park, is located between Mt. Morris and Letchworth Park. Francis Bellamy, author of the "Pledge of Allegiance to the Flag," was born in Mt. Morris. John Wesley Powell, explorer of the Grand Canyon, was also a native of Mt. Morris. The village is the site of the General William Mills Mansion.

MUSEUMS

COHOCTON VALLEY FARM MUSEUM

The Cohocton Valley Farm Museum is located in a 12,000 square-foot building in Cohocton, alongside the Cohocton River and adjacent to the old Erie Railroad depot. The museum is the idea of Stanley Clark, owner of the Keuka Maid tour boat and operator of the Bath-Hammondsport Railroad. The Cohocton Valley Farm Museum is one of the destinations of Clark's Bath-based railroad; Hammondsport is the other destination of the "Champagne Trail" railroad.

Dick Sherer, the Steuben County historian, is the historical consultant for the museum. Sherer read a 100-year farm saga, *The Phelps-Gorham Purchase* by Oramus Turner (1859), and decided to stretch the theme to 200 years. The typical farmstead of 1790, a one-room log cabin with an open hearth and a loft, is depicted in a 28-foot diorama on the second floor balcony of the two-story museum.

The 1840 diorama shows that the farmer has added a bedroom to the farmhouse, replaced the open hearth with a wood stove, plastered the inside of the walls, and cleared more fields. Rooms representing 1790 and 1840 kitchen settings are located across a drawbridge in the balcony of the museum.

In the 1890 diorama, oil-paper windows have been replaced by double-hung windows, and the dining area is decorated with wainscoting and wallpaper. The kitchen in the 1940 farmhouse has bright wallpaper and a Kelvinator refrigerator with a compressor on top.

The intent of the museum, which charges a nominal admission fee, is to be of interest to the entire family. It is completely accessible to the handicapped.

GENESEE COUNTRY MUSEUM

The Genesee Country Museum is located on Flint Hill Road in Mumford, which is a half-hour drive southwest of Rochester. A typical upstate community of the 1800s has been created by moving fifty-seven historic homes, shops, and other buildings from the surrounding area. Each building has been restored and authentically furnished to give visitors the impression that they are strolling through nineteenth century rural America. Daily demonstrations of blacksmithing, hearth cooking, printing, spinning, tinsmithing, weaving, and other occupations are provided.

The Genesee Country Museum shows the architectural changes that took place in western New York from a 1795 log cabin to a 1870 Victorian villa. Examples are the Victorian Italianate John Hamilton house, the Livingston-Backus house from Rochester's historic Third Ward, an octagon house, and an authentic village square. The museum has a nature center with four miles of interpreted trails; the nature center is open all year.

Also on the grounds is the Gallery of Sporting Life, the largest collection of sporting and wildlife art in North America. It contains hundreds of paintings and sculptures. The Carriage Museum has a notable collection of more than forty horse-drawn vehicles, from private stagecoaches to a twelve-horse brewery hitch wagon.

The Genesee Country Museum has a cafeteria, tavern, ice cream parlor, and picnic areas. Also, there are four gift shops and a bookseller's shop on the grounds. The museum is a not-for-profit educational living history museum chartered by the regents of the State University of New York.

NATIONAL WARPLANE MUSEUM

The National Warplane Museum, located off Route 63 in Geneseo, is a non-profit, tax-exempt organization incorporated and approved by the New York State regents in 1983. The museum's members are dedicated to the restoration and maintenance of World War II aircraft in flying condition. The museum's collection includes a Boeing B-17 Flying Fortress, a Curtis P-40 Warhawk, a Fairchild C-119 Boxcar, and a ME-109 Messerschmitt. It also contains a PBY-6A Catalina, a Spitfire, a Stinson V-77, and a Vultee BT-13.

The National Warplane Museum's over 2,700 square foot visitors' center features educational displays and historical artifacts. Annual events include the "1941 Wings of Eagles" Air Show, held the third weekend in August, with over 100 WW II-vintage aircraft, and a fly-in breakfast in June that is open to the public. The museum is open seven days a week.

NEW YORK MUSEUM OF TRANSPORTATION

The New York Museum of Transportation is located between the New York State Thruway and Scottsville-Rush Road (Route 251) at 6393 East River Road in Rush. It can be reached by taking Exit 11 of the I-390 expressway, traveling west on Route 251, turning right onto East River Road, and proceeding one mile north.

The museum collection of trolley cars includes the Rochester and Eastern 157, a wooden inter-urban car, and a sweeper used to clear streetcar tracks. Displays depicting the transportation history of the Rochester area include manual pump-type handcars, a baggage cart, lanterns, and signs. The archives of the museum include photographs and records of highway, local transit, and railway history. The museum has assembled a notable gallery of photographs; it also presents video programs, including a color film of the Rochester Subway in 1956.

The museum is operated by volunteers, who also maintain a gift shop containing railroad books, magazines, and photographs. The New York Museum of Transportation, which charges a nominal admission fee, is open on Sundays. From mid-May until the end of October, four-mile round trip track car rides are offered between this museum and the Rochester & Genesee Valley Railroad Museum.

ROCHESTER & GENESEE VALLEY RAILROAD MUSEUM

The Rochester & Genesee Valley Railroad Museum, a 1909 Erie Railroad depot maintained by the Rochester Chapter of the National Historical Rail Society, is located at 282 Rush-Scottsville Road (Route 251), Rush. The museum can be reached by proceeding west on Route 251 for two and a half miles from Exit 11 of the I-390 Expressway.

The museum displays restored cabooses, freight cars, and passenger cars. Rail excursions are offered at selected times during the summer from Webster to East Williamson on New York Central tracks, and from Sodus to Newark. The museum, which charges a nominal admission fee, is open on Sundays from June through mid-October. It is available for special events and for large groups at other times by appointment.

TIRED IRON TRACTOR MUSEUM

The Tired Iron Tractor Museum in Cuylerville, three miles west of Geneseo, has the largest permanent collection of antique farm machinery in New York State. Examples of the "tired iron" in the museum are a 1919 Fiat tractor (the only complete one in the world), the 1922 model 1816 International tractor used in the movie *The Natural*, a 1925 American LaFrance fire truck, and a 1937 Linn half track. The collection also includes twenty-five pieces of horsedrawn equipment, 110 antique tractors, and 180 farm toys.

This trip through yesteryear is open on Saturdays and Sundays from May through November and by appointment.

WILLIAM PRYOR LETCHWORTH MUSEUM

The William Pryor Letchworth Museum, located in the Middle Falls area of Letchworth State Park near the Glen Iris Inn, contains a collection representing the Indian and pioneer history of the Genesee Valley. The Museum, built in 1912 to expand the original Genesee Valley Museum, also houses archeological and natural history displays. It is open seven days a week.

PLACES OF INTEREST

ABBEY OF THE GENESEE

The Abbey of the Genesee is located one mile north of Route 63 on River Road, west of Piffard. The abbey, founded in May, 1951, was the fourth monastic foundation to be made from the Abbey of Gethsemani in Kentucky. About forty monks live a daily round of prayers, readings, and manual work (such as farming) in an environment of simplicity, silence, and fraternity. The excellent Monks' Bread baked at the abbey is distributed at supermarkets throughout the region.

Liturgical prayer is celebrated by the abbey community seven times a day from vigils in the middle of the night to Compline in the early evening. Eucharist is celebrated daily, and there is ample time for solitary prayer. Several hours are set aside each day for reading and study in a private room, the library, or the surrounding forest.

The Benedictine way of life is lived at the abbey according to Cistercian / Trappist patrimony. The monks adhere to the ancient Charter of Charity, as interpreted by the constitution of the Cisterian Order of the Strict Observance.

Each year many visitors and retreatants are welcomed to the abbey. Retreats are given Monday afternoon until Friday morning and Friday afternoon until Sunday afternoon. Two houses, Bethany and Cana, are available for those who wish to make a semi-private retreat (October-May). Reservations are required for the retreats.

LOOKOVER STALLION STATION

Lookover Stallion Station, headquarters of the Genesee Valley Breeders Association, is located south of Avon on Route 39. This major center for horse breeding had its beginnings in a stud farm for hunting and steeplechase horses established by Mrs. Herbert Wadsworth in 1914. By the 1970s, the station had 4,000 acres used for horse farming, and a horse population of 2,000 valued at over $3,000,000.

Lookover Stallion Station raises standard breds and thoroughbreds for the racing industry that are marketed at sales such as New York's Old Glory Sale. Appaloosas, Morgans, quarter horses, and Shetlands are also raised on the station. Also, breeding mares are shipped in from outside the county for a stay of two to six months.

The Genesee Valley Breeders Association has produced many national champions-- hunters, jumpers, and show horses. Dexter, a trotter that broke the time record for the mile, is one of the most famous; he was the subject of a Currier and Ives engraving.

NEW YORK STATE FISH HATCHERY AT CALEDONIA

The New York State Fish Hatchery in Caledonia, established in 1870, was the first fish hatchery in the United States. The hatchery started as a private enterprise in 1864 by Seth Green of Rochester on property that he purchased on Spring Creek. Green had observed female salmon depositing fertilized eggs in prepared nests in Canada. It is a wasteful operation since the male salmon eats as many of the deposited eggs as he can find.

Although Green had not heard of the artificial propagation of fish, he experimented with propagation techniques in the Genesee River. He knew that his methods were more efficient than nature's techniques. Although artificial propagation of fish had been done for centuries in China and by two Frenchmen and a Prussian army officer, Green was the American pioneer. In 1864, he began to propagate hundreds of thousands of trout fry in his hatchery on Spring Creek.

Green was one of the first three commissioners of the New York State Fish Commission when it was created in 1866. The other two commissioners were Horatio

Seymour of Utica, who had served two terms as governor of New York State, and Robert B. Roosevelt, an uncle of Theodore Roosevelt. Green and Roosevelt collaborated on a book, *Fish Hatching and Fish Catching*. Green sold his private hatchery on Spring Creek to the state, and became the first New York State Superintendent of Fish Culture, a position that he held for the rest of his life.

Green began the state program with 80,000 eggs from thirteen lake trout from Lake Ontario, and with whitefish eggs from the St. Clair River near Detroit. He also propagated salmon and shad. By 1974, the New York State Department of Environmental Conservation stocked 7.4 million trout and salmon from sixteen state hatcheries. Trout were stocked along 4,400 miles of 1,100 streams and in 700 lakes and ponds.

Seth Green died in 1888. The Isaak Walton league placed a bronze plaque at the State Fish Hatchery at Caledonia commemorating him as the father of fish culture and as a "world famous pioneer in conservation." The Caledonia hatchery is open to visitors daily, and appointments may be made for group visits. Picnic tables and barbecue grills are provided on the grounds of the hatchery.

SALT MINE AT RETSOF

The salt mine at Retsof, in the Town of York, is located several miles west of Geneseo, off Route 63. The Retsof mine, owned by the Netherlands corporation, Akzo, N. V., is the largest rock salt mine in the western hemisphere. The mine, one thousand feet below the surface, is part of a salt bed that extends from the Province of Ontario to Virginia, and from Michigan to Syracuse, New York. The mine shafts were sunk through Onondaga limestone and dolomite about 500 to 600 feet below the surface, bounded above by four types of shale, Cardif, Skaneateles, Ludlowville, Marcellus, and below by two types, Camillus and Vernon.

The mine extends for 6,000 acres under three towns; it has over 300 miles of tunnels and passageways. Salt mines are safer than other mines; salt is neither flammable nor subject to explosion, and is not considered a health hazard. Approximately half of the salt mined by Akso is rock salt, and the other half is classified as "table salt." In addition to seasoning food, table salt is used in the manufacturing of blue dye and elastic, in oil drilling, and as a filler in cosmetics, household cleaners, laundry detergent, and toothpaste.

The mine was established by the Empire Salt Company in 1885. It was named by the first president of Empire Salt, William Foster; Retsof is Foster spelled backwards. One of the early shafts was sunk at Cuylerville, and was subsequently closed. Is is considered to be the haunt of the "blue lady." Many consider the phenomenon of the blue glow to be escaping methane gas; others claim to have see the ghost of a woman carrying a lantern in search of her husband, who lost his life in the mine.

Akzo N. V. bought the Diamond Crystal Salt Company in 1988, merged it with International Salt, and renamed the merged companies Akzo Salt. Akzo Salt is the largest salt company in the world. The mine is not open to visitors.

HISTORIC SITES

BOYD-PARKER MEMORIAL PARK

The Boyd-Parker Memorial Park, on Route 20A in Cuylerville, is a memorial to two scouts from General Sullivan's army who were captured by Seneca Indians near here in 1779. General Washington ordered Major General John Sullivan to destroy Iroquois villages and crops to discourage the Indian confederation from joining with the British and attacking the Continental Army from the west during the Revolutionary War. Lieutenant Boyd and Sergeant Parker were killed in the westernmost advance of Sullivan's army.

In their movement west, the army camped near the Indian village of Conesus at the southern end of Conesus Lake. General Sullivan detailed Lieutenant Boyd to take a small scouting party of five or six men and one Indian scout to the Indian village of Chenussio (near present day Cuylerville). It was located on the west side the Genesee River near where the Canaseraga Creek flows into the river. Boyd was directed to look for signs of Senecas preparing for a battle or setting an ambush; he was told to engage the enemy only to protect his scouting party.

Boyd, an ambitious officer who had distinquished himself at Otsego Lake, left camp with a light mounted company of twenty-eight men, including Sergeant Parker and two Indian scouts. Boyd and his scouting party proceeded to Chenussio, which means "the beautiful valley" in the Seneca language. Although Chenussio was a large village, there were few Indians there. Those that remained were preparing to leave, as the Iroquois had done all along the route of Sullivan's army. Boyd sent three of his men and one of the Indian scouts back to the main camp of the army with the information that no large body of the enemy was preparing to fight them.

On the way back to rejoin Sullivan's army at Consesus, Boyd's party encountered four Seneca braves near the small Indian village of Coshequa, between Chenussio and Conesus Lake. Boyd sent eight men, led by Private Timothy Murphy, an experienced Indian fighter, to capture or kill the four braves. They killed one and wounded one, but the other two helped the wounded brave to escape. Boyd disobeyed his orders in attacking the four braves; he made another poor decision by deciding to rest where they were, instead of returning to the main body of the army. Since the army was heading west, he intended to let the army catch up with him instead of returning to them.

Boyd's men sighted the three braves who had escaped from them; they were now being used to lead Boyd into an ambush. Indian leader Joseph Brant, Chief Big Tree, and three hundred braves had moved into the area from Canawaugus to fight Sullivan's army. They decided against it, because they were outnumbered; when they heard of Boyd's party of twenty-four men, they decided to attack them instead. Brant and Chief Big Tree had just watched Sullivan's men burn the Indian village at Conesus, and the young braves in their party were ready for revenge.

Boyd's party didn't have a chance; they were surprised and quickly surrounded. Fifteen men were killed immediately, and most of the men except Lieutenant Boyd and Sergeant Parker were killed. Only Private Murphy and a few others escaped to tell their story to General Sullivan. The Senecas captured Boyd and Parker, and took them to Chenussio. They were tortured, mutilated, and killed.

As General Sullivan traveled westward toward Chenussio, he was awed by expanse of the valley below him. He exclaimed to his aide that "this has to be considered as being one of the most beautiful places in all of America." Sullivan found the Indian village at Chenussio deserted. His men found the bodies of Boyd and Parker nearby. They buried them with full military honors alongside Little Beard's Creek. The next morning, Sullivan's men burned the village, destroyed the crops, and began their long march east.

Boyd-Parker Memorial Park is the site of the "torture tree," a large oak tree where the two scouts were tortured. The park, near Cuylerville, commemorates the deaths of Lieutenant Boyd and Sergeant Parker.

CLARA BARTON CHAPTER NO. 1, THE AMERICAN RED CROSS

The Chapter House of Clara Barton Chapter No. 1, the American Red Cross, is located at 57 Elizabeth Street in Dansville. The first two organizational meetings of the American Red Cross were held at the Dansville Presbyterian Church on August 7, 1881, and at St. Paul's Lutheran Church on August 22, 1881. After its organization, meetings were held in the Bastian Pharmacy, the Village Building, Dansville High School, and in rented space.

In 1949, the sons and daughter of Emma Hartman Noyes, a charter member of the chapter, donated her home and many of its furnishings to the chapter in her memory. The dining room became the production room, the library is the meeting room, and the music room serves as the office. The pantry is now the canteen. A large second-floor bedroom is used as a classroom for training in first aid, home nursing, and mother and baby care.

Many of the items of historical interest were presented by Saidee F. Riccius, a grandniece of Clara Barton.

The Clara Barton Chapter No. 1 Chapter House is open Monday through Friday. It also welcomes visitors on Saturday mornings, except during June, July, and August.

COUNCIL HOUSE IN LETCHWORTH STATE PARK

The Iroquois Council House was originally built at Canadea (Ga-o-ya-deo) prior to the Revolutionary War. Canadea was the Western Door of the Longhouse of the six nations of the Iroquois Confederation. The Council House was well built; the French assisted the Seneca Indians with its construction. All of the important councils of the Senecas, "Keepers of the Western Door," were conducted in the house, including the planning for the massacre at Wyoming, Pennsylvania. That attack and the massacre at Cherry Valley, New York, were the two incidents that motivated General Washington to order the Sullivan Campaign to remove the Indian threat to the Continental Army from the west in 1779.

The Council House, which was falling into disrepair, was purchased by William Letchworth in October, 1871. It was disassembled at Canadea, eighteen miles southwest of Letchworth State Park, and transported by canalboat on the Genesee Valley Canal to a point opposite the present council grounds on the plateau behind the Glen Iris Inn. The house was moved across the ice during the winter of 1872, and reassembled on the council grounds that spring. A new roof of shakes and withes (a tough, flexible twig, e.g. willow, used to bind things together) was installed at that time.

The Sign of the Cross is carved on one of the interior logs, and another log contains the totem of the Snipe Clan. Originally, the house contained no fireplace. The Senecas built their council fire in the center of the earthen floor, and the smoke exited through openings on the ridge of the roof. The plot of land at Canadea containing the Council House was purchased by Joel Seaton in 1830. Seaton built a fireplace and chimney at one end of the house. A new fireplace and chimney were built into the Council House to fill in the hole in the roof, when the house was reassembled at Letchworth State Park

Mr. Letchworth decided to have one last Indian Council in the Council House on the Genesee River on October 1, 1872. He invited the descendants of the Iroquois Nation to attend. Senecas came from the Allegany and Cattaraugus reservations, and Mohawks came from the Grand River area in Canada. This "Last Council on the Genesee," the only one in seventy years, was attended by Col. W. J. Simcoe Kerr, grandson of the Mohawk chief Captain Brant; Nicholson H. Parker, grandnephew of Chief Red Jacket; Thomas Jemison, descendent of Mary Jemison; and William Tallchief. The Senecas and Mohawks adopted Letchworth into the Wolf Clan as a blood brother, and gave him the Seneca name for "the man who always does the right thing." The Senecas performed their rite of high honor before twenty-one guests, including former President Millard Fillmore.

GRAVE SITE OF MARY JEMISON

Mary Jemison, the "white woman of the Genesee," was born in 1743 on the sailing vessel, *Mary and William*, enroute from Ireland to Philadelphia. Her parents, Thomas and Jane Jemison settled near Gettysburg, Pennsylvania. During the French and Indian War in 1758, the Jemison home was attacked by a party of six Indians and four Frenchmen. They killed and scalped the Jemison family and a visting family. Fifteen-year-old Mary Jemison was spared, but was carried off by the Indians.

The Indians traveled west to Fort Duquesne and down the Ohio River by canoe. Mary was placed in the keeping of two Seneca women who had lost a relative in battle. They adopted Mary as a sister, gave her Indian clothing to replace her tattered dress, and named her Deh-Ge-Wan-Us, which means "Two Falling Voices." Initially, she missed the society in which she was raised, but she adapted well to Indian life. She had numerous opportunities to leave her Indian captors in her lifetime, but she chose to remain with them. Eventually, her light skin and blonde hair were the only things that distinguished her from the other Indian women.

When she was seventeen, Mary's Indian sisters told her that, according to custom, she must marry Sheninjee, a Delaware chief. Their first child was a daughter who died in infancy. Their second child was a son, who was named Thomas for her father.

Mary's two Seneca sisters returned to their home at the Indian settlement at Little Beard's Town on the Genesee River. Sheninjee left on an extended hunting trip, and told Mary he would join her at Little Beard's Town. Mary set out on the long eastward journey carrying her nine-month-old son, Thomas. She was accompanied by two foster brothers.

Mary's first home in Genesee country was at Caneadea, described by the Senecas as the place "where the heavens lean against the earth." At the end of the long trek, Mary rejoined her Seneca sisters at Little Beard's Town, thirty-five miles north of Caneadea. The following spring, she heard that Sheninjee had been killed. Her second husband was Hiakatoo, a six-foot tall, sixty-year-old Seneca chief. In battle, Hiakatoo was ferocious. He had a reputation for brutality, but he was always kind to his twenty-four-year-old bride. Hiakatoo and Mary had six children, four daughters and two sons.

Hiakatoo went off to fight General Sullivan's army in 1779. Mary and her children left the village before it was destroyed by Sullivan's men. She moved to the Gardeau Flats, south of Little Beard's Town, and built a cabin. Gardeau, which is now part of

Letchworth State Park, was her home for the next fifty years. The Indians were kind to Mary; they gave her four acres of land at Gardeau for raising crops.

At the great Council of Big Tree in 1797, the Senecas settled their land claims with Robert Morris, the Financier of the Revolution. Mary told Thomas Morris, the son and agent of Robert Morris, that she had cultivated many areas in the Gardeau Flats; she requested that her tract be expanded. Morris thought he was giving away about 150 acres, but Mary became the owner of almost 18,000 acres (twenty-seven square miles) of scenic Genesee country. It was known as the Gardeau Tract.

Mary sold her land in the Genesee Valley in 1831, and moved to the Buffalo Creek reservation. She attended an Indian mission school, and converted to Christianity at the age of eighty-nine. Mary lived to the age of ninety-one. Her sons all met with violent deaths; her daughters cared for her in her old age. She was buried in the cemetery on the Buffalo Creek Reservation.

William Letchworth had her remains reinterred on the plateau near Glen Iris with an appropriate ceremony on March 7, 1874. A monument, sculpted by Henry K. Bush-Brown, was dedicated at Mary's grave site on September 10, 1910. The sculpture is of Mary as a young woman with a papoose on her back, as she looked on her trek back from Ohio. The cottage that Mary had built for her daughter, Nancy, was placed on the Council Grounds near the statue.

GENERAL WILLIAM MILLS MANSION

The Mills Mansion, at 14 Main Street in Mt. Morris, was built in 1838 by General William Mills. He was the first permanent white settler in Mt. Morris. Mills was a prosperous grain farmer who was instrumental in establishing Livingston County, which was formed from part of Ontario County. He was the first Mt. Morris town supervisor. During the War of 1812, Mills formed the first state militia for Livingston County and surrounding counties. He attained the rank of Major General.

At the age of sixty, he built the fourteen-room Federalist-style Mills Mansion. The mansion, a museum of 19th century artifacts, has an elegant cantilevered staircase with a double bannister and solid cherry doors between the two parlors. It features period rooms with Empire / Pillar and scroll furnishings, and has collections of costumes, needlework, textiles, Pink Lustre, and Spode. The kitchen has a large bake oven and an open hearth.

Susan Mills Branch purchased the house from her father's estate when he died in 1844. Her son, Carlton Branch, lived in the home until his death in 1923. Subsequently, the house was a single family dwelling, an apartment house, and a warehouse. In 1976, it was purchased by the Mt. Morris Rotary Club, who presented the deed to the Mt. Morris

Historical Society. The Historical Society began to restore the mansion in 1977; it was listed in the National Register of Historic Places in 1978. The Mills Mansion is open Friday, Saturday, and Sunday afternoons from June 1st to September 1st and by appointment.

RESTAURANTS--HISTORIC

AVON INN

The Avon Inn, established in 1820 on Main Street in Avon, is one of the oldest inns in western New York state. Jonathan Gerry contracted to build what is now the Avon Inn as his home, but lost his fortune and could not afford to have the work completed. Among other uses, it was utilized to store grain for ten years. In 1882, it was purchased by Cyrus Allen and James Carson, Jr., expanded to include a third floor and a west wing, and operated as a health sanatorium with mineral springs. It contained both a bank and a post office, and was a gathering place for social events. The health spa was converted to an inn and restaurant in 1912 by Frank Hovey. Visitors to the inn included Thomas Edison, Henry Ford, and Eleanor Roosevelt.

The Avon Inn was gutted by fire in 1979, but was restored. In 1984, it was registered as a State Historical Landmark. The Avon Inn has a country theme in every room. The main room is the Bridal Suite; there is a Bridal Hall of Fame on one wall of the dining room with photographs of couples who had a reception or a wedding at the inn. The earliest photographs were taken in 1904.

THE BIG TREE INN

The Big Tree Inn, located at 46 Main Street in Geneseo, was built in 1833 as the home of Allen and Bethia Ayrault. They called their home Big Tree Lodge, named for the huge American white oak tree that stood on the banks of the Genesee River, just south of the Village of Geneseo. The principal meeting place for the Seneca Indians and early settlers was under the giant oak tree. The enormous tree, which had a thirty-six-foot circumference, died when the 1858 flooding of the Genesee River eroded its root system.

The mansion was purchased in 1885 by James Wadsworth. He enlarged it to provide travelers with food and lodging, and renamed it the Big Tree Inn. The Big Tree Inn serves brunch, lunch, and dinner; it offers full service catering. The Federal-style inn has large meeting rooms that may be used for special occasions, such as business meetings and wedding receptions.

GLEN IRIS INN

The Glen Iris Inn is located near the southern end of Letchworth State Park, about half-way between the Castile and the Portageville entrances to the park. The inn includes guest rooms, a restaurant, and a gift shop; it is open from April through early November. The Pinewood Lodge, which is located a short distance from the inn, provides light housekeeping units. The mailing address of the inn is: Glen Iris Inn, Letchworth State Park, Castile, NY 14427.

Glen Iris was purchased by William Letchworth in 1859, when he bought 1,000 acres on both sides of the Genesee River. He named the house Glen Iris (Glen of the rainbow), because of the rainbow that arched over nearby Middle Falls. The Seneca Indians named the location An-de-ka-ga-kwa meaning "the place where the sun lingers."

Letchworth remodeled the house, planted 10,000 trees and shrubs, and built an arboretum on the estate for educational purposes. He spent $500,000 improving the estate. In planning the arboretum, he visited many arboretums around the world, including the Royal Botannical Gardens at Kew on the Thames River near London.

William Letchworth granted the estate's original 1,000 acres to the New York State in 1907. Glen Iris served as the administrative center for Letchworth State Park after the death of Mr. Letchworth. In 1914, The American Scenic and Historic Preservation Society enlarged the dining room, and added twelve bedrooms and four bathrooms.

WINERIES

EAGLE CREST VINEYARDS, INC. / O-NEH-DA WINERY

Eagle Crest Vineyards and the O-Neh-Da Winery is located at 7107 Vineyard Road, one half mile off Mission Road in Conesus-on-Hemlock. O-neh-da is the Seneca Indian word for hemlock. The O-Neh-Da Vineyard was founded in 1872 by Bishop Bernard J. McQuaid, the first Catholic Bishop of Rochester, when he purchased a 527-acre farm above Hemlock Lake as a vacation retreat. It was maintained as a working farm on which fruits and vegetables were grown, and dairy cows and sheep were tended.

He began the winery to supply his priests with wine for church services. Bishop McQuaid wrote to a fellow bishop: "When we are both put on the retired list, ... we can retire to the peaceful slopes of Hemlock Lake and, in the cultivation of the grape, amuse ourselves, and help believing priests to say Mass with wine that is wine." By 1905, the winery maintained eighty acres of grapes, and bottled 20,000 gallons of wine each year. The cellar, with two underground levels, was expanded to a capacity of 150,000 gallons.

Bishop McQuaid died in 1909, and the farm was bequeathed to St. Bernard's Seminary, which he had founded in 1893. His successor, Bishop Thomas F. Hickey, ran the farm and winery until 1924, when it became too much of a burden. Two factors contributed to the sale of the winery: the legal restrictions of prohibition and that "the vintners had not yet succeeded in correcting the sourness of O-Neh-Da wines." Strict Canon law prevented ameliorating (adding water to reduce the acid content), or adding sugar to altar wine if the natural sugar content of the grapes was low.

Bishop Hickey sold the operation to the Society of the Divine Word, a missionary order, for $40,000. The winery was closed during prohibition. Only twenty acres of the vineyard were still being cultivated when the winery was reopened in 1936. Leo Goering, trained in enology and viticulture at the Geisenheim Institute in Germany, was placed in charge of the operation. The society, owners of the nearby St. Michael's Seminary, refurbished the winery, and resumed making O-Neh-Da wines. Goering corrected the "sourness" problem of the wine, probably by adding grape concentrate with a high sugar content to the fermenting juice. Subsequently, the St. Michael's Seminary buildings were sold to the Church of the Restitution, a fundamentalist church.

In 1968, the winery operation was leased to Cribari Vineyards of Fresno, California, a vintner of altar wines nationally. By 1972, over one hundred acres of grapes were under cultivation, and a sufficient amount of altar wine was being produced to supply the clergy throughout the eastern United States. Other wine varieties were distributed to wine stores in Buffalo, Elmira, and Rochester.

Today, Michael Secretan, originally from London, England, owns and runs Eagle Crest Vineyards, Inc., which also bottles wine with the Barry Winery label. Barry labels include Chablis, Mellow Burgundy, and Rose' as well as the native varieties Niagara, Pink Niagara, and Pink Delaware. Barry Winery also makes a dark amber, nutty cream sherry.

Ninety percent of the output of Eagle Crest Vineyards, Inc., is altar or sacramental wine. For over a century, these wines have been "ecclesiastically approved by the Bishop of Rochester." O-Neh-Da labels include Angelica, Chalice White, Concord, Haute Sauterne, St. Michael's Red, St. Michael's Rose', Cream Sherry, and Pink Tokay. White and rose' altar wine are more popular than red, because they do not stain the purificator used to clean the chalice during Mass. The altar wines are sold directly to churches, are not taxed, and cannot be purchased or sampled by visitors to the winery.

The winery is located in a rustic setting. The wine tasting room is open year-round, on Monday through Friday. Group tours and weekend tastings can be arranged by appointment.

WEST OF THE LAKE--PERSONS

CLARA BARTON

Clarissa Harlowe Barton, founder of the American Red Cross, was born in North Oxford, Masachusetts, on December 25, 1821. She was the youngest of five children born to Stephen Barton, chief town administrator and state legislator, and Sally Stone Barton. Clarissa, who preferred to be called Clara, was raised somewhat as an only child, since the next youngest child, Sally, was twelve years older than she was.

Barton's favorite brother was David, who taught her to ride when she was three. In July of 1832, she saw her brother David fall feet-first from the ridge post of a barn onto a pile of timber in the cellar. He developed a chronic headache, and, as the summer progessed, he contracted a fever. The only treatment the doctors recommended was to "bleed" him, because the fever was due to his having "too much blood" that was "too vigorous" for his constitution.

Ten-year old Barton became her brother David's nurse. In her words:

> From the first days and nights of his illness, I remained near his side. I could not be taken away from him, except by compulsion, and he was unhappy until my return. I learned to take all the directions for his medicines from his physicians ... and to administer them like a genuine nurse. My little hands became schooled to the handling of the great loathsome, crawly leeches who at first were so many crawly snakes to me, and no fingers could so painlessly dress the angry blisters, and thus it came about that I was the accepted and acknowledged nurse of a man almost too ill to recover.

Two other doctors told the Bartons that their son's condition was hopeless. Barton cheered him up, fed him with a spoon, bathed him, and read to him. She rarely left his side for two years.

Finally, a new doctor, Dr. Asa McCullum, examined David. He was a believer in "hydrotherapy," who thought that bleeding a patient was not only unnecessary but harmful. He moved David to his sanatorium twenty miles from North Oxford, and began water therapy. He discontinued the bleeding and all of David's medications. David was able to return home in three weeks, and was fully recovered in six weeks. He owed his life to his little sister, who gave him constant care and the will to live long enough to see his cure.

Barton came from a long line of teachers, and, after passing an oral examination before a clergyman, a judge, and a lawyer, she taught school in North Oxford at the age of seventeeen. She was an excellent teacher, and was known for her discipline. After teaching for twelve years, she enrolled in the Clinton Liberal Institute to further her education. Upon completion of the program at Clinton, she accepted a teaching position in Bordentown, New Jersey.

She built the school up to an enrollment of 600 students, and the board of education decided that it was too large a school to be run by a woman. The young man that they brought in as her superior was very critical of her. Eventually the emotional strain took its toll. She lost her voice, almost had a nervous breakdown, and resigned her position in 1854, at the age of thirty-two.

Barton moved to Washington, D. C., to live with her sister Sally. She was hired by Charles Mason, the superintendent of the U. S. Patent Office, to copy documents. She worked at the Patent Office until 1857, when an appointee of the new Buchanan administration replaced Mason. She moved back to Massachusetts, and supported herself by copying documents sent to her in the mail. She returned to her job in Washington in 1860, when Abraham Lincoln began his administration.

At the beginning of the Civil War, Clara asked the Washington Infirmary if she could be of any help. She heard that the 6th Massachusetts regiment from Worchester had been attacked by a mob of Confederate symphathizers while traveling through Baltimore. Four men had been killed, dozens were wounded, and all of their baggage was stolen. They were dressed in winter uniforms and woolen underwear unsuitable for the spring and summer in Washington.

Clara used her own money to buy the men summer underwear, eating utensils, food, pots, and pans. She also contributed hankerchiefs, needles, soap, thread, and towels. She advertised in *The Worchester Spy*, their hometown newspaper, that she would receive and distribute provisions for area servicemen. She received so many items that she had to ask the army quartermaster to find a warehouse for them. During 1862, she never had less than five tons of material in the warehouse.

Following the first disastrous Battle of Bull Run, Clara found that little had been done to provide medical care for the wounded. They weren't treated, and they were left without food or water. She encountered resistance when she offered her services as a nurse. In the 1860s, women weren't considered to be strong enough to deal with conditions at the front. Sense of propriety was an issue.

She returned home briefly to nurse her dying father, who told her: "I know soldiers, and they will respect your errand." Upon her return to Washington, she received the long-awaited permission from Dr. William Hammond, Surgeon-General of the U. S.: "Miss C. H. Barton has permission to go upon the sick transports in any direction--for the purpose of distributing comforts for the sick and wounded--of nursing them, always subject to the direction of the surgeon in charge."

She was introduced to battlefield nursing at the Battle of Cedar Run in Virginia. She arrived with a wagon load of supplies just as Brigade Surgeon James Dunn was addressing the dilemma of treating the wounded without supplies. He called her "the Angel of the Battlefield," a name that stayed with her. Her second battlefield service was dealing with the staggering casualties of the Second Battle of Bull Run in August of 1862.

At the Battle of Chantilly, she was up three nights in a row; she managed to get two hours of sleep on the fourth night, while lying in water from the heavy rains. On the way back to Washington, the train carrying the wounded was almost captured by the Confederate cavalry, who burned the station from which they had just departed.

At Antietam, when she arrived with supplies that were vitally needed, brigade surgeon Dunn was using corn husks for bandages. While she was giving a glass of water to a wounded soldier, a bullet passed through her sleeve, and the soldier fell back dead. Another soldier asked her to use his pocket knife to remove a musket ball from his cheek; he couldn't wait his turn for the surgeon. With a sergeant holding the wounded soldier's head, she removed the ball.

In the last year of the Civil War, Barton was superintendent of nurses for General Benjamin Butler's Army of the James. She organized hospitals and their staffs, and supervised their administration from Point of Rocks, near Petersburg, Virginia. After the war, she worked to find information on soldiers who were missing in action. As with her nursing jobs, she worked without pay. In four years, she located over 22,000 missing soldiers; finally, she was paid $15,000 by the government for her efforts. From 1866 until 1868, she went on the lecture circuit; she sometimes shared billing with Samuel Clemens and Ralph Waldo Emerson. She delivered 300 lectures during 1867 and 1868. One evening in 1868, she attempted to deliver her lecture, and found that she had lost her voice. Just like in 1856 in Bordentown, she was on the verge of a nervous breakdown.

She traveled to Europe to rest, and stayed with friends in Switzerland. Dr. Louis Appia of the Red Cross sought her out. He knew of her work during the Civil War, and asked her why the United States had rejected his offer three times to join the International Red Cross. Barton had not heard of the organization founded by Jean-Henri Dunant.

Dunant had witnessed the bloody Battle of Solferino, with 40,000 casualties, between Austria and a French-Italian alliance. He wrote *A Memory of Solferino* in which he proposed the formation of an international relief organization. The Swiss-based organization chose a red cross on a white background--the reverse of the design of the Swiss flag. Barton, who was influenced by what Dunant had started in Europe, began to think of a relief organization for the United States.

Barton received a visit from the Grand Duchess Louise of Baden, daughter of King Wilhelm I of Prussia, just after the start of the Franco-Prussian War. Louise asked her to organize the relief effort. Part of Barton's work was centered in Strasbourg, where she developed one of her relief concepts--rehabilitation. The people of Strasbourg were paid to rebuild their city, and she hired several hundred women to make much-needed clothing for an impoverished populace. She returned the people's self-respect to them by helping them to help themselves. They showed their appreciation by bringing her a large Christmas tree laden with candles for her 50th birthday on December 25, 1871.

Barton returned to the United States in 1873, and spent the next four years convalescing from a nervous disorder that caused migraine headaches and periods of blindness. She moved to Dansville, New York, in March 1876, to improve her health at a sanitorium called "Our Home on the Hillside." After a year's rest and wholesome food in a peaceful environment, Clara completely regained her health. She liked Dansville, and made many close friends. She bought a home there, and lived in Dansville for ten years.

While in Dansville, she began to work to bring the United States into the International Red Cross. She found that the principal reason the the U. S. didn't want to join the international organization was that it was viewed as a relief organization for wartime only. Clara began to push for its utilization in peacetime disasters as well, such as earthquakes and floods.

She went to Washington to talk with President Garfield's cabinet. However, President Garfield was assassinated in the summer of 1881, and Barton was faced with convincing a new administration of the importance of her cause.

Upon her return to Dansville, the people asked her to help form a local chapter of the Red Cross. The first American chapter of the Red Cross was established in Dansville on August 22, 1881. The first need addressed by the chapter was a forest fire in Michigan that took 500 lives and destroyed 1,500 homes. On March 16, 1882, Congress signed the Treaty of Geneva, making the U. S. a member of the International Red Cross. Barton, now sixty years old, was named the first president of the American Red Cross. She held the position until May, 1904. Barton died on April 12, 1912, in Washington, D.C.

WILLIAM LETCHWORTH

William Pryor Letchworth, businessman, conservationist, and philanthropist, was born in 1823 near Watertown, New York. His parents, Josiah Letchworth and Ann Hance Letchworth, also lived in Moravia and in Sherwood, both in Cayuga County, while he was growing up. Letchworth's first job, when he was fifteen, was as an apprentice for the Hayden and Homes saddlery hardware business in Auburn.

Hayden and Homes were both importers and manufacturers, and they dealt with retail and wholesale trade. In 1845, the firm sent Letchworth to New York City for further training in the business. Upon his return to Auburn in 1848, he was named a partner in an old, highly regarded Buffalo company, Pratt and Company. The firm was reorganized, and renamed Pratt and Letchworth. They, too, were importers and manufacturers, and served both retail and wholesale customers. They employed between 500 and 800 men, and owned all of the stock in an iron manufacturing company.

After six years with Pratt and Letchworth, and sixteen years of long work weeks, little social life, and no vacations, the toll on Letchworth's health began to show. His brother Josiah had joined the firm, and was able to shoulder the detail burdens of the job. Letchworth took a well-deserved vacation in Florida in 1854. In 1857, his interests broadened into art, literature, and social activities; he traveled to Europe for the first time. Upon his return from Europe, his brother, George, who had been with Hayden and Homes, joined Pratt and Letchworth.

Letchworth's first view of the Genesee River Gorge was in the spring of 1858, from the Portage railroad bridge spanning the gorge. He was considering buying a place in the country, and had searched for property in the Niagara Falls area. A friend suggested the Genesee River Valley to him. It was love at first sight; the scenic, peaceful forests with the mild roaring backdrop of Middle Falls captivated him. He felt tired at thirty-five, so he resolved to buy the area, and to establish a country home.

In February, 1859, his purchase offer to nine landowners for 200 acres was accepted. Instead of tearing down the homestead on the property, he remodeled it, and renamed it Glen Iris (Glen of the rainbow). Over the next fifty years, Letchworth spent $500,000 on landscaping. He purchased land in addition to his original 200 acres to protect the gorge and all three waterfalls--upper, middle, and lower--and to safeguard the property from utility companies, particularly the Genesee River Company. During the Civil War, he purchased an additional 500 acres. He had the foresight to place his estate under the jurisdiction of the American Scenic and Historic Preservation Society. Otherwise, the public might not have Letchworth State Park to enjoy today.

Letchworth announced his plans to retire from Pratt and Letchworth when he was forty-seven. In 1871, he sold his interest in the firm to his brother, Josiah, and retired at the end of the year. He declined a nomination to run for congress, but accepted an appointment as the Commissioner of the State Board of Charities. Other examples of his work in social reform were his support for the Craig Colony for Epileptics at Sonyea, Letchworth Village (a home for retarded children in Rockland County), and Industry, a detention home for boys near Avon.

In 1872, he had one of the remaining Seneca Buildings, the Council House at Caneadea, disassembled and reassembled near Glen Iris. He held the "Last Council of the Genesee" there, with dignitaries including ex-president Fillmore and American Indian representatives in attendance. The bronze statue of Mary Jemison, the "white woman of the Genesee" was unveiled near Glen Iris in September, 1910.

Letchworth died in December, 1910, and was buried in Forest Lawn Cemetery in Buffalo. His 1,000-acre estate had been deeded to the State of New York on December 31, 1906, and named Letchworth State Park. We can thank William Letchworth for preserving one the most scenic areas in the eastern United States. Letchworth provided proof that one person can make a difference.

JOHN WESLEY POWELL

John Wesley Powell, explorer of the Grand Canyon, was born in Mt. Morris on March 24, 1834. Powell was the son of the Reverend Joseph Powell, a Methodist minister, and Mary Powell, who had both emigrated from England in 1830 to spread the word of Methodism in America. In 1833, they supervised the construction of the first Methodist Church in Mt. Morris. The Powells moved from Mt. Morris to Ohio and Wisconsin. In his teenage years, Powell managed the family farm and taught school to earn college tuition money. He earned a degree in botany and zoology, and accepted a teaching position at Hennepin, Illinois.

He enlisted as a private with the 20th Illinois at the outbreak of the Civil War, and was commissioned second lieutenant a month later. He was wounded at the Battle of Shiloh, and his right forearm was amputated. He continued to serve with distinction at the Battles of Atlanta, Chattanooga, Meridian, Nashville, and Vicksburg. At the end of the war he was a brevet Lieutenant Colonel and Chief of Artillery of the Army of the Tennessee.

In 1865, he became a professor of geology at Illinois Wesleyan University at Springfield, Illinois. He advocated a balanced approach to learning by supplementing textbook learning with field trips. In 1867, he led a group of students on an expedition of the Rocky Mountains to collect specimens for museums, and to make topological measurements for the Smithsonian Institution. The trip was financed by an endowment from the state legislature for the Museum of the Illinois Natural History Society.

An expedition during the summer of 1869 made him a national figure. He traveled by boat down the Green River Valley and the Colorado River Valley to the Virgin River, just beyond the Grand Canyon in Arizona. Powell led a team of ten men in four small boats through the largest unknown region of the United States. His goal was to study the geology and geography of the canyons of the Green River and the Colorado River. He formed new concepts of drainage and erosion that became the foundation for "new geology," now called geomorphology.

Three men of the party became concerned with dwindling food rations on the trip, and decided to set out on their own. The men left the Powell expedition at Separation Rapids; they climbed to a plateau, where they were killed by the Indians. The remaining seven men successfully completed the expedition south of the Grand Canyon. The expedition made Powell a public figure. The combination of his war record, the hardships of the journey, the loss of three men killed by the Indians, and the public's fascination with the exploration of the West, made Powell a national hero.

The expedition made periodic determinations of altitude, latitude, and longitude, collected fossils, and sampled rock formations, but little scientific information was gained from the expedition. However, Powell's paper, *New Tracks in North America*, displayed his understanding of the interrelationship of erosion, uplift, vegetation, and water. He was eager to make another expedition to collect more scientific data.

A second expedition of the Colorado River Valley, sponsored by the Department of the Interior, was undertaken in 1871-72. Powell concentrated on the study of the regional geology, and the formulation of concepts about the interaction of land, water, people, and social institutions. Powell wrote monographs about his expeditions: *Geology of the Uinta Mountains* (1876), *Introduction to the Study of the Indian Language* (1877), and *Report on the Lands of the Arid Region* (1878).

Powell's recommendations led to the establishment of the United States Geological Survey in 1879. He initiated the establishment of the Bureau of American Ethnology of the Smithsonian Institution in the same year. Powell served as director of both agencies from 1881 to 1894. His interest in the development of the western lands led to the establishment of the Bureau of Reclamation.

In 1888, Powell helped found two societies for the advancement of science, the National Geographic Society and the Geological Society of America. Also, he was president of the American Association for the Advancement of Science that year. Powell died on September 23, 1902 at Haven, Maine. He was buried at Arlington National Cemetery.

High Falls and downtown Rochester

TABLE OF CONTENTS

CHAPTER 2

ROCHESTER: THE WESTERN GATEWAY

I. Rochester: The Western Gateway--Introduction
    A. Rochester: The Western Gateway--Description ... 59
    B. Rochester: The Western Gateway--Brief History ... 60

II. Rochester: The Western Gateway--Things ... 62
    A. Items of Interest ... 62
        1. Eastman School of Music Concert Series ... 62
        2. Ellwanger Garden ... 62
        3. Geva Theatre ... 62
        4. Lamberton Conservatory ... 63
        5. Rochester Americans Hockey Team ... 64
        6. Rochester Philharmonic Orchestra ... 65
        7. Rochester Red Wings Baseball Team ... 66

    B. Legends and Stories ... 66
        1. The Legend of Onnolee ... 66
        2. Rattlesnake Pete's Museum ... 67
        3. Sam Patch ... 68
        4. The Story of the Galvanized Tubs ... 69
        5. The Technology That Nobody Wanted ... 69
        6. William Morgan and the Masons ... 70

    C. Parks, Forests, and Trails ... 72
        1. Black Creek Park ... 73
        2. Braddock Bay Fish and Wildlife Management Area ... 73
        3. Churchville Park ... 73
        4. Durand-Eastman Park ... 73
        5. Ellison Park ... 74
        6. Genesee Valley Greenway ... 74
        7. Genesee Valley Park ... 74
        8. Genesee Valley Park West ... 75
        9. Hamlin Beach State Park ... 75
        10. Highland Park ... 76
        11. Lower Falls Park ... 76
        12. Manhattan Square Park ... 77
        13. Maplewood Park ... 77
        14. Maplewood Rose Garden Park ... 77
        15. Mendon Ponds Park ... 78
        16. Northampton Park ... 78
        17. Ontario Beach Park ... 78
        18. Powder Mills Park ... 79
        19. Seneca Park ... 79
        20. Webster Park ... 79
                                                80

    D. Shows and Festivals ... 80
        1. Clothesline Festival ... 80

CHAPTER 2

ROCHESTER: THE WESTERN GATEWAY

> Could I a beauty-sketching pencil wield
>> With all the witchery and magic skill
>> Of Gilbert's fingers I'd a picture fill
> With beauties of fair Rochester. What field
> Of Art could purer fascination yield?
>> I'd paint the "Flower City" growing still
>> From early germ near "Indian Allan's mill."
> The plant was set by men of whose faith revealed
> The trend of civic progress to their view.
>> They had persistent faith to work and wait;
> They nurtured well, aye, better than they knew:--
>> A wildwood region by auspicious fate
> From "Flour" to "Flower" and then ... grew--
>> The pride and glory of New York State.

Sonnet by Helen E. Lucas

ROCHESTER: THE WESTERN GATEWAY--INTRODUCTION

ROCHESTER: THE WESTERN GATEWAY--DESCRIPTION

Rochester, originally called the "Flour City" because of its flour mills at the waterfalls on the Genesee River, became known as the "Flower City" for its many flower nurseries. Contemporary Rochester is called the "World's Image Center" because it is home to the University of Rochester's Institute of Optics, Rochester Institute of Technology's College of Imaging Arts and Sciences, and over ninety imaging and optics firms, including Bausch & Lomb, Eastman Kodak, and Xerox. The imaging industry employs 100,000 people in the Rochester region; half of the U.S. workers who manufacture photographic equipment and supplies work in the area.

Rochester is located in Monroe County south of Lake Ontario, where the Genesee River empties into the lake. The city extends along the lower Genesee River to the Port of Rochester on Lake Ontario. Rochester has three exits from the New York State Thruway, Exits 45, 46, and 47, and an inner loop and an outer loop of expressways encircling the city. The City of Rochester has a population of 231,636 people, according to the 1990 census; the twenty Monroe County suburban towns have a population of 482,332, for a total Monroe County population of 713,968 people.

Rochester is ranked 66th in population of U. S. cities and is the 39th largest U.S. metropolitan area. The city has excellent medical facilites, and rates high nationally in health care. Area colleges include Monroe Community College, Nazareth College of Rochester, Roberts Wesleyan College, Rochester Institute of Technology, St. John Fisher College, State University of New York--College at Brockport, and University of Rochester. The county has an outstanding park system. Including village, town, city, county, and state parks, there are 119 parks in Monroe County.

Rochester has a nationally-ranked symphony orchestra, the Rochester Philharmonic Orchestra, and the top-ranked Eastman School of Music of the University of Rochester. Also, Rochester has a wealth of museums, including the Eastman House International Museum of Photography, the Memorial Art Gallery, Rochester Museum and Science Center, Strasenburgh Planetarium, and Strong Museum. The city is home to the American Hockey League Rochester Americans hockey team and the International League Rochester Red Wings Triple-A baseball team.

ROCHESTER: THE WESTERN GATEWAY--BRIEF HISTORY

Ebenezer "Indian" Allan, who settled near Scottsville in 1786, was the first settler in Monroe County. Oliver Phelps, land agent for the Phelps-Gorham Purchase, promised the Indians that he would have a grist mill and a saw mill built at one of the Genesee falls. He offered Allan 100 acres to fulfill that pledge. The mills were operating by November of 1789, just west of the present location of the Court Street Bridge. Among the next settlers were Israel and Simon Stone, who cleared land in Pittsford, sowed wheat, and convinced five families of their old neighbors to join them in 1791. Orringh Stone built a home and tavern, the Stone-Tolan House, on East Avenue about 1790.

Indian Allan sold his 100-acre tract in 1792, and his mills fell into disrepair. One of them was carried away in a flood. In 1803, three men from Maryland bought the 100-acre Allan property for $17.50 per acre. Nathaniel Rochester and his partners, Charles Carroll and William Fitzhugh, had a profound influence on an evolving Rochester. Hamlet Scrantom, from Lewis County, was the first settler on Colonel Rochester's 100-acre tract. Colonel Rochester petitioned the state to incorporate the settlement as a county in 1817. The state legislature rejected the petition, but granted a charter for the Village of Rochesterville. Finally, Monroe County, named for President James Monroe, was formed on February 23, 1821.

Rochester's second grist mill was built at Middle Falls in 1807. It burned in 1818, and the Phoenix Mill was built on its foundation. Phoenix Mill was one of the large flour mills that contributed to Rochester's reputation as the "Flour City."

The excavation for the Erie Canal began near Rome, New York, in 1817. The canal reached Busnell's Basin by 1821, and that village served as the temporary western terminus until 1823. The canal was finished in 1825, when the complex, multi-level locks at Lockport were completed. An 802-foot long aqueduct carried the Erie Canal over the Genesee River at Broad Street. The completion of the Erie Canal made Rochester, which had an 1825 population of 5,000, a boom town. Wheat flour was one of the principal Rochester area products that were shipped via the Erie Canal; corn was another. Rochester shipped 200,000 barrels of flour in 1826.

In 1834, Rochester, with a population of 12,000, received its city charter from the state legislature. Laying of railroad track was completed between Rochester and Batavia in 1837, and by 1842 it was possible to cross the state by rail. Ultimately, twenty-one flour mills along the Genesee River ground 500,000 barrels of flour each year. The first Rochester nursery and seed farm, Mt. Hope Nurseries, was established in 1834 by Patrick Barry and George Ellwanger.

By 1850, Rochester was the fourth largest city in the state, and had a population of 51,000. By the 1850s, over 4,000 acres of land in the suburbs were planted with flowers, shrubs, and trees. The area supplied almost half of the U.S. commercially produced trees by the 1870s and 1880s.

Susan B. Anthony began her participation in the Women's Rights Movement in 1851; she was arrested for voting in the 1872 presidential election, decades before women won the right to vote. Frederick Douglass, editor of the *North Star*, was a leader in the anti-slavery movement. Clothing and shoe manufacturing moved into the area, and Cyrus McCormick's reapers manufactured in Brockport revolutionized the agriculture industry in the late 1800s.

John Bausch and Henry Lomb began their partnership in the Reynolds Arcade, the same location in which Hiram Sibley planned the combining of many small, competing telegraph companies to form the Western Union. In 1878, George Eastman, a young bank clerk, founded the Eastman Dry Plate Company, which was the forerunner of the Eastman Kodak Company. The Haloid Company was founded at the turn of the century, and expanded rapidly once office copiers were introduced in volume in the early 1960s. It became the Xerox Corporation in 1961.

ROCHESTER: THE WESTERN GATEWAY--THINGS

ITEMS OF INTEREST

EASTMAN SCHOOL OF MUSIC CONCERT SERIES

The Eastman School of Music Concert Series is an outstanding series of concerts that is open to the public. Many of the concerts are free, admission is nominal to many other concerts, and the ticket price for the remainder is modest. Some of the concerts are in the Eastman Theatre, but most of them are in the adjacent 459-seat Kilbourn Hall, a performance hall with excellent acoustics. Representative of their offerings are:

ORCHESTRAS--Eastman Philharmonia, Eastman School Symphony Orchestra, and the Graduate Chamber Orchestra

CHAMBER MUSIC--Brass Chamber Ensembles, Chamber Percussion Ensemble, Contemporary Percussion Ensemble, Eastman Chamber Orchestra, Woodwind Quintets, Intermusica, and Musica Nova

JAZZ ENSEMBLES--Eastman Chamber Jazz Ensemble, Eastman Jazz Ensemble, Eastman New Jazz Ensemble, Eastman Studio Orchestra, and Saxology

OPERA AND CHORAL--Eastman Chorale, Eastman Opera Theatre, and Eastman Studio Theatre

In addition, there are Eastman-Ranlet Concerts, Faculty Artist Concerts, the Kilbourn Concert Series, Wind Ensemble Concerts, the World Music Series, and special offerings.

ELLWANGER GARDEN

Elwanger Garden, located at 625 Mt. Hope Avenue in Rochester, contains noteworthy collections of perennials, roses, and trees. The garden, a living museum, has been cultivated continuously since 1867 by the family of one of Rochester's most prominent horticulturists, George Ellwanger. It represents an historic period landscape.

GEVA THEATRE

GeVa Theatre, located at 75 Woodbury Boulevard, brings major city theatre to mid-sized Rochester. Although most of the actors, designers, and directors are from New York, Chicago, and Los Angeles, all of the work on costumes and scenery and all of the theatre's artistic work, including the selection of plays, is done in Rochester for the region's audiences. The theatre offers five plays each season. In addition, *A Christmas Carol* is staged each year from Thanksgiving through the Christmas season. GeVa has been gracing the Rochester stage since 1973.

The building that houses the Geva Theatre was built in 1868 as the Naval Militia Armory, home of the 54th Regiment. The initial role of the naval militia was to protect the Erie Canal from foreign invasion, a mission that became less relevant over the years. The armory was used more for conventions and shows than for military purposes. It was renamed Convention Hall in 1908. Enrico Caruso, Jascha Heifetz, Anna Pavlova, and Sergei Rachmaninoff all performed at Convention Hall. Franklin D. Roosevelt was nonimated for governor in the hall. The Great Depression reduced the need for Convention Hall; it was used by the welfare department in 1936, and eventually was closed. GeVa petitioned the State Division of Historic Preservations for Landmark status for the armory in 1982. They refurbished the building, and established a world-class 500-seat theatre.

The Backstage Bistro offers dinners in a theatre setting up to one hour before curtain. Reservations are required. Also, a light-fare menu is available in the cabaret. The Gift Shop offers threatre-related gifts one hour prior to each performance, during intermission, and after each performance. GeVa welcomes group tours by appointment. GeVa Theatre is accessible to the handicapped; wheelchair accommodations are available upon request.

LAMBERTON CONSERVATORY

Lamberton Conservatory, located at 180 Reservoir Avenue in Highland Park, was built in 1911 and renovated in 1987-88. Informational handouts are available in the Visitor Center, which has a large map displayed of the conservatory and the park. Drinking fountains, a public telephone, and restrooms are located in the Visitor Center.

The Courtyard Garden, accessible only from inside the conservatory, provides a protected area for growing special plant materials. Waterlilies and other submerged plants are grown in the rectangular pool in the center of the courtyard. The Lamberton Conservatory has six plant display areas:

THE SEASONAL DISPLAY HOUSE--the most colorful area in the conservatory. The show is changed five times a year. It features the following plants:

o Spring--azaleas, daffodils, tulips

o Summer--fuchsia, hydrangeas, lantana

o Fall--chrysanthemums

o Holiday display--poinsettias

o Mid-winter--calceolarias, cinerarias, cyclamen

EPIPHYTES, ORCHIDS, FERNS, AND EXOTICS--including birds nest fern, bromeliads, creeping fig, cut-leaf philodendron, ferns, orchids, spanish moss, and staghorn fern. Ephiphytes, plants that live upon (epi-) other plants (-phytes), require warm and humid conditions. Some ferns and many bromeliads and orchids are epiphytic.

THE TROPICAL FOREST--has plants such as baby tears, banana "tree," Benjamin tree, golden bamboo, Indochinese grape-ivy, shrimp plant, and snowflake tree. It is a combination of groundcovers, vines, medium-sized plants, and tall trees. The observation platform in the Tropical Forest gives visitors a view the foliage from above. Being above the foliage permits visitors to appreciate the various leaf shapes and colors.

DESERT ENVIRONMENT--including bunny ears cactus, carrion flower (star flower), century plants, cinnamon cactus, crown of thorns, and old man cactus. The Desert Environment display is separated into two areas with representative plants from the New World (cacti) and the Old World (euphorbias). Special adaptations of these plants that allow them to withstand dry conditions are lack of leaves, shape that minimizes surface to help prevent water loss, and waxy protective coating.

ECONOMIC PLANTS--those that furnish us with various usable products. Banana, mango, olive, passionvine, and pineapple provide us with fruit. Agave and sansevieria give us fibers; bay and ginger yield flavorings. Other economic plants are aloe, cassava, the coffee tree, and the macadamia nut.

HOUSEPLANTS--including lesser known plants, such as goldfish plant, pleomele, pony tail palm, and syngonium. These plants can tolerate the less than ideal growing conditions that exists in most houses. Some plants, spathiphyllum for example, will even flower in low light. Certain groups of plants, such as begonias and peperomias, are available in many different forms.

The Lamberton Conservatory is open Wednesday through Sunday year-round. Smoking is not allowed. No admission fee is charged, but donations are welcomed.

ROCHESTER AMERICANS HOCKEY TEAM

The American Hockey League (AHL) Rochester Americans, an affiliate of the Buffalo Sabres of the National Hockey League, play at the Rochester War Memorial, located at 100 Exchange Boulevard. Professional hockey was established in Rochester on July 2, 1956, when the Americans joined the American Hockey League. Local ownership of the Rochester Americans began in 1966. The affiliation with the Buffalo Sabres, who purchased the team in 1982, began in 1979.

Rochester has many avid hockey fans. The average attendance is about 6,000, whereas the average attendance at AHL games is approximately 4,000. The annual attendance at "Amerk" games is about 250,000. The Americans have won many Calder Cup championships, and they have the winningest percentage of all active AHL members at .5392, with 1362 wins, 1150 losses, and 297 ties. The "Amerks" bring exciting hockey to Rochester, and earn the support of the community.

ROCHESTER PHILHARMONIC ORCHESTRA

The Rochester Philharmonic Orchestra was established in the 1922-23 season, the first season of the 3,094-seat Eastman Theatre. The Rochester Philharmonic Orchestra, Inc., the corporation that supports the performing ensemble, was formed in 1930 as "The Rochester Civic Music Association." The Rochester Philharmonic Orchestra has always had a "core orchestra," which at the present time has fifty-nine members. At various times, the core orchestra has been augmented with part-time professional musicians, creating larger orchestras of varying sizes for a range of purposes.

The Rochester Philharmonic Orchestra (RPO) has always been a separate organization from the Eastman School of Music of the University of Rochester, both administratively and financially. Areas of cooperation have always existed, but with different missions-- one to "conduct concerts of an educational character" and "to conduct public programs," and the other to educate and train musicians.

From the time of its founding, the RPO has been committed to bringing music to all segments of the community. George Eastman's purpose in founding the orchestra was to ensure that all of Rochester had access to the great music of the world. Almost one third of the concerts of the RPO are related to education. Tens of thousands of Rochester's young people have access to the RPO's educational programs each year without charge.

The RPO has been fortunate to have many fine music directors, including Jose Iturbi, Eric Leinsdorf, David Zinman, and Mark Elder. Conductors and principal guest conductors have included Guy Fraser Harrison, Fritz Reiner, and Jerzy Semkow.

The educational programming of the orchestra has had a laudable history. The RPO has given high school concerts since 1929 and elementary school concerts since 1962. The Rochester Philharmonic Youth Orchestra has performed since 1970.

The Rochester Pops Orchestra is an augmented orchestra formed by adding five to fifteen part-time professional musicians to the RPO core orchestra, usually with a popular music or jazz background, to perform lighter programs. The summer home of the RPO is the Finger Lakes Performing Arts Center near Canandaigua.

The RPO brings world-class music, normally enjoyed only by the residents of major cities, to mid-sized Rochester. George Eastman had some thoughts on the subject of music that are still relevant today: "It is necessary for people to have an interest in life outside of an occupation ... What you do in your working hours determines what you have. What you do in your leisure hours determines what you are." Attending an RPO concert never fails to be an uplifting experience. The Rochester region is extremely fortunate to have an asset like the Rochester Philharmonic Orchestra.

ROCHESTER RED WINGS BASEBALL TEAM

The Rochester Red Wings, the Triple-A International League affiliate of the Baltimore Orioles, play in the 12,503-seat Silver Stadium at 500 Norton Street. The Red Wings have been associated with the Baltimore Orioles for thirty-four years, which is the longest affiliation between a triple-A minor league team and a major league team in baseball history. In 1993, attendance was 381,061, the second-highest in franchise history. The Red Wings have won nine Governor's Cups.

Bob Gibson, Stan Musial, and Jim Palmer are Major League Hall of Famers who have played for the Red Wings. Other former Red Wings include Don Baylor, Bobby Grich, Edddie Murray, "Boog" Powell, and Cal Ripken. Jr. General Manager Joe Altobelli managed two Red Wings teams to Governor's Cups. He was the National League Manager of the year with the San Franciso Giants in 1978. Also, he was named American League Manager of the year in 1983, when he guided the Baltimore Orioles to the World Series championship.

The Red Wings were an affiliate of the St. Louis Cardinals until 1961, when they began their association with Baltimore. The ballpark has been known as Silver Stadium since August 19, 1968, when it was dedicated in honor of Morrie Silver. Silver led the effort to keep professional baseball in Rochester. The largest attendance at 500 Norton Street was 19,006 on May 5, 1931.

An afternoon or evening at the ballpark is a good family pastime. Parking areas are designated for handicapped individuals, and there is wheelchair access behind the home plate screen. Handicapped seating can be reserved.

LEGENDS AND STORIES

THE LEGEND OF ONNOLEE

The legend of Onnolee predates the time that the Seneca Indians dominated the country just south of Rochester. Between 1350 and 1375, a small tribe of friendly Indians, the Munsees, lived in the area. They were surrounded by the Mengwees. The Mengwees were a warlike tribe, but the two tribes lived in peace. However, one night the Mengwees attacked the Munsees without warning, and annihilated them. Onnolee, whom some said was a maiden and others said was the wife of the bravest chief, was the only survivor. She was bound to the red belt of Mickinac, a Mengwee chief, and carried off.

At noon the following day, they rested at a spreading oak to eat their mid-day meal. While Mickinac was eating, Onnolee grabbed his knife from his belt, and swiftly buried it in his side. The young squaw knew that her life was forfeited, but she ran as fast as she

66

could while arrows whizzed by her from all directions. She reached a craggy bluff overlooking a small lake, and according to W. H. C. Hosmer:

> Regardless of the whizzing storm
> of missiles raining round her form,
> Imploring eye she then upcast,
> And a low, mournful death hymn sang;
> On hill and forest looked her last,
> One glance upon the water cast,
> And from that high rock sprang.

It is said that for over three hundred years after her leap into the lake and her death, the form of the once beautiful Onnolee could be seen rising out of the lake in the still of a summer night, and either disappearing into the sky or returning to her watery home.

RATTLESNAKE PETE'S MUSEUM

"Rattlesnake Pete" Gruber ran a saloon and museum at 8 Mill Street in Rochester from 1893 until his death in 1932. Pete was born in Oil City, Pennsylvania, one year before Colonel Drake discovered oil in nearby Titusville. Pete began his snake collection with rattlesnakes and spotted adders from the hills around Oil City. Indians from the Cornplanter reservation taught him how to capture snakes with a forked stick. Seneca Indian medicine men taught him how to extract snake oil. He added guns and Indian relics to his collection, and began to charge admission. He took his museum on the road to Pittsburgh, Jamestown, and Buffalo, prior to settling in Rochester.

He opened his museum on West Main Street near the Erie Canal in 1892, and moved to larger quarters on Mill Street eight months later. In addition to his many tanks of reptiles, Pete's museum housed many of nature's oddities, including two-headed calves, four-legged chickens, and eight-legged lambs. His museum also contained memorabilia such as John Wilkes Booth's meerscham pipe and the battle flag of Custer's last charge, as well as the first electric chair used in New York State and the skull of General Phil Sheridan's horse. Pete was a good customer for the taxidermists; his collection included a hairless cow from India and a 3,500-pound Percheron horse.

Pete was bitten by poisonous snakes thirty-three times: twenty-nine times by rattlesnakes and four times by copperheads. On one occasion, he was unconscious for nine days, and did not recover fully for nine months. He obtained his snakes from the Bristol Hills and from Pennsylvania. Pete employed many snake remedies, including poultices for blood poisoning. One of his most unusual remedies was to reduce a goiter by wrapping a rattlesnake tightly around the sufferer's neck. He brought new meaning to the words: "the cure was worse than the disease." Pete, an outgoing showman in a snakeskin coat and vest, was a Rochester institution.

SAM PATCH

Sam Patch was born in Pawtucket, Rhode Island, in 1807. In his teens, he lived with his widowed mother and worked at a cotton mill in Pawtucket. Sam became an excellent swimmer and jumper at at early age. He swam in the river and jumped from the bridge near the mill, but his biggest challenge was to jump from the roof of a paper mill, 100 feet above the river. In his early twenties, he moved to Patterson, New Jersey, to work as a spinner in a cotton mill there.

The first jump for which he gained notoriety was a seventy-foot jump off a cliff into the chasm near Passaic Falls. A crowd was gathered to watch the construction of a bridge over the chasm, when Sam eluded the town policemen and jumped. He made the same jump at Patterson again in July, 1828, and in August he jumped from a platform at the masthead of a schooner moored off Hoboken.

The ultimate goal for any jumper was to jump at Niagara Falls. On October 6, 1828, Patch made a 70-foot jump before a small crowd from the lower end of Goat Island. He planned a bigger event, and advertised a 120-foot jump on October 17th. The platform on Goat Island was about two-thirds of the way up the surrounding banks. He took off his coat and his shoes, tied a handkerchief around his waist, waved his hand, and jumped.

Patch became a national figure, and, although he was only twenty-two years old, he was famous. His income far exceeded that of a cotton spinner. He began to talk about leaping off the London Bridge. However, the Genesee Falls in Rochester was only seventy miles away. The jump at the 100-foot Upper Falls was scheduled for November 6th, and a crowd of 3,000 gathered to see him jump. He sent off his pet bear first; the bear jumped successfully, and swam to the shore of the river. Sam tied the handkerchief around his waist, waved to the crowds, and made his own successful jump.

He planned a higher jump for Friday, November 13th, 1829. A twenty-five foot platform was erected on the rock above Genesee Falls. Seven thousand people came from all over western New York to watch the jump. He wore a black handkerchief around his waist. Some observed that he didn't seem to have his usual confidence that day. One spectator thought that he swayed when he climbed the platform, but it was explained that he had had a glass of brandy to ward off the chill.

He made a speech before he jumped: "Napoleon was a great man and a great general. He conquered armies and he conquered nations. But he couldn't jump the Genesee Falls. Wellington was a great man and a great general. He conquered Napoleon. But he couldn't jump the Genesee Falls. That was left for me, and I can do it and I will."

Patch jumped, but his arms flailed, he lost control of his body, and he struck the river at an angle with his arms and legs apart. This was Sam's last jump. The river was dragged for his body, but it wasn't found. On March 17, 1830, a farmer breaking the ice in the river to water his horse at Charlotte found the body, which was identified by the black handkerchief around the waist. Sam was buried at a pioneer cemetery in Charlotte.

Sam's death was the subject of many editorials and sermons, and it triggered the writing of many poems and songs. Nathaniel Hawthorne wrote about him, and William Dean Howells told Sam's story in a novel, *The Wedding Journey*. In his book, Howells referred to Rochester as "the enchanted city." The temporary marker on Sam's grave read: "Here lies Sam Patch. Such is Fame."

THE STORY OF THE GALVANIZED TUBS

The Eastman Theatre was built in 1921-22; it opened on September 4, 1922. The main chandelier that is suspended over the orchestra section was installed in time for the opening performance, but the two small chandeliers for the balcony section, one for each side of the theatre, did not arrive. A quick decision was made to buy two galvanized laundry tubs, paint them, and decorate them to look like small chandeliers. The action was a stopgap measure to use until the ordered chandeliers were received.

For some reason, the two small chandeliers were never delivered, and the two decorated laundry tubs became permanent fixtures. In 1971, when the Eastman theatre was restored to its original condition, a decision was made to replace the laundry tubs with real chandeliers. However, those committee members who knew the story of the tubs indulged themselves in some nostalgia and voted to keep them in place. They prevailed, and the inverted tubs still are there as surrogate chandeliers.

THE TECHNOLOGY THAT NOBODY WANTED

Chester Carlson began experimenting with a dry copy process in 1935, and, on October 22, 1938, he produced the first crude copy using his electrophotography process. Carlson, a patent attorney, filed a comprehensive patent in 1939. He spent five years looking for a sponsor to finance the further development and commercialization of his new technology. Over a five year period, he was turned down by the National Inventor's Council, the U.S. Army Signal Corps, and thirty-two companies, including A. B. Dick, Eastman Kodak, IBM, General Electric, and Remington-Rand (Univac). Carlson said that they all displayed "an enthusiastic lack of interest."

In 1944, he found an interested sponsor, the Battelle Memorial Institute in Columbus, Ohio. Battelle was to receive sixty percent of future proceeds in return for helping to develop the technology. They suggested the use of selenium instead of sulphur in the process, as well as the use of a specific black toner powder. They, too, were unsuccessful in promoting of the product. An Ohio State University professor renamed the process "xerography," from the Greek words "xeros," meaning dry, and "graphos," meaning writing.

Finally, John Dessauer of the Haloid Corporation of Rochester, New York, saw an article about electrophotography in *Radio News*. Dessauer's boss, Joe Wilson, Jr., wanted to increase the $100,000 yearly earnings of the company, and had asked him to read technical journals to look for new products and / or processes. Haloid Corporation purchased the patent and rights to Carlson's technology from Battelle. They produced a flat plate copier in 1949 that required 3-5 minutes per copy, spent more on research and development than they earned each year, and, by 1956, received forty percent of their sales from xerography. They changed the name of the company to Haloid-Xerox.

In 1959, IBM was asked to manufacture copiers for Haloid-Xerox. IBM commissioned Arthur D. Little, a consultant from Cambridge, Massachusetts, to do a study of the market potential. The study identified a total potential market of 5,000 units of sales for Haloid-Xerox's new 914 copier. IBM declined the offer to participate in Xerography a second time, and Haloid-Xerox began to manufacture the model 914 copier themselves. By 1968, they had produced 200,000 of them. The fallacy in the Arthur D. Little study was in basing their recommendations on the estimate of the number of copies made at the point of origin, using the original. Most copies are made at the point of receipt from copies made elsewhere.

Haloid-Xerox changed its name to the Xerox Corporation in 1961. By 1988, three billion copies were being made each day worldwide, and the business of making copies had become a $22 billion a year business. The technology that nobody wanted made millionaires out of many people, and revolutionized the way in which we communicate with one another.

WILLIAM MORGAN AND THE MASONS

William Morgan was born in Culpepper County, Virginia on August 7, 1774. He served in army in the War of 1812, married Lucinda Pendleton in Richmond, Virginia, in the fall of 1819, and moved to Toronto, Canada, to work in a brewery. In 1823, he worked as a a mason-bricklayer on Aqueduct Bridge that carried the Erie Canal over the Genesee River. He lived on West Main Street near Bull's Head in Rochester. Later, he worked on other mason-bricklayer jobs in Batavia, Leroy, and Rochester.

He was admitted to the Wells Lodge of the Masons in Rochester as a visitor, and was awarded membership in the Royal Arch Masons in LeRoy. Morgan broke with the Masonic Order when he failed to obtain work on the Masonic Lodge building being built in LeRoy. He moved to Batavia with his wife and two young children in 1826, where he signed a petition for membership in a Royal Arch Masons chapter being formed. Officials of the Lodge knew Morgan as one who had more than an occasional drink and as a loose talker. They denied him membership; he was determined to get even with the Masons.

He decided to publish the secrets of the order with the help of David C. Miller, publisher of the Batavia *Republican-Advocate*. Miller had received the first degree of the Masonic order. The Masons became aroused by this threat to reveal the secrets of the first three degrees of the order, attempted to talk him out of it, and published an item in the *Canandaigua Messenger*: "If a man calling himself William Morgan should introduce himself to the community, they should be on their guard, particularly the Masonic fraternity. Morgan was in the village on May 1st, and his conduct here and elsewhere calls forth this note ... Morgan is considered a swindler and a dangerous man."

Both Miller and Morgan were prosecuted for debts, but both raised bail and stayed out of jail. Attempts were made to burn down the building that housed Miller's press. Morgan was served with a warrant on September 11, 1826, for the theft of a shirt and cravat from a Canandaigua tavernkeeper. He was taken to Canandaigua, where the charge was dismissed. Then he was jailed in Canandaigua for a debt of $2.69 owed to another Canandaigua innkeeper. Loton Lawson, accompanied by three other Masons, paid the debt and secured the release of Morgan.

The four men seized Morgan as he left the jail, and led him to a carriage. Morgan lost his hat in a minor scuffle, and was heard to cry out, "Murder." The carriage traveled through Victor and Pittsford, and was in Rochester before dawn. The men acquired a fresh team of horses at Hanford's Landing on the Genesee River. The carriage rolled westward along Ridge Road. The men stopped briefly at a house along the ridge, traveled through Clarkson, Gaines, and Ridgeway, and had a meal at Wright's Corners Tavern.

Morgan was taken to Fort Niagara, where he was kept in the powder magazine until arrangements could be made to send him into exile in Canada. His "guard" rowed him across the Niagara River, but the Canadians backed down--they didn't want him either. People were starting to ask, "Where is William Morgan?" An Anti-Mason movement began to build. Morgan's book was entitled *Illustrations of Masonry by One of the Fraternity Who Has Devoted Thirty Years to the Subject* . Sales were sluggish at best; people were more interested in what had happened to Morgan than they were in his expose' of passwords and secret grips.

Morgan's body was never found. With no *corpus delecti,* no proof of death, no one could be charged with his murder. However, Thurlow Weed, the Rochester editor, did manage to pry some information from John Whitney, one of Morgan's abductors. Whitney told Weed that Morgan was promised a farm in Canada, so he willingly went again in a rowboat on the Niagara river. When they were out on the river, his captors tied a rope around him with a weight at the other end. Morgan struggled and bit off the thumb of one of his captors, but they maneuvered him into the lake. Whitney never signed a confession of the incident; nothing could be proved in court.

However, Loton Lawson, along with Nicholas Chesebro, Edward Sawyer, and John Shelden, were all convicted of kidnapping Morgan from the Canandaigua jail. They received brief jail terms. There were twelve indictments at trials in Genesee, Monroe, Niagara, and Ontario Counties, and Sheriff Bruce of Niagara County spent two years and two months in jail. Whitney was jailed for one year and three months, and others received short jail terms. In all, sixty-nine Masons were involved in the abduction. Their actions had an unanticipated, adverse impact on their fraternal order.

A new political party, the Anti-Masonic Party, was formed, and 112 delegates, including eleven ex-Masons from eleven states, attended its initial meeting. In 1831, the Anti-Masonic Party met in Baltimore to pick a candidate for President of the United States. They were the first third party in the United States, the first party to hold a nominating convention, and the first to publish a platform of party principles.

William Seward of Auburn, Secretary of State in the Lincoln and Andrew Johnson administrations, began his political career as a member of the Anti-Masonic Party. He won State Senate elections in 1830 and 1832 as a member of the party. Eventually, the party merged with the Whigs. When the Republican Party was established in 1856, many of the Whigs became Republicans.

The number of Masonic lodges in New York State declined from 360 in 1826 to seventy-five in 1836; membership went from 22,000 to 4,000 over that ten year period. Morgan's wife, Lucinda, remarried, and moved west with the Mormons. She became one of the plural wives of Joseph Smith, the Mormon leader. The impact of this man, William Morgan, on the events of his era was significant, but was out of proportion to his deed.

PARKS, FORESTS, AND TRAILS

Monroe County is blessed with a varied selection of beautiful parks. The county may be without peer in its wealth of parks. There are 119 village, town, city, county, and state parks in Monroe County, which is too many to treat individually in an overview such as this. However, highlights are provided on some of them.

BLACK CREEK PARK

Black Creek Park, located south of Route 33A and west of Union Street in southwestern Monroe County, is a 1,505-acre park established in the 1960s. Access is from Chili-Riga Town Line Road, Route 33A, or Union Street. The park features group camping sites, a model plane field for use with non-fuel gliders, picnic areas, two small ponds, a rental lodge, and trails for cross-county skiing, hiking, and horse-back riding.

BRADDOCK BAY FISH AND WILDLIFE MANAGEMENT AREA

Braddock Bay Fish and Wildlife Management Area, located between the Lake Ontario State Parkway and Lake Ontario, is a shallow water bay-marsh complex comprised of five units along the Lake Ontario shoreline west of Rochester. Proceeding west from Rochester, these five units are Buck Pond, Long Pond, Cranberry Pond, Braddock Bay, and Rose Marsh. Excluding Braddock Bay, the ponds and the marsh are connected to Lake Ontario by channels that open and close intermittently as lake currents and wave action work on the gravel and sand bars.

Access to the Fish and Wildlife Management Area from the Lake Ontario State Parkway is via Island Cottage, Long Pond, Lowden Point, East Manitou, and Manitou Beach Roads. This bay-marsh area offers excellent waterfowl feeding, nesting, and resting habitats for blue-winged teal, puddle ducks (particularly mallards), and wood ducks. All waterfowl common to the Atlantic flyway, including uncommon species such as Barrow's goldeneye, brant, and harlequin duck, utilize the area.

The 2,125 acre Braddock Bay Fish and Wildlife Management Area was transferred to the New York State Department of Environmental Conservation in 1982. The transfer from the Office of Parks and Recreation did not include the 375 acres, including Beatty Point, Braddock Bay Marina, and Braddock Bay Park, that was leased to the Town of Greece in 1981. Braddock Bay Park has a education center, Hawk Lookout Tower, hiking trails, marina, nature center, picnic area, and a pavilion.

Public use opportunities include boating, canoeing, fishing, hunting, trapping (a permit is required), photography, and wildlife observation.

CHURCHVILLE PARK

Churchville Park, located north of Route 33 in the Village of Churchville in southwestern Monroe County, has an 18-hole and a 9-hole golf course, with a clubhouse, food concession, and a pro shop. Access to the park's rolling meadowlands along Black Creek is from Kendall Road and Main Street. The 742-acre park has a car-top boat launch

73

access to Black Creek for canoeists and fishermen. The park has five lodges, a playground, nine picnic shelters, five soccer fields, four softball fields, and tennis courts. Ice skating, along with a warming lodge, is available during the winter.

DURAND-EASTMAN PARK

Durand-Eastman Park is located along 5,000 feet of Lake Ontario shoreline between the Genesee River and Irondequoit Bay. It has an 18-hole golf course, with a clubhouse, food concession, and pro shop. Access to the 965-acre park is from Lakeshore Boulevard off Culver Road or at St. Paul Boulevard and King's Highway. The park has seven picnic shelters with tables and grills that can accommodate from thirty to fifty people, and trails over hilly terrain for cross-country skiing, hiking, and horseback riding.

The park, originally the estate of Dr. Henry Durand, was a gift to the city by Dr. Durand. George Eastman acquired adjacent land to increase the park's size. The combined property was dedicated as Durand-Eastman Park in 1909.

ELLISON PARK

Ellison Park, located east of Rochester in the Towns of Brighton and Penfield, has trails for cross-county skiing, hiking, and horseback riding. Access is from Blossom Road and Landing Road. The 447-acre park, which was the first Monroe County park, is adjacent to the Irondequoit Bay wetlands. Its natural beauty is formed by the combination of steep hills and the level flood plain of Irondequoit Creek.

Ellison Park has five lodges with electric stoves and fireplaces, as well as eight other picnic shelters with fireplaces and grills. Skaters who enjoy the park's winter ice rink use Creekside Lodge as a shelter. The park also has a playground, five softball fields, and eight tennis courts.

THE GENESEE VALLEY GREENWAY

The Genesee Valley Greenway, a multi-use trail, will utilize the towpath of the abandoned Genesee River Valley Canal and the bed of the Genesee Valley Canal Railroad, which became the Rochester Branch of the Pennsylvania Railroad. The 90-mile greenway, used for bicycling, birdwatching, cross-country skiing, hiking, horseback riding, jogging, and snowmobiling (in some areas), will extend from Genesee Valley Park in Rochester to Hinsdale, outside of Olean, New York. Among the goals of greenway are:

    o To protect canal features and significant green space along the Genesee River.

    o To develop a recreational trail along the canal and abandoned railroad right of way.

    o To increase access to and to encourage recreational use of the Genesee River.

o To link natural, cultural and historic attractions in the Genesee Valley.

The northern fifty miles of the trail, which will link Rochester with Letchworth State Park, will pass through the towns of Chili, Wheatland, Caledonia, York, Leicester, Groveland, Mt. Morris, Nunda, and Portage. For most of its length, the canal will follow the Genesee River. In Mt. Morris and Nunda, the greenway will traverse the Keshequa Creek Valley. The section of the greenway between Rochester and Letchworth State Park is scheduled to be completed in 1997-98. The 40-mile segment south of Letchworth State Park is near the villages of Fillmore, Houghton, Caneadea, Belfast, Cuba, and Hinsdale.

Among the recommendations of the Genesee Greenway Steering Committee are:

o To provide access to waterways such as the Genesee River and Black, Keshequa, and Oatka Creeks for boating, fishing, and picnicking.

o To provide linkages with other trails and resources such as the Finger Lakes Trail in Letchworth Park, and the Erie Canal, Lehigh Valley, and Seaway Trails in Monroe County.

o To identify high-priority locations for scenic, habitat, public access, and historic intrepretation purposes, and to develop strategies for protecting, managing, and using these areas.

An important connection in the north is the greenway's link with the Erie Canal Heritage Trail, which crosses New York State east to west. The Genesee Valley Greenway will traverse the state north to south. The City of Rochester's river trail system will extend through Rochester and north to Lake Ontario.

GENESEE VALLEY PARK

Genesee Valley Park, located along the east bank of the Genesee River in the City of Rochester, has two 18-hole golf courses, a clubhouse, a food concession, and a pro shop. Access is from Crittenden Road, Elmwood Avenue at Wilson Boulevard, and East River Road. The 800-acre park, designed by Frederick Law Olmstead, consists of rolling pastoral fields and scenic woods along the river. The park has cricket fields, soccer fields, and seven softball fields, as well as biking paths and hiking trails. Genesee Valley Park is one of the oldest parks in the Monroe County Parks System.

GENESEE VALLEY PARK WEST

Genesee Valley Park West is located off Elmwood Avenue along the west bank of the Genesee River opposite Genesee Valley Park. It has a baseball diamond, an ice skating rink, a public swimming pool, softball fields, and tennis courts. Access is directly opposite Plymouth Avenue South. Rental canoes are available for paddling in the river. Genesee Valley Park West shares a pastoral setting with Genesee Valley Park, and is joined to it by footbridges as well as by the Elmwood Avenue Bridge. The 79-acre park is a City of Rochester Park.

HAMLIN BEACH STATE PARK

Hamlin Beach State Park, located on the southern shore of Lake Ontario, twenty-five miles west of Rochester, is a popular recreational and camping facility. The park, accessible from the Lake Ontario State Parkway just west of Route 19, has swimming on life-guarded sandy beaches from late June through Labor Day. Hamlin Beach State Park has 264 tent and trailer campsites available from the last week of April through Columbus Day. Hot showers and electrical hookups are available in the park, as well as a camp store, laundry, and snack bar. Five picnic areas provide over 1,500 picnic tables and four enclosed picnic shelters.

The first phases of an Environmental Education Center in the Yanty Creek Marsh area were completed in 1977. This trail, which is just under a mile long, offers a view of the 200-acre Yanty Creek Marsh Environmental area at the eastern end of the park. It is a self-guided, informational trail with large print and braille signs along the path. The park also has trails for biking, cross-country skiing, and snowmobiling.

A car-top boat launch for small craft is available near the entrance to the park. Marine launch sites are available both east and west of the park off the Lake Ontario State Parkway. Fishing with a New York State license is allowed in all non-swimming areas of the park. Fishing is not permitted from rock jetties.

The park was developed as part of the Monroe County Parks System in 1928, and became Hamlin Beach State Park in 1938. Between 1935 and 1941, the Civilian Conservation Corps constructed six buildings in the park, and reclaimed ninety acres of swamp area in the east woods section.

The park is open every day. Swimming is permitted only in areas with lifeguards.

HIGHLAND PARK

Highland Park, located at the southern edge of the City of Rochester along Highland Avenue, is the home of Rochester's Lilac Festival. Access is from Highland Avenue, Mt. Hope Avenue, and South Goodman Street. Twenty-two acres of the 150-acre park are planted with 1,200 lilac shrubs of more than 500 varieties. The park also features a barberry collection, a Japanese Maple collection, thirty-five varieties of sweet-smelling magnolias, and a rock garden with dwarf evergreens. Highland Park also has andromeda, azaleas, horse chestnuts, mountain laurel, 700 varieties of rhododendron, spring bulb flowers, wildflowers, and many rare trees. The pansy bed has 10,000 plants arranged into an oval floral bed each year.

Highland Park, designed in 1888 by Frederick Law Olmstead, was the first of Rochester's city parks. Actually, it is a planned arboretum or "tree garden." The Lamberton Conservatory, opened in 1911 and reopened after restoration in 1988, is one of the assets of Highland Park, as is the Highland Bowl. The bowl, officially called the John Dunbar Memorial Pavilion, is an outdoor amphitheatre used for summer concerts by the Rochester Philharmonic Orchestra, which are sponsored by the City of Rochester.

Recreational facilities of the park include hiking paths, a pond used for ice-skating, a sledding hill and warming shelter, and a softball field. The Glass Pavilion, located near the corner of Highland and South Avenues, has benches, a brick patio, and a fountain; it is used for small receptions and weddings. The historic Warner Castle in the park is the headquarters of the Garden Center of Rochester. The castellated Gothic-style house was built as the residence of attorney and editor Horatio Gates Warner. Its display gardens include a courtyard garden, a fern bed, an iris and daylily bed, a miniature rose bed and a 13th-century herb garden. It also has a rock garden and a sunken garden.

LOWER FALLS PARK

Lower Falls Park, located on the west bank of the Genesee River in Rochester, overlooks the lower falls of the Genesee River. Access to the three-acre park is from Driving Park Avenue. The park offers a scenic vista of the falls and the river.

MANHATTAN SQUARE PARK

Manhattan Square Park, located in downtown Rochester at the corner of Chestnut and Court Street, has a "space frame" constructed of metal tubing above the performance area. The 4.5-acre park is popular summer spot for concerts and dancing. The summer basketball court becomes a winter skating rink--a convenient lunchtime gathering place for downtown workers. The park has a playground, a restaurant, tennis courts, and a wading pool for children.

MAPLEWOOD PARK

Maplewood Park, located west of the Genesee River in the northern part of Rochester, was designed by Frederick Law Olmstead. Access is from Driving Park Avenue at Lake Avenue. The 144-acre park offers biking paths, hiking trails, ice skating, and tennis courts.

MAPLEWOOD ROSE GARDEN PARK

Maplewood Rose Garden Park, located west of the Genesee River in the northern part of Rochester, has 3,500 roses of 260 varieties. Access is from Driving Park Avenue at Lake Avenue. The 14-acre park's rose collection includes floribunda, grandifloras, hybrid perpetuals, hybrid tea roses, and shrub roses. The third week of June is the peak blooming time; flowering continues through the first frost.

MENDON PONDS PARK

Mendon Ponds Park, located east of Route 65 in the Towns of Pittsford and Mendon, is a moraine-kame-kettle complex formed by the Wisconsin glacier about 11,000 years ago. This 2,514-acre park is a living natural museum of glacial geology. Mendon Ponds Park was named to the National Registry of National Landmarks in 1969. Access is from Route 65 and Pittsford-Mendon Center Road.

The moraine in the park is a ridge of glacial drift left at the front of the glacier; kames are mounded outwashed sediments. Kettles are hollows in which ice blocks were buried in outwash before melting, and eskers are long ridges of gravel and sand marking the courses of rivers on or under the ice. The "Devil's Bathtub" is the most well-known kettle in Mendon Ponds Park. Lost Pond and Round Pond are other examples of kettles.

Hundred Acre Pond has a supervised swimming area with a bathhouse. The park has fishing areas and a boat launch (motorized boats are not permitted). Deep Pond and Hundred Acre Pond are joined by a corrugated tunnel that canoeists and kayakers can paddle through--if they keep their heads down. Mendon Ponds Park, the largest Monroe County Park, has trails for cross-country skiing, hiking, and horseback riding. Also, the park has five lodges, many picnic areas, seven picnic shelters, playgrounds, two softball fields, and a group camping area that requires a special permit.

NORTHAMPTON PARK

Northampton Park, located in western Monroe County south of Route 31 and west of Route 36, has a ski area with a rope tow and a ski school. Access is from Colby Street, Hubbell Road, Route 36, Salmon Creek and Route 31, and Sweden-Walker Road. The 973-acre park has sledding hills and a warming shelter, in addition to trails for cross-country skiing, hiking, and horseback riding. Northampton Park also has two lodges, a playground, two softball fields, and group camping (with a special permit).

Springdale Farm, an educational farm, is operated within Northampton Park. It has beef cattle, chickens, dairy cattle, dairy goats, ducks, pigs, sheep, and turkeys. The farm also has field crops, a fruit orchard, herb gardens, hiking trails, pastures, a pond, vegetable gardens, and a five-acre wood lot. Springdale Farm is open all year. Admission is free; group tours can be scheduled.

ONTARIO BEACH PARK

Ontario Beach Park, located on the shore of Lake Ontario in the northern part of Rochester, has one of the Great Lakes' finest natural sand beaches. The sand is several hundred feet deep, and extends for over a half mile. Access is from Beach Avenue and Lake Avenue. The 39-acre park has supervised swimming from June through Labor Day. Ontario Beach Park has a restored 1905 Dentzel menagerie carousel and a performance pavilion that often features the Monroe County Parks Band.

Ontario Beach Park has a year-round boat launch, a lighted fishing pier, and an ice skating rink. The park has a bathhouse, a food concession, six picnic shelters, soccer fields, softball fields, and volleyball courts. The park also provides a good observation spot for watching the procession of boats that enter Lake Ontario from the Genesee River.

POWDER MILLS PARK

Powder Mills Park, located southeast of Rochester in the Town of Perinton, features a varied topography that ranges from flat creekside meadows and swamplands to steep hills. Access is from Route 96 south of Bushnell's Basin. The 380-acre park has a downhill ski area for beginner and intermediate skiers, and has equipment rental, a rope tow, ski lessons, and snow-making capability. Open skiing is held on Sunday afternoons and school holidays. The lift ticket charge is nominal.

Powder Mills Park has a fish hatchery in which 12,000 trout are raised each year for stocking in Irondequoit Creek. The hatchery is open all year, seven days a week. Specialized demonstrations, lectures, and tours can be arranged with advanced notice. The park has trails for cross-country skiing and hiking, and a sledding hill with a warming shelter. Also, Powder Mills Park has seven lodges, picnic areas with tables and grills, playgrounds, five shelters, and tennis courts.

SENECA PARK

Seneca Park, located along the east bank of the Genesee River in the northern part of Rochester, is a three-mile preserve of forested river gorge designed by Frederick Law Olmstead. Access is from St. Paul Boulevard, north of Route 104. The 297-acre park is best known as the home of the Seneca Park Zoo. Trout Lake in the park was created by damming a natural spring. Swan boats, propelled by men who pedaled the boats like bicycles, provided rides for visitors on Trout Lake until 1922.

Seneca Park, originally called North Park, was renamed Seneca in commemoration of its Indian heritage. It is a good observation point for spectactular vistas of the Genesee River. The park has hiking trails, open fields, picnic areas, and a public swimming pool.

WEBSTER PARK

Webster Park, located in the northeastern part of Monroe County along Lake Ontario in the Town of Webster, consists of rolling lakeshore meadows and woodlands. It has several waterfront areas and a fishing pier. Access is from Lake Road and Holt Road. The 550-acre park has five cabins, which can accommodate 30 to 35 campers; they are popular with youth groups and scout troops. Webster Park has thirty family campground sites, five lodges, and eight shelters. The park also has baseball fields, picnic tables and grills, soccer fields, and tennis courts, as well as trails for cross-country skiing and hiking.

SHOWS AND FESTIVALS

CLOTHESLINE FESTIVAL

The Clothesline Festival, which is held each year the first full weekend after Labor Day, is Rochester's oldest and largest arts and crafts festival. The first festival was held in 1957. It is held on the 17-acre campus of the Memorial Art Gallery at 500 University Avenue between Goodman and Prince Streets. The two-day festival attracts crowds of over 60,000 and contributes ten percent of the Memorial Art Gallery's annual budget. A recent festival had over 600 exhibitors from 23 countries including artists, basket makers, ceramicists, floral designers, glass artisans, jewelry designers, and leather crafters. Also represented were metal crafters, painters, photographers, printmakers, sculptors, textile artists, and woodworkers.

The Paint Pen gives children the opportunity to create things from scrap material, model with clay, or paint at an easel. They may also go to the "Fun Faces" booth to have their faces painted. The Clothesline Festival has something for all ages and for every taste. The admission fee is nominal, and includes admission to the Memorial Art Gallery.

CORN HILL ARTS FESTIVAL

The Corn Hill Arts Festival is held in early July in Corn Hill, Rochester's most historic neighborhood. Corn Hill, bounded by Exchange Boulevard and Ford Street, is a short walk from downtown Rochester. The Corn Hill Arts Festival attracts 200,000 visitors and over 500 artists and craftsmen from most states and from Canada. They exhibit in categories such as drawing, glass, graphics, jewelry, leather, painting, photography, pottery, sculpture, and wood. The show has earned recognition as one of the top 200 shows in the country, and as one of the top selling shows.

A variety of food is offered by forty concessionaires. The festival has entertainment for all ages and interests; a sampling of music from a recent festival included Boston-style jazz, classical music, classic rock, contemporary jazz, dixieland, Latin jazz, and Reggae. Some of the groups that performed were the Baroque Chamber Trio, Draper Dance Theatre, Kids Koncert Band, Rochester Children's Theatre, and the Rochester Scottish Pipe Band.

The festival sponsors a 5K race on Sunday morning. Rugby matches are scheduled featuring teams such as the Batavia Creamers, Buffalo Old Boys, Lockport Old Green, Rochester Aardvarks, Rochester Colonials, and Syracuse Chargers. There are also special events such as the Rochester Police Community Exhibition, which features the K-9 unit and the SCUBA Diving Rescue Team. Proceeds from the festival are used for neighborhood beautification and preservation projects.

LILAC FESTIVAL

The Lilac Festival, which is held in late May each year in Highland Park along Highland Avenue, is the largest celebration of its kind in North America. At the center of the festival are Highland Park's over 1,200 lilac bushes--more than 500 varieties from pure white to deep purple. The Lilac Parade has over twenty floats, and is accompanied by bands such as the champion Teen Tour band of Canada, Rochester's national champion Empire Statesman drum and bugle corps, and Rochester's New Horizons Band.

The Lilac Festival has concerts at the Downtown Festival Tent adjacent to Geva Theatre, and at the Highland Bowl off South Avenue. The types of musical groups that performed at the festival in recent years were blues, country music, jazz, new wave, and rock. A variety of food is available at stands; also, food is available from rolling carts.

More than ninety exhibitors display baskets, hand-made clothing, jewelry, leather items, paintings, photographs, pottery, and stained glass. Local artists showcase drawings and prints of Rochester scenes and historical homes. Craft demonstrations offer the opportunity to watch artisans at work.

MONTAGE: INTERNATIONAL FESTIVAL OF THE IMAGE

The first annual Montage: International Festival of the Image was celebrated in Rochester in 1993. Montage 93 proved that Rochester's slogan,"the World's Image Centre," is more than a slogan. The city on the Genesee became a "river of images." The

French word "montage" was chosen to represent the festival because it describes the artristic technique of gathering discrete and contradictory elements into a single composition. The festival was held during the last three weeks of July and the first week of August.

Many different elements made up this festival of the image, including:

o Exhibitions--18 exhibitions, including 13 premiering at the festival, and the works of more than 300 artists from around the world. On display at over eleven sites around Rochester.

o Arts and Technology Exposition and Book Fair--interactive exhibits and demonstrations of the latest technologies, e.g. new applications using electronics and computer technology for animation, drawing, illustration, painting, and photo-manipulation

o Trade Show--showcase for cutting-edge technologies and previews of new products

o International Film and Video Festivals--new works by independent film and video producers

o International Student Festival--hands-on demonstrations and seminars by leading artists, educators, and photographers

o Media Arts Workshops--special hands-on sessions designed especially for children and teachers to explore the world of images

o Kaleidoscope of Special Events--concerts, dance, plays--the performing arts

Montage brings together innovators and pioneers in the field of imaging from all over the world. The festival provides a taste of the future for everyone, from the casual observer to the imaging professional.

ROCHESTER HARBOR AND CAROUSEL FESTIVAL

The Rochester Harbor and Carousel Festival is held in June each year at Ontario Beach Park. The festival features amusement park rides, concerts, crafts, and storytelling. Other activities include sand sculpture contests, lighthouse tours, and volleyball tournaments. The festival also has parades and fireworks. Admission and most activities are free.

WALNUT HILL FARM DRIVING COMPETITION

The Walnut Hill Farm, located just north of the New York State Thruway overpass on West Bloomfield Road (off Route 64), has been the site of the Walnut Hill Farm Driving Competition since 1972. The carriage driving competition is held during the third week in August each year. Two hundred horsemen from Canada, Europe, and the United States come to Walnut Hill Farm for a full schedule of competitions in coaching, cross-country obstacle, pleasure, and reinsman classes. The Walnut Hill Driving Competition sets the standard for carriage competitions.

The driving competition was organized in 1972, when a group of local carriage enthusiasts scheduled an informal drive followed by a picnic. Their initial gathering led to the formation of the Pittsford Carriage Association, which now sponsors the six-day international carriage competition. Interest in carriage sports has had a healthy renaissance in recent years, both in the United States and abroad. The driving competition provides a showcase for horse-and-carriage enthusiasts to practice their sporting art. The Pittsford Carriage Association's carriage festival promotes public awareness of the history of the horse and carriage.

Simulating the conditions of the 1890s is one of the challenges in planning the competition. For example, the cross-country course has natural obstacles that include an abandoned sugar shed, farm animals, farm machinery, open country, water hazards, and woods. The courses are challenging, but can still be driven by a novice or a once-a-year driver. Many of the rules and regulations used in driving competitions originated at Walnut Hill, particularly those that involve safety.

Many antique vehicles participate in the competition, from pony carts to four-horse road coaches with polished brass and silver harnesses. On the first day of the competition, competitors present their carriages in an unhorsed carriage concourse; they display their carriages in the stable area. Activities during the six-day competition include:

o Ascot Pairs Scurry Obstacle Competition--designed to test the speed, agility, and teamwork of the horses and ponies through an obstacle course. In past years, this event has been accompanied by a picnic supper and the music of the Rochester Philharmonic Orchestra.

o The Jack Russell Terrier Races--considered to be a form of organized chaos

o The Coaching Division--features a challenging and unique class called the "Coaching Putting-To." The scene is a coach-and-four arriving at an inn. The passengers disembark for some liquid refreshment, the driver and groom replace the spent horses with a fresh foursome, and the passengers remount and continue on.

o Victorian County Fair--spectators sample turn-of-the-century food and drink at "Ye Whip and Horn," while enjoying the music of the Walnut Hill Band. They stroll through the English Garden or browse at the "carriage lane boutiques."

o Exhibitions of the City of Rochester's Mounted Police--demonstrations of the training and use of police horses

o Rochester Pipe Band performances

o Presentation Pleasure Drive--exhibitors take their horses and carriages for an eight-mile drive through Mendon Ponds Park and the surrounding area.

    o Special events, such as performances by the Morrisville College six-horse hitch of champion Belgians, each of which weighs more than a ton. The drivers demonstrate how freight was delivered through narrow streets at the turn of the century.

TOUR BOATS

COLONIAL BELLE

The 221-passenger *Colonial Belle*, operated by Colonial Cruise Lines, Inc., offers scenic cruises on the Erie Canal. The *Colonial Belle*, which operates from Packett's Landing on Main Street (Route 250) in Fairport, offers daily two-hour cruises at noon and mid-afternoon, as well as two-hour lunch and dinner cruises. The *Colonial Belle* serves both American and oriental cuisine.

The tour boat has an experienced crew, licensed captains, and is Coast Guard certified. The *Colonial Belle* is also available for business meetings, charters, weddings, and all special occasions. A minimum number of passengers is required for all cruises.

EMITA II

Mid-Lakes Navigation Company, Ltd., Skaneateles, NY, offers spring cruises on the Erie Canal from Fairport. Four cruises are offered from Fairport's Packet's Landing Dock from mid-May until mid-June:

    o Erie Canal Afternoon--a two-hour afternoon cruise on the *Emita II* from Fairport east to Macedon or West to Pittsford on Monday through Friday.

    o Prime Rib Dinner Cruise--a three-hour evening cruise from Fairport through Bushnell's Basin and Pittsford to Lock 32 at Clover Street on Thursday, Friday, and Saturday. A five-course meal is served after the *Emita II* locks through the twenty-five-foot high lock.

    o Sunday Excursion--a four-hour cruise departing Fairport in late morning on Sunday. A continental breakfast is served; the *Emita II* locks through Locks 32 and 33 and continues toward the Genessee River. A hearty barbecue is served at lunchtime.

    o Sunset Cruise--a three-hour evening cruise from Fairport on Sunday through Wednesday. The *Emita II* cruises to Lock 32 at Clover Street, locks through, and returns to Fairport after sunset.

SPIRIT OF ROCHESTER

The *Spirit of Rochester*, owned by Riverview Cruise Lines, Inc., operates from their dock at 18 Petten Street Extension, off Lake Avenue in Charlotte. The *Spirit of Rochester* offers two-hour lunch and dinner cruises along the shore of Lake Ontario on Monday through Saturday. A late morning / early afternoon and a mid-afternoon brunch cruise are scheduled on Sundays.

The tour boat has a capacity of 250; a minimum of fifty passengers is required for a cruise. The *Spirit of Rochester* also offers moonlight cruises. Reservations are required for all cruises.

SAM PATCH

The 54-foot *Sam Patch* is operated by the Corn Hill Waterfront & Navigation Foundation at 250 Exchange Boulevard in Rochester. They provide lunch and dinner cruises, as well as cruises without meals, on the upper Genesee River and the Erie Canal. The authentic canal boat, which operates from May to October, carries up to forty-nine people.

The *Sam Patch*, which was built in 1991, was named after the daredevil waterfall jumper who lost his life jumping from High Falls in Rochester in 1829. The tour boat operates Tuesdays through Sundays. On Mondays, the *Sam Patch* is available for charters of groups, meetings, and special events. Moonlight cruises are offered on Friday and Saturday evenings. Reservations are required for meal cruises; reservations are recommended for other cruises, but are not necessary.

ROCHESTER: THE WESTERN GATEWAY--PLACES

COLLEGES AND UNIVERSITIES

MONROE COMMUNITY COLLEGE

Monroe Community College, located at 1000 East Henrietta Road in Rochester, offers more than sixty different programs of credit courses. The college, one of thirty community colleges within the State University of New York, serves more than 13,000 full-time and part-time students. Another 20,000 students enroll in courses at Monroe Community College through community education programs and corporate training. The college also offers evening and summer courses at high schools throughout Monroe County.

The Community College, located on an eleven-building, 314-acre campus in the Town of Brighton, provides two-year programs of higher education to all members of the community. It is primarily a teaching institution that was developed in response to the community's demand for extended educational opportunities. Monroe Community College is committed to the ideals of democracy, comprehensiveness, community-centeredness, and life-long education.

A top priority of the faculty and administration of Monroe Community College is providing the best educational opportunities to all students; this is reflected in the quality of instruction, and the flexibility and multiple purposes of the institution. Monroe Community College offers a range of opportunities in career education, continuing education, developmental education, non-traditional education, and preparation for further study.

NAZARETH COLLEGE OF ROCHESTER

Nazareth College of Rochester, located at 4245 East Avenue, is an independent, coeducational liberal arts college founded by the Sisters of St. Joseph in 1924. The college, on a 75-acre campus with seventeen modern buildings, offers more than forty majors and concentrations. The college's full-time undergraduate enrollment is over 1,400 students; almost as many part-time students are enrolled in both undergraduate and graduate study.

Nazareth College offers a wide range of academic programs, including majors in art, language, and literature, as well as computer and information science and business administration. Students are encouraged to combine programs. Nazareth College serves students who wish to pursue academic programs that combine a strong liberal studies experience with concentrations in a chosen field to prepare them for both professional careers and graduate study.

The college promotes the articulate use of language, informed and alert thinking, and self-motivated learning that extends throughout a lifetime. Nazareth College places emphasis on personal achievement and fulfillment as well as service to others. The curriculum cultivates skills of listening, thinking, writing, and speaking analytically and critically.

The Nazareth College Arts Center, with its academic programs in fine arts and special programs, provides an extra dimension of aesthetic experience for students at the college. The Casa Italiana and two other languge houses are important assets for the study of language. Also, many opportunities for internships to supplement a student's education with work outside the classroom are available.

ROBERTS WESLEYAN COLLEGE

Roberts Wesleyan College, located at 2301 Westside Drive in suburban Rochester, is an independent, coeducational, liberal arts college in the Christian tradition founded by the Free Methodist Church of North America. The college offers a quality education for students of all denominations and a program designed to facilitate development of all dimensions of its students' lives. Roberts Wesleyan admits academically qualified students of any race, color, sex, handicap, creed, or national origin.

The college serves the needs of both traditional and non-traditional students. The college has a commitment to foster lifetime learning that includes services to any who are pursuing personal and professional development goals. In earning a liberal arts education, the student is exposed to the historic, philosophic, and scientific methodologies, and behaviorial, historical, and scientific investigation. The divisions within the college organize the content, materials, and methods used in their particular disciplines. Students are given the opportunity, via the cooperative effort of the divisions, to become liberally educated, professionally prepared, and fitted for service to the community and to society.

The educational philosophy is based upon the assumption that education must address the entire person as a physical, psychosocial, rational, and spiritual being. Both the academic program and the curriculum are designed to encourage honest inquiry into various fields of knowledge, and to prepare students for creative leadership and productive community involvement. The academic programs offered include:

o Management of Human Resources   o Fine Arts

o Natural Science and Mathematics   o Nursing

o Religion and Humanities   o Teacher Education

o Social Science and Business

ROCHESTER INSTITUTE OF TECHNOLOGY

The Rochester Institute of Technology, located on Jefferson Road near the Genesee River, is a privately endowed, coeducational university. The institute, which emphasizes career education, has over 8,500 undergraduate students and 1,400 graduate students. More than 4,000 students study part-time. All fifty states and over sixty-three foreign countries are represented in the student body. The modern 1,300-acre campus is located in suburban Rochester.

The institute, which was founded in 1829, offers a variety of masters, bachelors, and associate degrees as well as certificate and diploma programs. The first doctoral program, in imaging science, was established in 1990. Rochester Institute of Technology is the fourth oldest and fifth largest cooperative education institution in the country. Each year it places over 3,400 students in co-op positions with approximately 1,300 employers.

The Colleges of the university include:

o College of Applied Science and Technology   o College of Business

o College of Continuing Education   o College of Engineering

o College of Fine and Applied Arts   o College of Liberal Arts

o College of Graphic Arts and Photography   o College of Science

Some of the course offerings are unique or unusual, such as microelectronic engineering, packaging science, printing, and programs for the School for American Craftsmen. In addition, over 1,000 students are enrolled in the federally-funded National Technical Institute for the Deaf.

ST. JOHN FISHER COLLEGE

St. John Fisher College, located at 3690 East Avenue in suburban Rochester, is an independent, liberal arts college in the Catholic tradition of American higher education. The college was founded in 1948 as a Catholic college for men by priests of the Congregation of St. Basil. The first women students were admitted in 1971. The institution emphasizes liberal learning both for men and women in traditional academic disciplines and in more directly career-oriented fields. In addition to its baccalaurate degrees, St. John Fisher College offers a Masters of Business Administration degree and a variety of continuing education opportunities.

The principal goals of the college are to help students develop intellectual skills, a foundation in the liberal arts, and proficiency in a major. The liberal arts are emphasized because they are intrinsically valuable, and also because they prepare students for life-long learning and for an ever-changing work environment. Intellectual growth begins by emphasizing both verbal and quantitative skills.

St. John Fisher College welcomes qualified students, faculty, and staff, regardless of cultural or religious background. The college's commitment to students from varied backgrounds and with differing educational needs reflects an emphasis on life-long learning and a direct involvement with the community of which the institution is a part. A dual emphasis placed on intellectual and personal growth derives from a belief that learning is valuable for its own sake, for the sake of the student, and for society as a whole.

SUNY--COLLEGE AT BROCKPORT

The State University of New York--College at Brockport, located sixteen miles west of Rochester in the Village of Brockport, is a liberal arts college supported by public funds. It is a comprehensive college of arts and sciences that offers balanced and integrated programs in the arts, humanities, professional studies, sciences, and social sciences at the baccalaureate and master's levels. The college also offers certificate programs in selected professional areas.

The college educates students in the liberal arts and professional skills, fosters an understanding of global interdependence and cultural diversity, and encourages post-graduate study and lifelong learning. The liberal disciplines and professional studies have a close relationship that stimulates students to develop strengths in applied skills, critical and creative thinking, and communications. A balance of practical and theoretical studies prepares the graduate for advanced education in a profession, informed citizenship, leadership in the community and the workplace.

The student body is from every region of New York State, twenty other states, and more than twenty foreign countries. Two thousand graduate students are seeking advanced degrees, pursuing teacher certification, or otherwise upgrading their professional skills. Three quarters of full-time and part-time faculty members at SUNY--College at Brockport hold doctoral degrees, and more than fifty have received the prestigious Chancellor's Award for Excellence in Teaching since the award began in 1973. The 591-acre campus has sixty buildings.

The college offers thirty-nine majors for baccalaureate degrees, and has sixteen provisional and thirteen permanent certification programs. In addition, twenty-five programs of graduate study and two certificates of advanced study programs are offered.

UNIVERSITY OF ROCHESTER

The University of Rochester, located off Elmwood Avenue, is one of the leading private universities in the United States. The university, which was founded in 1850, has approximately 4,800 full-time undergraduate students, 3,400 full-time graduate students, and 1,500 part-time students. The University of Rochester has a low faculty to student ratio with 1,200 faculty members. Out of 3,000 colleges and universities in the country, the university is one of fifty-eight members of the prestigious Association of American Universities.

The University of Rochester's motto is "Meliora," which signifies "always better." The 90-acre campus is at the southern edge of Rochester along the Genesee River. The University Medical Center is adjacent to the campus. The University has eight schools and colleges:

- o College of Arts and Science
- o College of Engineering and Applied Science
- o Eastman School of Music
- o Graduate School of Education and Human Development
- o School of Medicine and Dentistry
- o School of Nursing
- o William E. Simon Graduate School of Business Administration
- o University College of Liberal and Applied Studies

The University of Rochester offers ninety master's programs and over fifty doctoral programs. The university awarded its 5,000th Ph.D. degree in 1990. The first Ph.D. degree was awarded in 1925, and one of the first three candidates to earn the degree became a Nobel laureate. Among the university's special laboratories are the Nuclear Structure Research Laboratory, the Laboratory for Laser Energetics, the C. E. K. Mees Observatory, and the New York State Center for Advanced Optical Technology. Other facilities of the university include the Memorial Art Gallery, the Eastman Theatre, and Kilbourn Hall.

MUSEUMS

EASTMAN HOUSE INTERNATIONAL MUSEUM OF PHOTOGRAPHY

The Eastman House International Museum of Photography, located at 900 East Avenue in Rochester, is one of the most important repositories of photographic apparatus, films, photographic literature, and photographs in the world. Permanent exhibits portray over 150 years of the history of photography, and changing exhibits showcase important photographers and photographic movements.

The Eastman House houses the world's finest still photography collection of over 500,000 fine art and historical prints, and the works of over 8,000 international photographers from 1839 until the present. The museum also has a motion picture collection of over 7,000 titles, as well as 3,000,000 still photographs and celebrity portraits. Video playback stations provide the opportunity to view the movie stars, including Clark Gable, Greta Garbo, and Lillian Gish.

The museum's technology collection includes over 11,000 historic cameras, photographic accessories, and pieces of photographic equipment. The Discovery Room provides the opportunity to create your own images, to examine vintage cameras and photographs, and to view demonstrations and entertaining videos.

The International Museum of Photography's comprehensive film and photographic library also includes many exceptional books and rare manuscripts. Four rotating exhibits display many rare, original photographs. Access to historic archives is provided by research appointments.

The Dryden Theatre offers regular screenings of their 7,000 movies on Tuesday through Saturday evenings. The theatre also offers a free weekly Hollywood classic matinee on Thursdays for senior citizens. The Museum Shop features books, collector's items, gifts, and posters that meet a wide variety of visitors' interests.

The Eastman House was built from 1902 to 1905 under the close supervision of George Eastman, founder of the Eastman Kodak Company. The 35,000 square foot home has fifty rooms and formal gardens. The Eastman House, a National Historic Landmark, has been restored to its original grandeur. A tour of the Eastman House and grounds gives visitors a glimpse of:

- classic wood detailing
- decorative art
- elaborate moldings
- exquisite Oriental rugs
- hand-painted window glass
- intricate landscaping
- marble floors
- period furnishings
- plaster relief ceilings

The Eastman House International Museum of Photography is open Tuesdays through Saturdays, and Sunday afternoons. It is closed Mondays, New Year's Day, Thanksgiving Day, and Christmas Day. Tours of the museum are conducted every day; groups must schedule their tours in advance. An admission fee is charged. The entire museum complex is accessible to the handicapped. The facility is equipped with special devices to assist hearing impaired visitors.

MEMORIAL ART GALLERY

The Memorial Art Gallery, located at 500 University Avenue in Rochester, provides a panorama of the world's art from the relics of history to works in the vanguard of contemporary art. The gallery's permanent collection of over 10,000 items includes masterworks by Cassat, Cezanne, Homer, Matisse, and Monet. Represented in the museum are the cultures of Egypt, Greece, Rome, Africa, and Asia. Pre-Columbian art and medieval treasures are displayed, as well as the work of 19th-century American landscape painters.

The permanent collection is particularly strong in works that include medieval and 17th-century art, 19th- and early 20th-century French and American paintings, American folk art, and European and American prints and drawings. The gallery has a year-round schedule of temporary exhibitions, both popular and scholarly, intended to promote interest in specific artists, movements, and periods of art history.

The Memorial Art Gallery, founded in 1913 as a publically supported teaching museum, has many activities, programs, and resources that allow visitiors to discover and explore art. Also, concerts, gallery talks, guided tours, and illustrated lectures are offered throughout the year in addition to the exhibitions.

The gallery offers hands-on workshops and performances for children and parents throughout the school year. Childspace, a children's discovery room, offers families the opportunity to explore art concepts through participatory displays all year round. Self-guiding tour books are also available for families with children.

The Creative Workshop, the gallery's studio art school, offers classes for children and adults at all skill levels. Year-round courses are offered in art history, ceramics, drawing, jewelry making, and weaving. Day and evening classes are conducted for adults, and credit for some courses can be arranged. There are Saturday daytime classes for children; classes for preschoolers are offered during the week.

The art library, the Charlotte Whitney Allen Library, houses more than 20,000 books, catalogs, indexes, and periodicals about art auctions, art history techniques, the history of architecture, and museum management. The library is open to the public for reference work.

The Gallery Cafe, located on two levels overlooking the indoor sculpture garden, offers luncheons, dinners, and Sunday brunch. It is closed Mondays and Sunday evenings. The Gallery Store provides a selection of artwork and gifts as well as art books, educational toys and games, exhibition catalogs, jewelry, and reproductions. No Memorial Art Gallery admission fee is required for either the Gallery Cafe or the Gallery Store.

The Memorial Art Gallery is open all day Wednesday through Friday, Tuesday and Sunday afternoons, and Tuesday evenings. It is closed Mondays and major holidays. Admission is charged. Handicapped access to the Memorial Art Gallery and the Gallery Cafe is via the main entrance on University Avenue.

ROCHESTER MUSEUM

The Rochester Museum, located at 657 East Avenue in Rochester, is part of the Rochester Museum and Science Center that also includes the Eisenhart Auditorium, the Gannett School of Science and Man, the Strasenburgh Planetarium, and the Cumming Nature Center near Naples. The Rochester Museum reveals the many facets of upstate New York's past via permanent and changing exhibits that focus on the cultural and natural heritage of the Finger Lakes Region and the lower Genesee Region.

Major traveling exhibits and changing displays from the museum's own collection are highlighted on the first floor. Permanent exhibits include colorful dioramas of area flora and fauna, the City of Rochester in 1838, fossil seas from 300 million years ago, and an Iroquois village. The permanent exhibit, *At the Western Door*, displays the finest examples of the museum's widely-acclaimed Seneca Iroquois collection. The museum offers family-oriented, hands-on programs during weekends and vacations that help to bring history and science to life.

The museum also houses a 28,000 volume Museum Research Library as well as 1.5 million objects for use in interpreting the region's prehistory, history, natural history, and ethnic diversity. The Collections Division acquires, documents, and conserves the objects; the Research Division conducts archaeological field work and research to provide the information used in exhibits, programs, and publications.

The Gannett School of Science and Man provides access to the entire Rochester Museum and Science Center through classes, expeditions, and workshops. It includes Rochester's only museum-based preschool. The Eisenhart Auditorium, home of the annual International Folk Festival, offers programs that range from antique shows to children's theatre to films and lectures.

The museum also houses the Fruit and Salad Company Restaurant and the World of Science Gift Shop. The museum is open Monday through Saturday, and afternoons on Sundays and holidays. An admission fee is charged.

STRASENBURGH PLANETARIUM

The Strasenburgh Planetarium, a component of the Rochester Museum and Science Center complex, unites the worlds of theatre and the science of astronomy for 200,000 visitors each year. The Zeiss Mark VI projector, hundreds of other projectors, and a superior sound system, transport the visitor through space and time. The star projector cost $250,000, is seventeen feet long, weighs two and three quarter tons, and contains 120 single and double projectors. The planetarium, which opened in 1968, was the gift of Mr. and Mrs. Edwin Strasenburgh.

Full-length star shows and seasonal sky mini-shows are projected on the great domed ceiling of the star theatre, which seats 240. The exhibition hall of the planetarium has many displays and the Space Tunnel shows objects in the universe and their relationships to one another and with the earth. The Space Shop offers many educational items, such has books, charts, games, photographs, and space kits.

Shows at the Strasenburgh Planetarium are on Monday through Friday evenings. Shows on Saturdays, Sundays, and holidays are presented in the early afternoon, late afternoon, and evening. An admission fee is charged.

STRONG MUSEUM

The Strong Museum, located at One Manhattan Square in downtown Rochester, houses over a half million objects that grew out of the vast, eclectic collections of Margaret Woodbury Strong (1897-1969). These objects provide a visual index of popular activities, interests, and tastes in the United States from 1820 to 1940, including books, diaries, clothing, home furnishings, household tools, journals, magazines, ornaments, playthings, and sporting goods.

The mission of the Strong Museum is to collect, exhibit, and preserve popular materials with which it interprets the cultural and social development of the United States, particularly the Northeast, during our industrialization. The collections are used to advance the understanding of customs, lifestyles, and traditions of ordinary Americans from 1820 to 1940. The museum's study collections include:

o an internationally-acclaimed doll collection
o American furniture
o American art pottery
o automobiles, boats, and fire engines
o ceramics and glass tablewares
o export trade goods from China and Japan
o housekeeping and food processing tools
o lighting devices

o mechanical banks
o silver and silver-plated tablewares
o Staffordshire figures
o timekeeping equipment
o toy steam locomotives
o toys, dollhouses, and miniatures
o Victorian home crafts

The museum library, which houses over 29,000 books, catalogs, and periodicals concerning the nineteenth and twentieth centuries, is a unique resource for collectors, history enthusiasts, and students. City directories of major northeastern cities from 1820-1940 are available on microfiche and microfilm. The museum also has collections of children's books, miniature books, and fore-edge paintings.

Margaret Woodbury Strong, the daughter of early Kodak investors John Woodbury and Alice Motley Woodbury, collected objects that fascinated her, and which she perceived to have educational and historical value. She collected items whose value was not understood by her contemporary collectors. She left her collection and an endowment for the establishment of a museum that opened in 1982.

The Strong Museum is designed for self-guided tours; all group tours are greeted and given an introduction to the museum. The museum is fully accessible to people with disabilities; wheelchairs are available. The museum auditorium is equipped with an induction loop for the hearing-impaired. Strollers are available for infants, and changing tables are provided in first-floor restrooms. Visitors may use hand-held cameras and electronic flashes inside the museum.

The Museum Shop is open during regular museum hours. The museum is open Monday through Saturday and Sunday afternoons. It is closed on New Year's Day, Thanksgiving Day, and Christmas Day. The Tuckaway Cafe, which offers light fare and beverages, is open Monday through Saturday from late morning until mid-afternoon and is closed Sundays. The museum charges an admission fee.

VICTORIAN DOLL MUSEUM

The Victorian Doll Museum, located at 4332 Buffalo Road in North Chili, near the intersection of Routes 33 and 259, has hundreds of collector dolls on display in floor-to-ceiling glass cases. The collection includes many contemporary dolls by Madam Alexander, Effanbee, and Ginny dolls by Vogue. Also exhibited are dolls representing well-known personalities in advertising, comics, fashion, history, literature, medicine, and movies. The dolls are made of bisque, china, felt, ivory, metal, papier mache, wax, and wood. Displays also include an action puppet theatre, Kewpie dolls, Noah's Ark, paper dolls, and Schoenhut dolls and circus.

A "doll hospital" associated with the museum repairs all types of dolls, from antique to modern dolls, for individuals and museums. The repair workroom used in doing expert doll restoration is not open to the public, but visitors can view the various parts used in doll repair. Antique dolls are appraised by appointment.

The gift shop includes a wide variety of dolls by well-known dollmakers, as well as authentic ethnic dolls, baby dolls, bride dolls, doll lamps, porcelain and musical dolls, and storybook dolls. Other doll items offered by the shop are books, calendars, costume patterns, doll houses, gift wrap, magazines, notes, patterns,and price guides.

The museum is open Tuesday through Saturday and Sunday afternoons. It is closed Mondays, holidays, and during the month of January. A nominal admission fee is charged; reservations may be made for group tours and school tours.

PLACES OF INTEREST

SEABREEZE AMUSEMENT PARK

Seabreeze Amusement Park and Raging Rivers Waterpark, located at 4600 Culver Road in Rochester, overlooks Lake Ontario. The amusement park has over seventy-five rides, including the barnstormers, bobsled coasters, flying scooters, Jack Rabbit roller coaster, scenic train rides, the sea dragon, and the yo-yo.

Raging Rivers Waterpark has body flumes, pint-sized kiddie slides, a tube slide, and a speedslide. Two new waterslides were added in 1994. Less rigorous activities include a cruise on the New Adventure River or stopping at Paradise Island for a tropical drink.

The admission fee provides access to all rides for the day. Also offered are "admission plus", "nite rider," and special kiddie passes. Special rates are available for groups of twenty-five or more people. Seabreeze Amusement Park and Raging Rivers Water Park are open Saturdays and Sundays from early May until mid-June, and seven days a week from mid-June until Labor Day.

SENECA PARK ZOO

The Seneca Park Zoo, located at 2222 St. Paul Street, north of Route 104 in Rochester, is home to over 600 animals, representing more than 200 species. The zoo, established in 1894, features weekend educational programs such as:

- o Animal of the month--A different animal is highlighted each month through photographic displays, visitor handouts, and handstamps.
- o Elephant Works--Trained volunteers answer questions about elephants and their management.
- o Live Animal Presentations--Animal behavior and conservation are discussed as visitors touch and ask questions about animals such as hedgehogs and snakes.
- o Touch Table--The Touch Table provides an informative look at items such as antlers, skulls, snake skins, and turtle shells.

The zoo offers school groups slide shows with names like, "Growing and Changing," "Hi, Polar Bear!," and "Vanishing Species." A Zoo Explorer Program is active at the zoo; registration and orientation are offered each fall through the Boy Scouts of America. Boys and girls fourteen years old and older receive hands-on experience in animal care by working with Seneca Park Zoo attendants.

The zoo has a snack and beverage shop and a gift shop. The Seneca Park Zoo is open every day of the year. An admission fee is charged, except on Mondays.

HISTORIC SITES

CAMPBELL-WHITTLESEY HOUSE MUSEUM

The Campbell-Whittlesey House Museum, located at 123 South Fitzhugh Street, is one of the finest examples of Greek Revival architecture in the United States. It is the restored home of Benjamin Campbell, a prosperous merchant / miller. The museum represents the prosperity the Erie Canal brought to Rochester during its boom-town years of 1835-1850. A visitor can listen to melodies made by musical glasses, see dolls and children's toys of the period, and get a glimpse of the private life of a wealthy family from 1835-50.

The Campbell-Whittlesey House is listed in the National Register of Historic Places. The museum is open Friday, Saturday, and Sunday afternoons. A nominal admission fee is charged. The museum is closed during January and February. Group tours of six or more are scheduled daily, except Monday. Special group services are available. The Campbell-Whittlesey House is accessible to the handicapped.

HIGH FALLS

High Falls, located at 60 Brown's Race in the Brown's Race Historic District, is Rochester's riverside educational and entertainment center. At High Falls, visitors can:
   o Watch the Genesee River rush over a 96-foot waterfall
   o Walk through Rochester's past including:
      --multi-level views of actual 1816 factory ruins at Triphammer Forge, an early iron forge
      --authentic ruins of the old Granite Flour Mill's foundation (circa 1850) and the millstone from the Moseley and Motley Milling Company
   o Walk across footbridges and look beneath the street at a replicated 240-foot section of the original raceway used to power mill wheels
   o Walk over the Genesee River Gorge on the 858-foot long Pont De Rennes bridge
   o Picnic or just relax in the park at Granite Mills Commons
   o Enjoy fireworks, a laser light show, and music
The Center at High Falls, designed as a high-pressure water system to quench fires, has been renovated into a modern educational and entertainment showplace. A simulated raceway and thundering falls are examples of the interactive three-dimensional exhibits that portray how creativity, culture, geology, and technology influenced early Rochester at High Falls. Activities at the Center at High Falls include pressing a button and meeting famous people who have lived in city, setting a water wheel in motion, and sitting in a taxi and getting to know Rochester.

Brown's Race Market houses the Triphammer Grill Restaurant, a 40-foot atrium with spectacular views of the Genesee River Gorge, and a gift shop. Banquet and meeting rooms occupy the second floor of Brown's Race Market. The terraced decks on each floor of the market offer open-air views of the Genesee River Gorge and the *River of Light* laser, light, and sound show with accompanying fireworks. The *River of Light* is a thirty-minute show projected on a 500-foot section of the Genesee River Gorge. It relates the story of a Seneca Indian spirit, Jonesho, who tells the history of the river and Rochester to Chester, a young bear whose great, great, great, great-grandfather jumped over the falls with daredevil Sam Patch in 1829.

Admission is free to High Falls; tours are self-guided. Advanced reservations are required for groups of ten or more. The Center at High Falls is handicapped accessible.

STONE-TOLAN HOUSE MUSEUM

The Stone-Tolan House, located at 2370 East Avenue, is a Federal-style farmhouse believed to be the oldest surviving structure in Monroe County. It recreates the private and public activities of a household and rural tavern in Brighton, New York, between 1790 and 1820. Orringh and Elizabeth Stone operated a tavern and raised nine children--all in the same house. Pioneer settlers gathered in the tavern to plan town governments and establish churches.

The museum displays clothes, tools, and utensils that represent how the Stone family managed their farm and operated their tavern. An early 19th century landscape is represented by an apple orchard, an herb garden, and over 200 varieties of plants. The Stone-Tolan House is listed in the National Register of Historic Places. The museum is open Friday, Saturday, and Sunday afternoons. A nominal admission fee is charged. The museum is closed during January and February. Group tours of six or more are scheduled daily, except Monday. Special group services are available. The Stone-Tolan House is accessible to the handicapped.

SUSAN B. ANTHONY HOUSE

The Susan B. Anthony House, located at 17 Madison Street in Rochester, was the home of the women's rights leader from 1866 until her death in 1906. She shared this house with her sister, Mary, and had many meetings here with reformers Frederick Douglass and Elizabeth Cady Stanton. It was the center for her organizing and writing efforts in support of the women's rights movement.

Also, it was at this house that Susan B. Anthony was arrested for voting in the presidential election of 1872, well before the Constitutional Amendment was passed granting women the right to vote. In her third-floor workroom, she contributed to the monumental work, *The History of Woman Suffrage,* along with Elizabeth Cady Stanton and others.

Today, the Susan B. Anthony House is a museum with National Historic Landmark status. The museum has a large display of memorabilia and photographs. The women's suffrage movement is portrayed by the comprehensive collection on the second floor. The Susan B. Anthony House is open Thursday through Saturday afternoons and at other times by appointment. It is closed Sundays and holidays. Group tours are scheduled by appointment. A nominal admission fee is charged.

WOODSIDE MANSION

Woodside Mansion, located at 485 East Avenue in Rochester, is the headquarters of the Rochester Historical Society. The mansion, a Greek Revival-style home built in 1839, is furnished as a period home. Woodside Mansion's extensive collections feature a large quantity of material about Rochester, as well as costumes, furnishings, paintings, and toys. The mansion houses many artifacts, including portraits of 500 Rochester pioneers. It also houses a detailed reference library. Woodside Mansion is open Monday through Friday. A nominal admission fee is charged.

RESTAURANTS-HISTORIC

DAISY FLOUR MILL

The Daisy Flour Mill, located at 1880 Blossom Road in Penfield, was originally a sawmill built by Samuel Rich in 1846; he built it to produce lumber for the grist mill that began operation in 1848. Initially, a mill race on Irondequoit Creek powered the stone mill wheels, but a Diesel engine provided the power after a flood in 1934. Flour and grain were produced at the mill until 1972. The Daisy Flour Mill is on the Register of Historic Places. It is the only existing mill of the sixteen that once lined Irondequoit Creek.

The grain bins and the heavy machinery with leather drive belts are still in place in the restaurant. They, along with the view of Ellison Park and the post and beam structure visible from the dining areas, contribute to the atmosphere of the restaurant.

The Daisy Flour Mill offers an extensive menu of contemporary cuisine and traditional favorites, including a wide selection of beef, fish, fowl, and game. The restaurant offers early bird and night owl specials; meals are accompanied by hot loaves of bread. As the season changes, the Daisy Flour Mill features American favorites from Cajun country, the seashore, and other regional specialties.

The Granary, the private dining room, accomodates thirty-six, and the three Grain Bins each seat ten for private dinners. The Indian Landing offers banquet facilities for up to 150 for celebrations, meetings, presentations, receptions, and weddings. A separate entrance and coatroom offers privacy from the restaurant, and there is a private lounge adjacent to the banquet room. The Indian Landing is equipped to provide visual aids; business meetings with special requirements can be arranged.

The Mill Race Bar has dancing to the area's finest jazz musicians on Friday and Saturday nights. It can accommodate cocktail parties of up to 125. The Daisy Flour Mill is open seven days a week. Valet parking is available.

RICHARDSON'S CANAL HOUSE

Richardson's Canal House, located at 1474 Marsh Road in Pittsford, is the oldest Erie Canal tavern surviving in its original form that is still on canal water. The tavern was built in 1818, restored in 1979, and is now listed in the National Register of Historic Places. Museum-quality antiques and artifacts help to capture the atmosphere and style of the tavern in its early days.

The restaurant features a seasonal menu inspired by French country and American regional cooking. Diners may chose a multi-course candlelit dinner in one of the restaurant dining rooms or an informal supper in the Cobblestone Pub or the Canalside Terrace (in season). Richardson's Canal House serves dinner Monday through Saturday. Reservations are recommended.

Oliver Loud's Inn, adjacent to the Canal House Tavern, is an historic country inn built in 1812. It has museum-quality paintings, china, and furnishings. Guest rooms, such as the Garland Room, have luxurious appointments that recall the private quarters of a country manor.

SPRING HOUSE

The Spring House, located at 3001 Monroe Avenue, is a beautiful four-story, Southern Colonial brick mansion, surrounded by a garden and patio. The restaurant was built as a hotel in 1822; it accommodated guests and visitors arriving by Erie Canal packet boat and stagecoach to take the waters of the Spa. The Spa was the famous Monroe Mineral Springs on the present site of the Oak Hill Country Club across Monroe Avenue. The old ballroom in the Spring House has a spring floor in which the resiliency is still evident. Many customers associate the spring floor with the origin of the name "Spring House."

The Spring House, one of the best preserved of the Erie Canal inns, is listed in the National Register of Historic Places. Its timbers were hand hewn; many natural woods were used in the floors, framing, and interior molding, including ash, birch, hickory, oak, and pine. In the center of the top floor is a "thunder room," which has no outside windows or skylights. Early inhabitants of the mansion went to the fourth floor to escape their apprehension of summer thunderstorms. The mansion still has all nine of the original wood-burning fireplaces.

The Spring House has four dining rooms and a patio surrounded by gardens for outside dining during the summer months. Separate banquet rooms are available for entertaining friends or business guests. The restaurant has an extensive winecellar, and the moderately-priced menu includes freshly baked goods and signature foods developed in its kitchens. The traditional menu offers a wide variety of beef, fowl, and seafood. The Spring House is closed Mondays; reservations are advisable.

WINERIES

CASA LARGA WINERY

The Casa Larga Winery is located fifteen miles south of Rochester at 2287 Turk Hill Road in Fairport. It has the appearance of a Tuscan villa, with Italian marble, light yellow stucco walls, sturdy arches, and vaulted ceilings. The winery sits atop Turk Hill, one of the highest points in Monroe County, and has a commanding view of the Rochester skyline.

The owners, Andrew and Ann Colaruotolo, specialize in wine made from *Vitis Vinifera,* or European-style grapes, such as Cabernet Sauvignon, Chardonnay, Gewurtztraminer, Pinot Noir, and Riesling. They also grow French-American hybrid grapes including Aurore, DeChaunac, and Vidal Blanc. The Colaruotolos planted their first vines in 1974, and by 1990 had twenty-five acres planted; annual yield was 20,000 gallons, with the use of some purchased grapes. Their son, John, is the vineyard manager.

Andrew Colaruotolo, who is also the winemaker, is a successful Rochester area builder. He grew up in Gaeta in the Frascati grape-growing region of Italy and spent twenty years of his youth working in the family vineyard, also known as Casa Larga. He still works in the vineyard--the "new" Casa Larga vineyard.

Casa Larga also makes champagne, including their award-winning Blanc de Blancs (both brut and *Naturel),* champagnes of Chardonnay, and Brut d'Ottonel, a champagne made from Muscat Ottonel. In addition to their varietal wines, Casa Larga makes blends including: Estate Blush, a blend of Aurore, DeChaunac, and Vidal; Estate Red, a blend of

Chelois, DeChaunac, and Rougeon (a teinturier that adds color to the wine); Estate White, a blend of Aurore and Vidal; and Tapestry, a blend of Cabernet Sauvignon and DeChaunac.

Casa Larga is open seven days a week for sales, tastings, and year-round tours (off-season tours on Saturday and Sunday only), but is closed on most holidays. The winery has banquet / meeting facilities for groups by reservation. During the spring, summer, and fall, the winery provides picnic tables and complimentary grape juice for children. Casa Larga offers a service of personalized wine labels for a nominal charge. Some of the most popular are "Bottled Especially for ...," and "Bottled to Celebrate the Anniversary (or Birthday) of ..."

Casa Larga offers world-class quality wine. The winery received three medals at the New York Wine Competition for its first vintage in 1978, and has received over 100 medals in regional, state, and international wine competitions since then.

ROCHESTER: THE WESTERN GATEWAY--PERSONS

SUSAN B. ANTHONY

Susan B. Anthony supported three causes: temperance, abolition of slavery, and women's rights. Initially, women's rights were third in that list of priorities, and she did not attend the first Women's Rights Convention in 1848 in Seneca Falls, New York. In fact, she did not meet women's rights leader Elizabeth Cady Stanton until March, 1851. They met on a street corner in Seneca Falls after attending an anti-slavery meeting. Their meeting was a momentous occasion, and was the beginning of a friendship and a working relationship that lasted over half of a century.

Anthony's attention to detail and her organizational skills were a perfect match with Stanton's strengths as a philosopher and policy-maker. In later years, Stanton's perception of their working relationship was:

> In thought and sympathy we were one, and in the division of labor we exactly complemented each other. In writing, we did better work together than either of us could have done alone. I am the better writer, she the better critic. She supplied the facts and statistics, I the philosophy and rhetoric and together we have made arguments that have stood unshaken through the storms of thirty long years ... Our speeches may be considered the united product of two brains.

Anthony had a sharp mind. One example of her quick thinking is her exchange of unpleasantries with Horace Greely, editor of the *New York Tribune*. Greely asked, "Miss Anthony, you are aware that the ballot and the bullet go together. If you vote, are you also prepared to fight?" Susan replied, "Certainly Mr. Greeley, just as you fought the last war-- at the point of a goose-quill."

The fifteenth Amendment to the Constitution, which was adopted in 1870, states that "The right of citizens of the United States to vote shall not be denied ... on account of race, color, or previous condition of servitude." The suffragettes would like to have seen the words "or sex" in the fifteenth Amendment. However, the words weren't there; women began to test the interpretation of their rights as citizens. Anthony wasn't the first woman to test this intrepretation of the Fifteenth Amendment, but she certainly received more newspaper attention than any other.

On November 1, 1872, Anthony decided that she would register to vote. The election judges told her that according to New York State law, she would not be permitted to register. Susan quoted to them from the Amendments to the Constitution, and insisted that she, as a citizen, had a right to vote. She was allowed to register. Anthony voted in the general election on November 5th, although she realized that she might have broken the law, and therefore be liable for a $500 fine. She received wide newspaper coverage, including articles in the *Chicago Tribune* and the *New York Times*. On November 18th, a marshall came to her home in Rochester and arrested her.

Anthony was arraigned, and her bond set at $500. She refused to pay it. Her lawyer, Henry Selden, who did not want to see his client go to jail, paid her bail. Unfortunately, by posting bail for her, he had inadvertently prevented her from appealing to higher courts. Posting bail indicated that she was not contesting the lawfulness of her arrest. Anthony made many speeches describing what was happening to her, including speeches in her home county, Monroe County, where her case was to be tried. The trial location was moved to Ontario County, south of Rochester, which was considered to be neutral ground.

On June 17, 1873, her trial began in Canandaigua, the county seat of Ontario County. The judge appointed to try her case was Judge Ward Hunt, an inexperienced judge who had just recently been appointed to the bench. Selden conducted a skillful defense, pointing out that Susan sincerely believed that she had been given the right to vote by the Fourteenth and Fifteenth Amendments. Judge Hunt refused to let her speak in her own defense.

Judge Hunt said that it didn't matter what Anthony's beliefs were; she had broken the law. Then he took a note from his pocket and read it to the jury. The note concluded with, "If I am right in this, the result must be a verdict ... of guilty and I therefore direct you to find a verdict of guilty." Henry Selden reminded the judge that he did not have the right to so instruct the jury, and demanded that the jury be asked for their own verdict. Judge Hunt ignored Selden, instructed the court clerk to record the verdict, and dismissed the jury.

This example of poor justice was widely covered by the press. Even people who did not agree with Susan's act of voting came over to her side because of this unjust treatment. Judge Hunt's actions were widely believed to have been politically motivated; Hunt's mentor was Roscoe Conkling, U. S. Senator from New York, who was a known foe of the women's rights movement. On the following day, Selden requested a new trial on the basis that his client had been denied the right to a fair trial by jury. Judge Hunt denied the request and fined her $100. Anthony responded, in part: "I shall never pay a dollar of your unjust penalty." The fine was dropped; she didn't have to pay it.

In 1880, Anthony began work on the monumental project, *A History of Woman Suffrage,* with Matilda Joslyn Gage and Elizabeth Cady Stanton. Ida Husted Harper wrote the final volume of the multi-volume series, which provided the history of the movement through 1920. Ida Husted Harper was also Susan's biographer; her *Life and Work of Susan B. Anthony* was published in 1898.

Anthony never really retired from her lifelong efforts to promote women's rights. The International Woman Suffrage Alliance was formed in 1904, and she, at the age of eighty-four, was recognized as their leader. At their convention in 1906, she commanded the delegates: "The fight must not stop. You must see that it doesn't stop." At a dinner in her honor on her eighty-sixth birthday, she concluded her speech with, "Failure is impossible."

In 1920, the Nineteenth Amendment to the Constitution was ratified. It included the statement that "the right of citizens of the United States to vote shall not be denied or abridged by any state on account of sex." It was called the "Susan B. Anthony Amendment." Anthony was right; failure was impossible. She was further honored in 1976 by the United States Government with the minting of the Susan B. Anthony dollar.

FREDERICK DOUGLASS

Frederick was born in February, 1818, in Talbot County, on the Eastern Shore of Maryland; he wasn't sure of the actual date of his birth. His mother, Harriet Bailey, was a slave and his father, whom he never met, was a white man. His master was Captain Aaron Anthony. In March, 1826, Frederick was sent to live with a member of Anthony's family, Hugh Auld, in Baltimore. Initially, Hugh's wife, Sophia, was very kind to Frederick. Frederick asked her to help him learn to read and write; she did so willingly until her husband heard what she was doing. Then the lessons stopped, and Sophia was no longer friendly to Frederick. However, living in Baltimore was a good experience for him, and he had many opportunities to learn.

Thomas Auld, Frederick's legal owner, brought him back to rural slavery in 1833. Frederick did not like Auld or his new wife, Rowena. He was not completely obedient, so Auld hired him out to Edward Covey, who had a reputation as a "slave breaker." Frederick endured six months of flogging and mistreatment, and then turned on Covey in a two-hour fight that Frederick won. After that, Covey did not bother him, but Frederick was even more committed to obtaining his freedom. He began to help his fellow slaves with reading lessons.

In April, 1836, Frederick and five other slaves made plans to escape. However, one of the five told authorities of their plans, and they were jailed in Easton. Instead of selling Frederick, Thomas Auld sent him back to Hugh and Sophia in Baltimore. Frederick became an experienced caulker in a boatyard, where there was considerable competition for jobs between poor white immigrants and slaves. Frederick was badly beaten because he was perceived to have taken a job from a white immigrant.

Frederick continued his self-education with a membership in the East Baltimore Mental Improvement Society, a debating club. He met Anna Murray, a freed slave who was barely literate, at one of their meetings. They became engaged in 1838. They both saved money and made plans for an escape to the North. An argument with Hugh Auld motivated Douglass to board a northbound train and escape. The conductor asked to see his free slave papers, which he didn't have; Frederick showed him his seaman's papers instead. Despite some tense moments when he saw two local men who could identify him as a slave, he arrived in Philadelphia safely and proceeded on to New York City.

He stayed with David Ruggles, publisher of the anti-slavery quarterly, *The Mirror of Slavery*. He sent for Anna Murray, and they were married on September 15, 1838. Ruggles, who was active in the underground railroad, suggested to Frederick and Anna that they move farther north. They moved to New Bedford, Massachusetts, where Frederick hoped to find work as a caulker. They lived with Nathan Johnson and his wife. Johnson suggested that since Frederick was an escaped slave he should change his name. Johnson had just finished reading Sir Walter Scott's *Lady of the Lake;* he suggested the surname of "Douglass," the name of the Scottish lord and hero. Frederick Bailey became Frederick Douglass.

When Douglass began to look for work as a caulker, he found that prejudice existed in the North as well as the South. The white caulkers didn't want to work with blacks. He was forced to take odd jobs as a common laborer. Anna helped by doing domestic work. One day he found a copy of William Lloyd Garrison's anti-slavery newspaper, the *Liberator,* and it changed his life. Garrison was a strong-willed abolitionist. In addition to being an editor, Garrison helped to found the New England Anti-Slavery Society. Douglass subscribed to Garrison's paper, and was moved by it.

Douglass attended the annual meeting of the New England Anti-Slavery Society in New Bedford on August 9, 1841, and a meeting on the next day on the island of Nantucket. Douglass was called upon to speak. He was nervous, but he spoke about his life as a slave, and was well received. Douglass was asked to become a full-time lecturer for the organization. He reluctantly accepted a three-month assignment, and stayed for four years. He improved his speech delivery techniques, and became one of the most popular lecturers.

Douglass had to learn to overcome hecklers; the life of an abolitionist was not easy. On September 15, 1843, he was severely beaten in Pendleton, Indiana. He escaped with a broken wrist and bruises. Abolitionist newspaper editor Elijah Lovejoy was killed in Alton, Illinois, while defending his press from an incensed mob. Garrison was dragged through the streets of Boston with a rope around his neck, and almost lost his life.

During the winter and early spring of 1844-45, Douglass took time out from the lecture circuit and wrote an autobiography, the *Narrative of the Life of Frederick Douglass, An*

American Slave. In August of 1845, he traveled to England, and went on a successful lecture tour of England, Ireland, and Scotland.

One month after his return to America, Anna and Ellen Richardson of Newcastle raised money and negotiated to buy Douglass' freedom. They went through American agents to buy his freedom from the Aulds for $711.66. The deed of manumission was filed at the Baltimore Chattel Records Office on December 13, 1846, and Douglass was a free man.

He returned to England for another lecture tour in 1847. Upon his return to America, he proceeded with plans to publish an anti-slavery newspaper. His British friends raised $2,000 to help him get started. He was surprised when Garrison advised against it. Garrison, who did not want competition for his *Liberator,* said that there were already too many newspapers of that type.

Douglass started his newspaper in spite of Garrison's counsel against it. He knew that he would have to choose a base far from Garrison's in New England. Douglass chose Rochester, a booming city of 30,000 on the Erie Canal, where he had been well received in 1842 and 1847. The leading abolitionist of central New York, Gerrit Smith, supported him, and gave him the deed to forty acres of land near Rochester. Douglass moved his family there on November 1, 1847.

The first edition of his newspaper, *North Star,* was published on December 3, 1847. He named the paper *North Star* because the north star was the guide that the slaves used when escaping from the south to freedom. In 1851, the *North Star* merged with the *Liberty Party Paper,* which was financed by Gerrit Smith; the resulting paper was called *Frederick Douglass' Paper.* In 1858, he began publishing *Douglass' Monthly* for British readers. The weekly ran until 1860, and he stopped the monthly in 1863. He had had a sixteeen-year publishing career.

Douglass also supported the Woman's Rights Movement. His *North Star* carried this announcement on July 14, 1848: "A convention to discuss the Social, Civil, and Religious Condition and Rights of Women, will be held in the Wesleyan Chapel at Seneca Falls, New York, the 19th and 20th of July instant." The masthead that Douglas used for the *North Star* was: "RIGHT IS OF NO SEX--TRUTH IS OF NO COLOR."

In January, 1871, President Grant appointed Douglass to a commission to Santo Domingo (Dominican Republic). He moved to Washington. D.C., because he thought that more federal appointments would be forthcoming. In 1877, President Rutherford Hayes appointed him United States Marshall for the District of Columbia. He served in that position until 1881, when President James Garfield appointed him recorder of deeds for the District of Columbia. He held that position until 1886.

Douglass' wife, Anna, died in August, 1882. He married Helen Pitts, his secretary in the office of the recorder of deeds, in January, 1884. The mixed marriage caused controversy, but Helen said, "love came to me and I was not afraid to marry the man I loved because of his color." Douglass' response to critics was that his first wife "was the color of my mother, and the second, the color of my father."

In September, 1889, President Benjamin Harrison appointed Douglass minister-resident and consul-general to the Rebublic of Haiti. He resigned the office in July, 1891. Douglass, one of the strongest anti-slavery voices of his time, died of a heart attack in Washington, D. C., on February 20, 1895.

GEORGE EASTMAN

George Eastman, founder of the photographic industry, was born in Waterville, New York, on July 12, 1854. He was the third child and first son of George W. Eastman and Maria Kilbourn Eastman. Eastman's father established a business school, Eastman's Commercial College, in Rochester in 1842. The school prospered in the thriving Erie Canal community, but George W. Eastman didn't move his family from Waterville to Rochester until 1860.

George W. Eastman died in 1862, leaving the family in reduced economic circumstances. Maria Eastman had to take in boarders to supplement her meager income. Young Eastman's first job was a part-time job with an insurance agency. His first substantial job was as junior bookkeeper for Rochester Savings Bank in April, 1874.

The first reference to photography in Eastman's diary was in 1869. His interest began in earnest in the summer of 1877, when he purchased almost $100 worth of "sundries and lenses," and arranged for a local photographer to teach him "the art of photography." Taking photographs in 1877 was a complex process requiring considerable equipment. The glass plates had to be exposed in the camera while wet, and development had to be completed before the emulsion dried. Eastman was bothered by the cumbersomeness of the process. He commented, "... the bulk of the paraphernalia worried me. It seemed that one ought to be able to carry less than a pack-horse load."

His thinking was given direction by an article in the *British Journal of Photography* that provided a formula for a sensitive gelatine emulsion for glass plates that could be used when dry. He spent long hours experimenting until he found a combination of gelatine and silver bromide that had the photographic qualities that he sought. Initally, he experimented to support his hobby of photography, but he soon realized that there was commercial potential in what he was doing. He decided to resign his job at the bank, make dry plates, and market them.

By June 1879, he was manufacturing quality photographic plates, and had designed and built equipment for coating them. He sailed to England, the center of the photographic industry, and obtained his first patent on July 22, 1879. His patent attorney, George Selden, submitted an application to the U. S. Patent Office for him on September 9, 1879 for "an Improved Process of Preparing Gelatine Dry Plates for Use in Photography and in Apparatus therefor." In April, 1880, he leased the third floor of a building on State Street in Rochester, and began to produce dry plates in quantity.

One of the first investors in the Eastman Dry Plate Company was Colonel Henry Alvah Strong, who, with his wife, boarded with Maria Eastman. Strong was a partner in Strong, Woodbury and Company, a successful manufacturer of whips. During the winter of 1879-80, Eastman formulated four business principles upon which to build his enterprise:

o Production in large quantities by machinery

o Low prices to increase the usefulness of the products

o Foreign as well as domestic distributrion

o Extensive advertising as well as selling by demonstration

A near-fatal catastrophy struck the new business in 1881--photographers complained that Eastman Dry Plates were no longer sensitive, and did not capture an image. Customers discovered something that wasn't realized until then: passage of time lessened the sensitiveness of the emulsion on the plate. The distributor in New York City had placed the newly received plates on top of the older plates, and had sold the new plates before using up all of the old. By the time the older plates were sold, they had lost their photographic sensitivity. At significant expense for a small company, Eastman recalled all plates and promised to replace them.

Then, Eastman encountered a second staggering blow--he could no longer make a satisfactory emulsion. During many weeks of sleepless nights with his factory shut down, Eastman conducted 469 unsuccessful experiments to produce a usable emulsion. On March 11, 1882, Eastman and Strong sailed for England. They discovered in England that the problem was due to a defective supply of gelatine received from the manufacturer; it was not a problem with the emulsion formula or Eastman's equipment. They returned on April 16th, conducted sixteen more unsuccessful experiments, and were successful on the seventeenth try. Eastman learned two lessons from this experience: to test samples of material received and to control the supply, whenever practical.

Next, Eastman searched to find a material to replace the fragile, heavy glass as a support for the emulsion. He experimented with collodion, which was made from gun-cotton (nitro-cellulose) and nitric acid. He filed his first patent application for photographic film on March 4, 1884. Then, Eastman worked on a mechanism to hold film in the camera. Both he and Wiliam H. Walker, who later joined Eastman's company, designed a roll-holder in a wooden frame.

The Eastman Dry Plate and Film Company was incorporated October 1, 1882, with $200,000 capital stock. Henry A. Strong was president and Eastman was treasurer of the new company, which purchased the plant and stock of the Eastman Dry Plate Company. The first commercial film was manufactured by the new organization on March 26, 1885.

Eastman used Dr. Samuel Lattimore, head of the department of chemistry at the University of Rochester, as a consultant. The first chemist hired by Eastman was Henry Reichenbach, one of Dr. Lattimore's assistants. Eastman was too involved with the operation of the business to devote much time to experiments; however, he continued to work on mechanical developments such as roller mechanisms. A patent for manufacturing transparent nitro-cellulose photographic film in rolls was granted to Reichenbach on December 10,1889. Joint patents were granted to Eastman and Reichenbach on March 22, 1892, and July 19, 1892.

Another early setback to the company was a serious fire on February 10, 1888, that destroyed most of the interior of the State Street factory and shut it down for two months. He was back in business in April, and by June he had his first camera on the market. Eastman came up with the name "Kodak" as a trademark for his products. He liked the letter K, the first letter of his mother's maiden name. "Kodak" was registered as a trademark in the United States on September 4, 1988. The first camera was the "No. 1 Kodak." Eastman explained the origin of the word to the British Patent Office:

> This is not a foreign name or a word; it was constructed by me to serve a
> definite purpose. It has the following merits as a trade-mark work:
> First: It is short.
> Second: It is not capable of mispronunciation
> Third: It does not resemble anything in the art and cannot be
>   associated with anything in the art except the "Kodak."

The company continued to expand to meet market demand. Brackett Clark, a director of the company, purchased several farms in the Town of Greece in August, 1890, which were to become Kodak Park, the world's largest film manufacturing complex. Camera and film development continued as Kodak strove to make a simple product that lived up to the slogan: "You press the button and we do the rest."

The next challenge that Eastman faced was one that he least expected--employee disloyalty. Reichenbach and two other employees secretly formed a rival company using the film-making formulae and processes of the Eastman company. Eastman investigated the charges and found them to be true. He also found that they had made 39,400 feet of unusable film and had let 1,417 gallons of emulsion spoil. Eastman discharged them.

The Eastman Photographic Materials Company, Ltd., was incorporated in London on November 28, 1889, to represent the company in all areas of the world except the western hemisphere. In December, 1889, the Eastman Company was incorporated in Rochester with $1,000,000 capital to represent the company in the western hemisphere. On May 23, 1892, the name of the company was changed to the Eastman Kodak Company, and the capitalization increased to $5,000,000.

Eastman established an organization in 1912 that was vital to the continued growth of the company. He founded the Eastman Kodak Company Research Laboratories, and brought Dr. C. E. Kennth Mees from England to serve as its head. Mees and his chief assistant, S. E. Sheppard, were both products of the University of London. They made significant contributions to the progress of the company. Motion pictures were introduced in the early 1920s, Kodacolor film was announced in the late 1920s, and many significant film improvements followed. These included Technicolor film, Kodachrome film, and the replacement of nitrate-based film with acetate-based product.

Eastman never married; he lived alone in his large mansion on East Avenue. He was instrumental in the founding of the Eastman School of Music at the University of Rochester, and the Eastman Theatre. He gave over sixty million dollars to educational institutions, including the University of Rochester, the Massachusetts Institute of Technology, Hampton Institute, and the Tuskegee Institute. In addition, he funded the Eastman Visiting Professorship at Oxford University, and gave $5,500,000 to establish dental clinics in Brussels, London, Paris, Rome, and Stockholm.

George Eastman took his own life on March 14, 1932 at his East Avenue home. He left a note which read: "To my friends: My work is done. Why wait? G. E." His death shocked the community. Karl T. Compton, president of the Massachusetts Institute of Technology, wrote in the April 15, 1932 issue of *Science* magazine:

> ... Consider for a moment the full significance of his last words. He had invented the modern photographic plate; he had invented the photographic film; he had made the Kodak a household object throughout the entire world; he had created a business; he had created a great research laboratory which had strikingly fulfilled his faith in it; he had selected certain fields of education, health, and art to which he had devoted his fortune for the benefit of the entire world; he had satisfied his distinctive desires for the excitement of exploration and big game hunting; he had no close relatives; the infirmities of old age had come upon him and were about to master him. He who had always been his own master remained so to the last.

Chimney Bluffs, east of Sodus Bay on Lake Ontario

TABLE OF CONTENTS

CHAPTER 3

NORTH OF THE LAKES

CHAPTER 3

NORTH OF THE LAKES

Ye hills of Wayne! Ye hills of Wayne!
Ye woods, ye vales, ye fields of grain!
Ye scented morns, ye blue-eyed noons!
Ye ever unforgotten moons!
No matter where my latest breath
Shall freeze beneath the kiss of death,
May someone bear me back again
To sleep among the hills of Wayne.

From *Hills of Wayne* by Mary Ashley Townsend

INTRODUCTION--NORTH OF THE LAKES

NORTH OF THE LAKES--DESCRIPTION

The principal features of the area north of the Finger Lakes are the northern boundary, Lake Ontario, with its beautiful natural bays, Sodus Bay and Little Sodus Bay; the glacial-formed drumlins that dominate the landscape; and the Erie Canal that crosses the entire region. The New York State Thruway parallels the Erie Canal through the northern Finger Lakes Region. The Ontario Lake shoreline has notable examples of erosion, particularly at Chimney Bluffs State Park.

Lake Ontario is the easternmost and smallest of the Great Lakes, but it is not the shallowest; it is deeper than Lake Erie and Lake Huron. The lake is one of the largest influences on the weather in the region. The area is known for its fruit production, particularly of apples, because of the moderating influence of Lake Ontario on the temperature.

The region contains one of the largest drumlin fields in the world. The field is bounded by Lake Ontario in the north and the Finger Lakes in the south; it extends from Syracuse in the east to about twenty-five miles west of Rochester. Drumlins, smooth ridges or hills of glacial drift, extend inland from Lake Ontario, both north into Canada and south into New York State. They were formed when the lake was the center of spreading Wisconsin Ice Age glaciers. Drumlins were molded by the ice movement above them, and were elongated in the direction of the movement of the glacier.

The Erie Canal extends across the approximate north-south midpoint of the region north of the lakes, except at the northern end of Cayuga Lake where it bends southward and then curves back again to the north. From west to east, Rochester to Syracuse, the canal passes through the Wayne County villages of Macedon, Palmyra, Newark, Lyons, and Clyde, and north of the Cayuga County villages of Port Byron and Weedsport and the Onondaga County village of Jordan. The Erie Canal is no longer used for commercial traffic; it is used for recreational purposes only.

NORTH OF THE LAKES--BRIEF HISTORY

In June 1687 in Montreal, Marquis Denonville, the Governor of New France, assembled a military expedition comprised of 2,000 French army regulars and 600 Indian allies. The expedition traveled down the St. Lawrence River and across Lake Ontario to Irondequoit Bay in 200 bateaux and 200 canoes. Another force of 180 Frenchmen and over 300 Indians, commanded by La Durantaye and Tonty, met the larger force at Irondequoit Bay. Denonville left 300 men to build a small fort to protect the canoes and barges, then marched overland to annihilate the Seneca Indians to reduce the French competition in the fur trade.

Denonville followed the Indian trail to Gannagaro, which was south of the present Village of Victor. As he approached the major Seneca village through a ravine on July 13, 1867, his expedition was surprised by a Seneca ambush and was almost overwhelmed. Some of his Indian allies fled, but his Mohawk allies held. Denonville ordered the sounding of trumpets and the roll of drums, while executing a flanking movement to rout the Senecas. In retreating, the Senecas burned their village, but not their store of corn. Denonville's men tore down the Seneca's palisades, and completed the destruction.

One hundred Frenchmen and eighty Senecas were killed. Denonville's men burned three other Seneca villages, and destroyed their stored corn and beans. His expedition then marched to their boats at Irondequoit Bay, and returned to Canada. No lasting benefit came to the French from this military venture. Gannagaro wasn't rebuilt; the Senecas merely moved farther inland, away from Lake Ontario. A negative result for the French was that the Senecas were driven into alliances with the English.

The War of 1812, a war for which the fledgling United States was woefully unprepared, included skirmishes along the southern shore of Lake Ontario. President Madison's Secretary of the Navy chose Commodore Isaac Chancey to command the naval forces on the lakes. Chancey was based at Sacket's Harbor at the eastern end of Lake Ontario, and that lake and Lake Erie were two of his major responsibilities. Chancey's British counterpart was Commodore Sir James Yeo.

At the beginning of the war, both Chauncey and Yeo had six ships on Lake Ontario; however, the Americans were outgunned thirty guns to one hundred. Chauncey's naval forces on Lake Ontario included the *Oneida* and the schooners *Conquest, Growler, Julia,* and *Pert.* Yeo's tactics were to cruise along the southern shore of Lake Ontario in his flagship, the *H.M.S. Royal George*, looking for an undefended port. He then seized the supplies stored there, either by force or by promising not to molest the settlers if they delivered their supplies willingly.

Five ships of Yeo's fleet were sighted off Sodus Point on June 19, 1813. The Redcoats landed from Yeo's ships, and were opposed by sixty militia. The British seized the stores in the warehouses; however, much of it had been hidden in nearby ravines. They burned all of the buildings in Sodus Point, except the Mansion House.

The British revisited the region on May 15, 1814, and landed in Pulteneyville. General John Swift's militia was ready for the British when they landed, but he was persuaded to negotiate. Swift agreed to allow the British to take 100 barrels of flour from the local warehouse, if the village was left alone. The highest quality flour had already been hidden in the woods. The *H.M.S. Royal George* fired a few cannonballs at the town as a parting gesture. The Selby house at the corner of Jay and Washington Street and the Legasse home at the bend in Lake Road were both struck by British cannonballs.

The building of the Erie Canal was the next major event in the region. Construction began to the east, at Rome, in 1817. In 1825, the Erie Canal was completed through the region north of the lakes from Albany to Buffalo; this opened up trade between the East and the Midwest. The canal was enlarged and upgraded in the mid-1800s, and again early in the twentieth century in an attempt to compete with the railroads. Initially, the railroads acted as feeders to the Erie Canal; eventually they went where the canals could not go. By 1850, rail transportation extended throughout the state.

Many short railroads were combined into one line across the state when the New York Central Railroad was formed in 1870. The Erie Railroad, completed in 1851, connected New York City with Dunkirk on Lake Erie via its roadbed across the southern tier of the state. Eventually, the railroads replaced the canal systems as the principal means of transporting both people and material.

In the late 1950s, the New York State Thruway was completed from New York to Albany, across the northern part of the state to Buffalo, and then south to the Pennsylvania State line. The four-lane divided highway replaced the two-lane Routes 5 and 20 as the main east-west route through the region north of the lakes .

NORTH OF THE LAKES--THINGS

ITEMS OF INTEREST

AUTO RACING

Elbridge--The Rolling Wheels Track is located eight miles east of Auburn on Route 5 in Cayuga County. It is a Drivers' Independent Race Tracks (DIRT) track with a five-eighths mile clay oval.

Weedsport--The Cayuga County Fair Speedway is located at the Cayuga County Fairgrounds on Route 31, one mile from New York State Thruway exit 40. It is a DIRT track with a three-eighths mile clay oval.

Williamson--Apple Valley Speedway is located two miles west of Williamson in Wayne County on Route 104. It is a National Association for Stock Car Racing (NASCAR) track with a paved half-mile oval.

THE ERIE CANAL

....
Low bridge! Ever'body down!
Low bridge, for we're coming to a town.
You always know your neighbor,
You always know your pal,
If you've ever navigated on the Erie Canal.
....
--Traditional

Between Rochester (Monroe County) and Syracuse (Onondaga County), the Erie Canal traverses the Wayne County villages of Macedon, Palmyra, Newark, Lyons, and Clyde.

Macedon--West of Macedon, the canal parallels the old New York Central Railroad. The canal widens in three places in this section, because the present canal was routed alongside the earlier canal that it replaced. Just west of the Wayneport bridge, the Fairport Yacht Club moors its boats in the old Erie Canal. East of the Canandaigua Road bridge, the old and new canals are separated by small islands. The 1862 canal route, south of the present canal, was closer to the Village of Macedon. Lock 30 in Macedon is near the end of Railroad Avenue. The site of lock 61 on the 1862 Erie Canal is just east of Route 350.

Palmyra--The old canal and the new canal are parallel to one another; the old canal is closer to the village. The ruins of the aqueduct that used to carry the Erie Canal over Ganargua Creek are located at lock 29, the site of Aqueduct Park. Biking and hiking trails link up with the towpath on the south side of the canal between lock 29 and the Division Street bridge. East of the village, a spillway made from an 1840s aqueduct channels excess water to Ganargua Creek, which is just north of the canal at this point. Swift's Landing County Park is just east of the spillway. East of the park, the canal passes though a narrow cutting, rounds Galloway Hill, turns southward for two miles, and then widens again near the Village of Port Gibson.

Newark--Lock 28B is in downtown Newark, near the railroad bridge over the canal. Adjacent to the lock is the powerhouse that used to supply the power for its operation. Lock 59 from the 1862 Erie Canal, a double lock that allowed two-way traffic, is located just east of Lock 28B. The canal passes through marshes for three and a half miles east of Newark between hills with a 600-foot elevation. The old canal can be seen from the new canal in this section.

Lyons--Dry-dock lock 28A is just west of the village. It is a New York State Department of Transportation waterway depot, and usually contains maintenance vessels undergoing repair. The canal utilizes the bed of Ganargua Creek from the point of its entry to the canal to lock 27 in the village. Canandaigua Creek enters the canal east of lock 27; it joins with Ganargua Creek to form the Clyde River, which is used by the Erie Canal for the next three miles. The three generations of the Erie Canal each took a separate route from Lyons to Clyde. The original canal looped to the north and back via Pilgrimport and Lock Berlin roads, the enlargement built between 1835 and 1862 took an eastwardly course, and the present canal turns south following the course of the Clyde River. The Clyde River and the canal separate three miles east of Lyons; the canal follows man-made channels while the river meanders.

Clyde--The Erie Canal and the Clyde River rejoin just west of Clyde. The remains of lock 53 from the second generation of the canal is just west of the village. Lock 26 on the present canal is two and a half miles east of the village. Lock 26 has a pivoted taintor gate used to control to water level. The gate is required because the canal uses the Clyde River in this section, and the water level is subject to fluctuations. The canal runs southeast from Clyde; the Clyde River moves in and out of the canal three times.

The canal passes through the 6,432-acre Montezuma Wildlife Refuge, and the canal and the Clyde River separate again one mile west of lock 25 at Mays Point. The Seneca-Cayuga Canal joins the canal one and a half miles east of lock 25 for three miles. The Seneca-Cayuga Canal, a 17-mile-long waterway with four locks, joins the Erie Canal with the two largest Finger Lakes, Seneca Lake and Cayuga Lake. To the north, the Erie Canal bypasses two Cayuga County villages, Port Byron and Weedsport, and the Onondaga

County Village of Jordan, that were on the original canal. North of Jordan, the Erie Canal passes through Cross Lake on its way eastward to Syracuse.

LAKE ONTARIO

Lake Ontario, the northern boundary of the region north of the lakes, is 193 miles long, 53 miles wide, and its area of 7,550 square miles is the smallest of the Great Lakes. It is 802 feet deep at its deepest point, and contains 393 cubic miles of fresh water. The lake is elliptical in shape, and is the easternmost of the Great Lakes. Its drainage area is 27,300 square miles--15,200 square miles in the United States and 12,100 in Canada.

Lake Ontario's shore line is regular and free of islands and navigational hazards, except for the northeast section that has diverse scenery with headlands and islands. The Thousands Islands area is just east of where the St. Lawrence River enters Lake Ontario.

ROBERT E. GINNA NUCLEAR POWER PLANT

The Robert E. Ginna Nuclear Power Plant Unit 1, located sixteen miles east of Rochester on the south shore of Lake Ontario, is owned and operated by the Rochester Gas and Electric Corporation (RG&E). The Ginna station has a pressurized light-water reactor system that generates electricity through the use of nuclear energy. The nuclear steam system, rated at 515 gross--490 net mw, was manufactured by the Westinghouse Corporation. The reactor system consists of three major components: the primary loop, the secondary loop, and the condensing cycle.

The reactor system is fueled with uranium in pellet form. The pellets are placed in zirconium fuel rods that are built into fuel assemblies. The reactor core contains 121 fuel assemblies, each containing 179 fuel rods, for a total of 21,659 rods. Two vertical shell, inverted U-tube steam generators each has 3,260 tubes. The turbine generator is a three-element turbine rated at 496,322 kw.

Commercial operation of the Ginna Nuclear Power Plant began on June 1, 1970. RG&E conducts tours of Ginna station, but visitors must plan ahead. Because of the obvious need for security, visitors must meet the following requirements:

  o Tours must be arranged six weeks in advance with the RG&E Speakers and Tours Bureau

  o Only group tours (10 to 25 people) are given.

  o No one under the age of eighteen is permitted in the Ginna plant. Simulator tours are provided in the training center for those under eighteen.

  o All visitors must be citizens of the U. S., and must have some form of picture identification with them. Simulator tours can be provided for non-U. S. citizens.

o Names and addresses of visitors must be submitted to the RG&E Speakers and
   Tours Bureau at least one week before the tour.

WILD WATER DERBY

The first Annual Wild Water Derby sponsored by the Twin Cities (Manchester and Shortsville) Lions Club was held in April, 1976. The Derby is held on three and a quarter miles of whitewater of the Canadaigua outlet between Littleville and Manchester, on Route 21 south of the New York State Thruway. This stretch of the outlet is whitewater rapids for only a few days in the early spring, when the floodgates between Canandaigua Lake and the outlet are opened to reduce the high lake level. When the lake level has dropped and the floodgates are closed, the course provides an easy canoe trip. Later in the summer, the water is too low for good canoeing.

However, in early April, the whitewater over the course of the derby is rated Class III, and is possibly Class IV at the peak rapids at Shortsville. Classification of rapids varies from Class I (easy) to Class IV (possible risk to life). In his book written over forty years ago, *Canoeable Waterways of New York State*, canoeing authority Lawrence Grinnell described the stretch of the outlet used for the Derby:

> Just before the bridge at Littleville, one and one-half miles above
> Shortsville, is a partly destroyed dam, which still backs up water. Below
> this dam are impassable cataracts. Between Littleville and Manchester, the
> stream descends sharply from a plateau in a succession of steep, boulder-
> strewn rapids, some definitely too shallow, or otherwise impossible to run
> at this stage. Steep banks make line-downs impractical. The descent could
> be dangerous at high water. The stream is still too steep and rocky to put in
> at Manchester bridge and re-embark one-quarter mile below this bridge,
> thus making the total portage from Littleville of about three and one-quarter
> miles.

There are five classes of Derby participants:
o kayaks (the smallest class)
o two-man canoe--men's class
o mixed canoe class--male-female or all-female teams
o inflatables--plastic and rubber manufactured craft and inner-tube rafts
o home-made rafts

The fifth class, home-made rafts, has the most variability--from well-built craft to a platform tied to fifty-gallon barrels that originally contained apple concentrate from South America. Beer barrels, casks, and kegs are also used as flotation devices. Some participants pay great attention to the artistic quality of the raft. Entries have included a craft decorated as a sea monster with a crew dressed as Vikings.

121

Personal flotation devices (life jackets) are required for all entrants, and kayakers must wear helmets. Many entrants wear wet suits. The derby is the principal fund-raising event for the Twin Cities Lions Club. The Ladies Auxiliary of the club provides a chicken barbecue. The awards committee provides trophies for the three fastest entrants in each category. Time to complete the race ranges from twenty to just under thirty minutes.

LEGENDS AND STORIES

THE ASTRONOMER IN THE LITTLE RED HOUSE

William Brooks was born in Maidstone, England, in 1844, into a Baptist minister's family. The family immigrated to America by way of Australia when William was thirteen. He became interested in astronomy while watching the ship's navigator make his daily observations of the sky with his sextant. Upon his arrival in the United States, William made his first telescope, which he used to observe Donati's comet in 1858. By the age of seventeen, he was giving lectures in astronomy in his father's church. He married, and moved to Phelps at the age of twenty-four.

He continued to build larger, more sophisticated telescopes, and in 1881 discovered his first comet--in the constellation of Leo. Brooks moved to a little red house on Lester Road outside of Phelps; he mounted his telescope on a platform, which he called the Red House Observatory. He discovered three comets in one month in 1886, using his fourth home-made telescope. Eventually, Dr. William Brooks discovered twenty-seven comets and became known as "the comet finder." He discovered the first eleven at his Red House Observatory in Phelps; the remaining sixteen he discovered at an observatory built for him by Hobart College in Geneva, where he was professor of astronomy.

He was the first scientist to become a member and a Fellow of the American Association for the Advancement of Science at the same time. Dr. Brooks died on May 3, 1921 in Geneva. The little red house no longer exists in Phelps, but the memory of its astronomer lives on.

THE COVERED RAILROAD

The Syracuse and Auburn Railroad, which ran parallel to Route 5 between the two cities, was completed in the 1830s. The route of the railroad was five miles north of the Village of Skaneateles. The Skaneateles village fathers built a wooden railroad to connect their village with the Syracuse and Auburn Railroad at Skaneateles Junction, halfway between Skaneateles Falls and Elbridge. It was replaced by a plank road in 1850, and by a steam railroad in 1867.

The president of the Skaneateles Railroad attended periodic meetings in New York City with the presidents of the major railroads to discuss matters of common interest. At one meeting, the subject was discussed of removing snow from the rails to keep the railroad traffic moving. The man from Skaneateles admitted that it was a major problem for his railroad. The president of one of the major railroads asked him how long his railroad was. He told the big railroad man that his road was five miles long. The president of the major railroad responded: "Hell, build a roof over it."

THE FOX SISTERS

John Fox, his wife, Margaret, and his two youngest daughters, Margaret and Katherine, moved to Rochester from Bath, Canada, in 1844. In December, 1847, the blacksmith and his family moved into a house on the corner of Parker and Hydesville Roads in the hamlet of Hydesville, which is located one mile north of Newark. Michael Weekman, who lived in the house in 1846 and 1847, had moved out because his family heard mysterious noises, and his eight-year-old daughter had felt cold, clammy hands on her face. The neighbors considered the house to be haunted. John Fox and his wife were devout Methodists, and did not believe the rumors.

In early 1848, the family heard mysterious rappings in the walls for the first time. Margaret and Kate both felt cold hands pass over their faces. On March 31, 1848, the two teenage girls, one sixteen and one fourteen, decided that they would try to communicate with the source of the rappings. Kate called out, "Here Mr. Splitfoot, do as I do," and snapped her finger three times. Three raps were heard in response. Margaret clapped her hands four times and said, "Do just as I do." Four raps were heard on the wall near her. Then Kate held up four fingers and asked, "How many fingers am I holding out?" They heard four raps. Kate pointed out to her mother that the source of the knocking could see as well as hear.

They received no response from the question, "Are you a man?" However, they received a multiple-rap response to the question, "Are you a spirit?" William Duesler, a neighbor who devised a code by assigning a number to a letter of the alphabet, learned that the spirit's name was Charles B. Rosma. He also learned that he was a peddler who had been murdered in the house, and buried in the cellar. When Duesler and several other neighbors dug in the cellar the next morning, they found a human skull, human hair, and quick lime.

Some people believed that modern Spiritualism was born that evening of March 31, 1848. They believed that the "conversation" that night with the spirit of Charles Rosma was the first communication between this world and the next. That spring the rappings became more frequent, and people began to visit the house. One day there were 500 visitors.

The girls' older sister, Leah Fox Fish, decided to capitalize on the attention that her family was receiving in the press. Leah, a widow who lived in Rochester, rented Corinthian Hall for public demonstrations of her sisters' ability to communicate with the next world. Leah moved her young sisters into her home on Troup Street in Rochester's Third Ward.

Several physicians from Buffalo learned that there were no raps if the girls' feet, while they were seated, were placed on chairs in front of them, and their knees were held firmly. Leah explained that the spirits didn't respond, because they thought that the girls were being mistreated. Leah took the girls on a tour of Albany, Troy, and New York City. The demonstrations in New York were attended by James Fenimore Cooper, William Cullen Bryant, and *Tribune* editor Horace Greeley, who offered to finance Kate's education. What began as the "Rochester rappings" continued as a growing cult of Spiritualism; there were 2,000 mediums in the United States by 1852.

Margaret Fox met the Arctic explorer Elisha Kent Kane in Philadelphia in 1852, fell in love, and married him. When he died at the age of thirty-seven, she gave up her spiritualistic demonstrations; she joined the Catholic Church to comply with her husband's wishes. However, Margaret later went on a tour to England with Kate, and, while there, demonstrated her psychic powers to Thomas Carlyle.

Upon their return home, they renounced the methods by which they had inspired the Spiritualistic movement. On October 21, 1888, at the Academy of Music in New York, Margaret gave a demonstration of how she and her sister had made the rapping sounds. She removed the shoe and stocking from her right leg, and showed the audience how she made the noises with her big toe. She said that her sister Leah had urged her two younger sisters not to reveal the secret.

In 1889, Margaret recanted and said that she really did have psychic powers, but that she had been talked into saying that she and her sister made the rapping sounds with their big toes. They were welcomed back into the Spiritualism movement, and remained active in it until their death. The movement was forty years old at that point, and had many followers. Later, the Hydesville house was moved to the Spiritualist camp at Lily Dale in the Chatauqua region.

THE LEGEND OF THE DISCOVERY OF MAPLE SYRUP

The Indians called the early spring the time of the Maple Moon. One brisk March morning, Woksis, an Iroquois chief, went hunting. He pulled his tomahawk out of the tree in which he had imbedded it the previous day. The sun came out, and it became a pleasant spring day. Woksis' squaw had left a wooden container below the gash her husband had made in the tree trunk. By the time the sun was overhead in the sky, her wooden bucket was full. She tasted the sweet watery sap, and decided to cook their dinner in it; she saved herself a long walk to the spring for fresh water.

That evening, the family of Woksis ate their meal cooked in the flavored water, and the use of maple syrup began. Other Indian families cooked with it, and maple syrup became so popular that the Indians started a maple festival with ceremonies and dances. All of the food at the festival was maple-flavored. They stored their maple syrup in boxes of white birchbark called "mokuks." The Iroquois used curved pieces of bark or hollow reeds to drain the sap from the tree. They collected it in bark buckets to bring to the boiling vessels made from hollowed-out hardwood logs. At other times, they didn't bother to boil the sap; they froze the sap they had collected, threw away the ice cap, and ate the residue under the ice.

THE MESSAGE THAT WASN'T RECEIVED

Fred Locke was the railroad telegraph operator in the Village of Victor in the early 1890s. One day the Buffalo office of the railroad sent a message to its station in Victor. In accordance with railroad procedures, Locke transmitted an acknowledgement of the receipt of the message. Several days later he received a stern rebuke from the Buffalo office for not acknowledging the message. Locke was a conscientious individual who paid attention to details, and he knew he had acknowledged the message.

He asked himself why the acknowledgement had not been received. He investigated the problem, and found that the cause was the poor quality of the insulators on the telegraph lines. The insulators in use at the time allowed sufficient current leakage that by the time Locke's dashes and dots reached Buffalo, there wasn't enough current left to activate the receiving key. He developed an improved insulator that would allow a minimum of current leakage.

He experimented making insulators with clay, and eventually developed the first porcelain insulator. They worked well, and were a great improvement over the insulators in use. Locke established a facility in Victor for the manufacture of insulators that permanently changed the insulator industry. He sold his insulator business in 1915 to concentrate on the development of new products, such as heat-resistant glass. A dish made with his glass could withstand intense heat without breaking. He became a pioneer in glass cookware.

THE STORY OF THE VICTORIOUS ADMIRAL

William Thomas Sampson was born in Palmyra in 1840. He lived with his Scotch Presbyterian parents at the corner of Johnson and Vienna Streets, until he left for the U. S. Naval Academy at Annapolis at the age of seventeen. Sampson served as an ensign on a U. S. Navy frigate during the Civil War, and returned to Palmyra to marry his school sweetheart, Margaret Aldrich. He attended the Naval War College, and became an authority on naval tactics.

By 1898, when the United States declared war on Spain, Sampson was a Rear Admiral. He was placed in charge of the North Atlantic Squadron. When the Spanish and U. S. fleets clashed in Santiago Bay, Admiral Sampson was eight miles away, steaming toward a conference with his U. S. Army counterpart, General Shafter. The squadron engaged the enemy, and Sampson's second-in-command, Admiral Winfield Schley, won an overwhelming victory. Controversy ensued as to whether Sampson or Schley should be given credit for the victory. A compromise was reached. Sampson was given credit for planning the battle; Schley received recognition for the successful execution of the plan. Both were victors.

Sampson returned to a hero's welcome in his hometown in 1899; it included bands, banners, speeches, and a large parade. Admiral Sampson died in Washington, D. C., in 1902. In 1902, the Navy Department sent to Palmyra a fourteen-centimeter gun that the Admiral's fleet had captured from a Spanish warship. The town fathers mounted the gun in the village park. Sampson Naval Training Base, later Air Force Training Base, on Seneca Lake, was named for Admiral Sampson.

WINSTON CHURCHILL'S NEW YORK STATE ANCESTORS

Most people are aware that Winston Churchill's parents were Lord Randolph Churchill of England and Jennie Jerome of New York. However, many people aren't aware that his wife's grandfather and father were from the region north of the lakes. One of Churchill's maternal grandfathers, Ambrose Hall, was a State Assemblyman from Wayne County and a highway commissioner in Palmyra in the 1820s.

Churchill's father-in-law, Leonard Jerome, was born south of Syracuse in Pompey, lived on Canal Street in Palmyra, and later resided on a farm in Marion. Ambrose and Clarissa Hall had two daughters, Katherine and Clarissa, who married two brothers, Lawrence and Leonard Jerome from Marion. Leonard Jerome studied at Princeton University for two years, transferred to Union College, and graduated in 1839.

Upon his graduation, he read law in his uncle Hiram Jerome's law office in Palmyra. Hiram moved to Rochester in 1842, and, in 1844, employed Lawrence and Leonard in his law office there. Lawrence Jerome and Katherine Hall were married in August of 1844; Leonard Jerome and Clarissa Hall were married in Palmyra in April of 1849. Both Lawrence and Leonard left the law in 1845 when they bought part interest in the *Rochester Daily American*, a Whig newspaper. They sold their interest in the newspaper in 1850.

Leonard Jerome moved to Brooklyn in 1850, and worked in the fastgrowing telegraph industry. Since his daughter, Jennie Jerome, who married Winston Churchill, was born in Brooklyn, that city is usually associated with the Jerome family; the memory of Churchill's Wayne County heritage has faded.

PARKS, FORESTS, AND TRAILS

CHIMNEY BLUFFS STATE PARK

Chimney Bluffs State Park, an undeveloped state park known as a "natural park," is accessible off East Bay Road, two and a half miles east of Sodus Point. The natural park, which consists of pinnacles and spires that have been carved out by hundreds of years of water and wind erosion, extends along the Lake Ontario shoreline for over a mile.

The park can be viewed from a hiking trail inland from the bluffs, and from a narrow strip of beach between the bluffs and Lake Ontario. Since the chimney bluffs can be easily damaged by foot and vehicle traffic, hiking on the bluff faces and off-road vehicle use is discouraged by park officials.

FAIR HAVEN BEACH STATE PARK

Fair Haven Beach State Park is located on 865 hilly, rocky acres one mile north of Fair Haven on Route 10A. Elevation in the park ranges from 245 feet to 360 feet. The park has a beautiful lakeshore, lakeshore bluffs, flat and wide expanses, inland Sterling Pond, and woodlands. Fair Haven Beach State Park contains thirty-two cabins, 191 campsites (44 electric, 147 non-electric, RVs allowed), three pavillions (two reservable), and picnic areas with tables and fireplaces. It also has playing fields, a playground, and hiking trails, including self-guided nature trails.

The park has a boat launching ramp, boat rentals, a camp store, concession stand, and pay telephones, as well as fishing, swimming at the lakeshore, and bathhouse facilities. There are hot showers, flush toilets, a marine sewage pumpout station, and a trailer dumping station. Camping is permitted from mid-April to the first weekend in November; a camper recreation program is provided. The recreation building is available for use all summer, and can be reserved in the off-season. Fair Haven Beach State Park is open all winter for cross-country skiing, hiking, and snowmobiling. Six cabins with wood-burning stoves are available during the winter.

Cayuga and Seneca Indians who canoed and fished on Little Sodus Bay in the mid-1600s called it "Date-ke-a-shote." In the last half of the Seventeenth century, French traders used it as a landing site from which to trade with the Indians for furs. The French called Little Sodus Bay, "Chroutons," or passage that leads to the Cayugas. Commercial activity in the area increased significantly in 1873, when the the harbor was developed and the Southern Central Railroad was completed. Coal was brought in by rail for shipment via Lake Ontario, and outgoing shipments included apples, ice, milk, and wood products.

Many cottages were built along the lake around 1900, and the area became a popular resort area. The Parks Commission was formed in 1923, and the building of park buildings and roads began in 1927; the Civilian Conservation Corps built additional buildings, campsites, roads, and trails in the 1930s.

The park contains two examples of wave-eroded drumlins, which are hills formed by glacial drift. Beaches separate Sterling Marsh, Sterling Pond, and other backwater areas from Lake Ontario. The sheltered wetlands are home for amphibians, beavers, ducks, fish, geese, muskrats, and aquatic plants.

GALEN WILDLIFE MANAGEMENT AREA

The Galen Wildlife Management Area, located two miles southwest of the Village of Clyde, consists of two parcels. The 562 acres in the larger parcel can be reached by River Road; the smaller parcel of 179 acres on Creager Island can be reached by boat or canoe from either the Clyde River or the Erie Canal. The Galen Wildlife Management Area has extensive frontage on the Erie Canal.

The management area consists of agricultural fields, marshes, upland woodlots, and wooded flood plains. It provides a habitat for deer, ducks, geese, great blue herons, songbirds, raccoons, and woodpeckers. Hunting, trapping, and fishing for bass, bullhead, and walleye pike are popular activities.

The Galen Wildlife Management Area was purchased in 1980 with funds from the Wetland Preservation category of the 1972 Environmental Quality Bond Act. It provides protection for a portion of the Galen Marsh, known locally as the Marengo Swamp. Camping, off-road vehicle use, motorized boating, snowmobiling, and swimming are prohibited in the Wildlife Management Area. Permitted activities are:

o Birding	o Fishing	o Nature Study
o Canoeing	o Hiking	o Picnicking
o Cross-country Skiing	o Hunting	o Trapping

HOWLAND ISLAND WILDLIFE MANAGEMENT AREA

The Howland Island Wildlife Management Area, located in north central Cayuga County, three miles northwest of Port Byron, can be reached by traveling north from Port Byron to Howland Island Road. The 3,600-acre Wildlife Management Area is divided into three units: Howland, 3,100 acres; Bluff Point Unit, 388 acres; and the Way-Cay Unit, 114 acres. The Erie Canal and the Seneca River are the water boundaries for Bluff Point Island and Howland Island. The topography varies from low-lying flood plains to gently rolling hills or steep drumlins.

The Wildlife Management Area contains a secondary growth of ash, basswood, black locust, hickory, oak, and willow, as well as shrubs such as alder, arrowwood, dogwood, spicebush, and sumac. Farm fields, meadows, water impoundments, wetlands, and woods provide a habitat for 220 species of birds and forty-six types of mammals, including deer, foxes, opossums, rabbits, raccoons, skunks, and squirrels.

Farmers settled Howland Island in the early 1800s, and cleared the elm, maple, and oak trees to raise crops. Farming was discontinued in the 1920s; the land was idle until 1932, when it was purchased for a game refuge. The area was managed for migrating waterfowl after the Civilian Conservation Corps created 300 acres of water impoundments by constructing eighteen earthen dikes. The area has been managed primarily for the natural production of waterfowl since 1962.

Public fishing is allowed, hunting and trapping are permitted under special regulations, and waterfowl hunting is controlled via a lottery and reservation system on Howland Island. Wildlife, particularly deer, songbirds, and fall migrations of shore birds and waterfowl, offer the birdwatcher and photographer many opportunities. Maintenance roads are available for use as hiking trails for the bird watcher, hiker, horseman, and naturalist. An observation tower offers a commanding view of the region. A launch site allows fishing boats access to the Erie Canal.

Rules for public use:

o Howland Island Wildlife Management Area is open except from April 1st through May 31st, the peak waterfowl nesting season.

o Camping is prohibited.

o Recreational boating and overnight mooring or storage of boats is not permitted.

o Off-road vehicular travel, including mopeds, motorcycles, motor scooters, snowmobiles, and trail bikes is prohibited.

o Swimming is not permitted.

o Fishing is permitted in season, except for April 1st through May 31st.

LAKE SHORE MARSHES WILDLIFE MANAGEMENT AREA

The Lake Shore Marshes Wildlife Management Area is located between Sodus Bay and Fair Haven Beach State Park in northeastern Wayne County. It consists of several parcels bounded on the north by Lake Ontario, and contains 6,179 acres of wetlands and adjacent uplands. The area provides a combination of bay-lake-marsh environments that offer habitats for fish, mammals, shorebirds, songbirds, and waterfowl, such as black ducks, mallards, teal, and wood ducks.

Popular activities are: fishing for largemouth and smallmouth bass, northern pike, and panfish; hunting for deer, pheasants, rabbits, squirrels, and woodcock; and trapping for mink and muskrats. Birdwatching is another popular pastime in the Wildlife Management Area. Developments include boat access sites and trails for fishermen, hikers, hunters, and naturalists. Also, small water impoundments and parking areas at scenic locations overlooking areas used by migrating waterfowl have been constructed in the Wildlife Management Area.

SHOWS AND FESTIVALS

HILL CUMORAH PAGEANT

The Hill Cumorah Pageant is held during the second week of July at Hill Cumorah, four miles south of Palmyra on Route 21. The pageant, recognized as America's largest outdoor drama, is attended by over 100,000 people from all around the world. The pageant features a costumed cast of 600, and the voices of the Mormon Tabernacle Choir. The pageant has notable special effects, including 15-foot water curtains, a quality outdoor sound system, and ten light towers using more than 500,000 watts of power. Critics have made the following observations of the pageant:

o "A pageant performed with the spirit of a George Lucas techno-dazzler and the scope of a Cecil B. DeMille epic." --*The New York Times*

o "And above all, it delights the senses." --*Rochester Democrat and Chronicle*

o "One of the most dramatic moments in the production takes place when the resurrected Christ appears 30 feet in the air, and slowly descends to the highest point of the gigantic seven-level stage." --*The Buffalo News*

o "As always, the pageant promises glittering exotic costumes and an extensive sound and light show." --*Denver Post*

The Hill Cumorah Pageant has been presented by the Church of Jesus of Latter Day Saints since 1935. The performance begins at dusk. There is no admission charge, parking is free, and there is seating for 10,000 (or bring blankets or lawn chairs). There are interpreters for the hearing impaired, and French, German, and Spanish earphone translations.

SAUERKRAUT FESTIVAL

Phelps, the home of the annual Sauerkraut Festival since 1967, was a center for cabbage growing and sauerkraut factories for much of its history. The annual Sauerkraut Festival is held at the Phelps firemen's field on Ontario Street in early August. The festival has food, music, parades, and plenty of sauerkraut.

Previous years' festivals have included an early evening children's parade and children's night on the midway on Thursday. Friday's activities were midway rides and a block dance at the American Legion on Main Street with music of the 1950s and 1960s. Saturday's activities have included:

o Arts and crafts	o Midway rides
o Festival parade	o Chicken barbecue
o Cutting of the sauerkraut cake	o Continuous live music
o A 20K race over country roads from Phelps to Clifton Springs and back	o Special music events, such as bagpipers and cloggers
o Disc Jockey music	o fireworks

Events scheduled for Sunday were a custom car show and a chicken barbecue at the American Legion.

SHAKER DAY FESTIVAL

One day every other summer, a farm south of Sodus Point returns to its heritage as a Shaker Community, a nineteenth-century utopian society. Members of the United Society of Believers in Christ's Second Coming were known as Shakers, because of the shaking and quivering dances they performed during religious services. They bought the tract of over 1,300 acres in 1826, and built the Shaker Dwelling House in 1834. The house, inhabited by sixty people, had an ice-house wing on the east side. The cluster of simple white buildings is located on a ridge overlooking Sodus Bay, south of Sodus Point and east of the hamlet of Alton on Shaker Road.

Alasa Farms, the current name for the farm, is a contraction of the names of two former owners, Alvah Strong and Asa McBride. It is a working farm owned by the Mangan family of Rochester, who host the Shaker Day Festival on a day in late July in even-numbered years. The Shakers lived simply; they were known for the simplicity of the design of everything they built, from early washing machines to dressers, ladder-back chairs, and tables. They sold baskets, brooms, brushes, and furniture, and are credited with being the first to market seeds in packets commercially.

In 1836, the Sodus Shaker Community moved to Groveland, which is south of Mt. Morris. Until 1892, 150 Shakers lived on 1,800 acres of rich Groveland farmland containing over thirty buildings, including barns, homes, mills, and a church. Their community was sold in 1893 to the Craig Colony for Epileptics. It is now the Livingston County Correctional Facility.

Past Sodus Shaker Day Festivals at Sodus Point have included craft demonstrations in the Shaker barn, Shaker dancers, a movie about Shaker life, story tellers, and talks about Shaker communities and Shaker furniture-making. Craft demonstrations have included broom making, chair taping, weaving, and the making of Shaker oval boxes. An antique sale has been held on the grounds. An admission fee is charged; parking is free.

STERLING RENAISSANCE FESTIVAL

The Sterling Renaissance Festival is located at 15431 Farden Road in Sterling, east of Fair Haven. It recreates festival time at the English village of Warwick during the reign of Queen Elizabeth I, about the year 1585. The comedies of Shakespeare and other playwrights of the period are performed on the Bankside Stage and Wyldwood Stage.

The festival, which was established in 1977, features period arts and crafts, entertainment, food, and music in a thirty-five acre natural, wooded setting. The period artisans and craftspeople demonstrate the making of books, glass objects, hair garlands, historic wax seals and ornaments, jewelry, leather crafts, prints, and stained glass. Over fifty artisans display their crafts. The grounds are populated with beggars, jugglers, knaves, lords, ladies, minstrels, monks, puppeteers, shopkeepers, and wenches. There are over 600 actors, crafters, entertainers, food people, and gamers.

Visitors may come in their own Elizabethan costumes, rent costumes from the village seamstress, or stay dressed as they are. Entertainment includes fire eating, juggling, magic, music, and dancing and jousting in the lanes and on the stages. Examples of English food are fish and chips, marinated steak-on-a-stick, peasant bread, spinach pies, turkey legs, and hot apple dumplings with ice cream.

Admission is charged, but once inside the grounds there is free entertainment, outdoor theatre, and street performances, including live jousting. Other activities are Shakespearean plays, street theatre, and children's productions, such as puppet shows, storytelling, and the Theatre of Fools. Over sixty stage and street performances are ongoing at no extra charge. The season is from early July until mid-August. The day's events open with Queen Elizabeth's parade at 10:00 AM.

TOUR BOATS

LIBERTY ERIE CANAL CRUISES

Cruises are provided on the 49-passenger *Liberty* from Village Park in Lyons. Several cruises are offered:

- o a "coffee and danish" cruise lasting an hour and a half
- o excursions to Creagger's Island, Newark, or Port Gibson, of two to four hours duration
- o a buffet dinner and evening cruise
- o a narrated canal study trip--covering Ganargua Creek, Clinton's Ditch, Erie Canal, Barge Canal, and the dry dock

Almost all public cruises pass through a canal lock, either at Lyons or Newark. The *Liberty* is available for charter cruises.

MID-LAKES NAVIGATION, LTD.

Mid-Lakes Navigation, Ltd., based in Skaneateles, offers cruises that originate in Syracuse and pass through the area north of the lakes. The Syracuse to Buffalo cruise on the 149-passenger *Emita II* departs from Cold Springs Harbour near Syracuse. Highlights of the cruise include:

- o the Montezuma National Wildlife Refuge and six locks
- o docking at Newark overnight--lodging at the Quality Inn
- o stopping at Palmyra to inspect the 1825 aqueduct
- o docking at Brockport's Harvester Park overnight--lodging in Rochester
- o Medina Aqueduct and double locks at Lockport
- o docking at North Tonawanda--return to Syracuse by chartered motorcoach

Mid Lakes Navigation also offers cruises from Buffalo to Syracuse, Syracuse to Albany, and Albany to Syracuse via the Erie Canal on the *Emita II*. They also offer cruises on Onondaga Lake and the Erie Canal near Syracuse on the *City of Syracuse,* and cruises on Skaneateles Lake

NORTH OF THE LAKES--PLACES

MUNICIPALITIES

CLIFTON SPRINGS

Clifton Springs is located on Route 96, five miles east of New York State Thruway Exit 43. Benjamin Shekell of Frederick County, Maryland, explored the area around Clifton Springs in 1799, and returned in 1800 to become the first settler. Benjamin's father, John Shekell, Sr., and his brother, John Shekell, Jr., moved to the area and built the first log house on East Hill in 1802. They built just above the sulfur springs that gave the village its first name, Sulphur Springs.

William Powell of Geneva moved to the area in 1806 to build a large hotel on East Hill. John Shekell, Sr., was one of the first hotel keepers. Dr. Henry Foster, of the New Graefenberg Water Cure located five miles south of Utica, visited the area in the fall of 1849 to check out the sulphur springs as a potential site for a "water cure" sanitarium. Foster, a devout Methodist, felt that he had a call to found a Christian sanitarium at Clifton Springs. He opened the Clifton Springs Water Cure Company on September 13, 1850.

Dr. Foster was current with the medical advances of his day, and was receptive to new therapy. He introduced the use of dry electricity, hand massages, salt baths, and Turkish baths. Card playing was not allowed, and dancing was reserved for special occasions. The Water Cure Company was renamed the Clifton Springs Sanitorium Company in 1871.

The hotel on East Hill was enlarged in 1865 to become an "air cure" facility that competed with Dr. Foster's "water cure" sanitorium. It provided a bar, entertainment, and a contrast to Dr. Foster's approach. It was very popular until it burned down; it was not rebuilt. Dr. Foster purchased the property to expand his operation. Today the facility begun by Dr. Foster is known as the Clifton Springs Hospital and Clinic; its excellent reputation is known well beyond the region.

CLYDE

The Village of Clyde is located at the intersection of routes 31 and 414. The original name of the village was Block House, when it was founded as a fort to protect the route of the British fur trade. In 1815, Frederick DeZeng, the "Father of Clyde," settled at the site of the Block House, which was named Lauraville for one of Lord Pulteney's daughters. It was renamed Clyde in 1818 by Andrew McNab, since it reminded the Scottish land agent of Scotland. A replica of the 1700s Block House was constructed in 1975; it contains local artifacts. The building of the Erie Canal contributed significantly to the development of the village. The canal flows through Clyde; lock 26 is just southeast of the village.

DeZeng donated land to Clyde for a village park. DeZeng's great-grandson, DeLancey Stowe, authorized the drilling of a well in the park that yielded mineral water instead of the fresh water he had expected. Townspeople initially hoped that the mineral springs would lead to the building of a spa, but they decided to forego the commercialism that would have resulted.

The Galen Historical Society museum is located on Sodus Street in Clyde. It is housed in the old Ketchem and Maloy mill, and contains some of the original milling equipment. Black Brook County Park in the Town of Galen is east of Clyde on old Route 31.

LYONS

Lyons, the county seat of Wayne County, is located at the intersection of routes 14 and 31. Charles Williamson, land agent for a group of English land speculators that was headed by Lord Pulteney, explored the area around Lyons in 1794. Williamson named the site of the joining of Ganargua Creek and the Canandaigua Lake outlet Lyons, because it reminded him of a smaller version of the confluence of the Saone and Rhone Rivers at Lyons, France. In 1789, Nicholas and William Stansell and their brother-in law, John Featherly, became the first settlers in the area. They built a log cabin where the Canandaigua Lake outlet flows into Ganargua Creek to form the Clyde River.

In 1830, area farmers began to grow mint, and, by 1868, there were 300 acres of mint under cultivation. H. G. Hotchkiss began his peppermint and essential oils business on Water Street in 1841; by 1877, his facilities in Lyons were the largest in the world. He shipped his product worldwide, but most of his exports went to England. Hotchkiss became known as the "peppermint king." He was awarded prizes for his products in America, and his peppermint extracts won medals in expositions in London, Paris, and Vienna. Peppermint cultivation shifted to the midwest, principally to Indiana and Michigan, but the leaves were still shipped to Lyons to be processed and bottled in the familar amber bottles.

Included among Lyon's favorite sons are Admiral Willard Bronson, who was Commandant of the U. S. Naval Academy; Admiral Bradley Fiske, who fought with Admiral Dewey at the Battle of Manila Bay during the Spanish-American War; and William Stewart, U. S. Senator from Nevada and promoter of the Comstock Lode.

Erie Canal Lock 27 and the Barge Canal Dry Dock Marina are located in the village. Lyons is also home to Abbey Park on Water Street and the hiking trails of the Blue Cut

County Nature Center, which is located west of the Village on Route 31. Lock Berlin County Park is located east of Lyons at Newark and Gansz Roads in the Town of Galen.

NEWARK

The Village of Newark is located in the Town of Arcadia at the intersections of routes 31 and 88. The first settlers of Newark cleared land along Ganargua Creek in 1791. Three Lusk brothers bought a one-square-mile tract that included the present site of Newark in 1806; however, the real development of the village began with the construction of the Erie Canal. The father of Newark is considered to be Joseph Miller; he bought 100 acres in 1819 from the Lusks, laid out streets, and sold lots. Miller had the contract for building one and a quarter miles of the Erie Canal through the area.

The hamlets of Lockville and Miller's Basin were consolidated in 1823 into the Village of Newark, which was named for Newark, New Jersey. Some Newark natives claim that the village was named for the English Viscount Newark, who was co-proprietor of the site under the royal grant of the King of England.

For a century beginning in 1873, Newark was one of the rose capitals of the United States. C. H. Stuart and his father-in-law, Albert Jackson, founded the Jackson-Perkins nurseries of the C. H. Stuart Company in 1873. At its peak, the nurseries had 400 employees planting, cultivating, packing, and shipping 12,000 plants per year, which consisted of 400 varieties and a multitude of colors. The Jackson-Perkins two-acre experimental garden was visited by thousands of people. The nurseries were closed in the 1970s, when the company was consolidated with another nursery on the west coast.

The Newark Canal County Park is at the intersection of Route 88 and Van Buren Street. Erie Canal lock 28B is in the village. Widewaters County Park is west of Newark on Route 31 in the Town of Arcadia. The Hoffman Antique Clock Museum is a gem of a museum that is housed in the Newark Public Library. The Wayne County Extension Center of Finger Lakes Community College is located in the Maple Building of the Newark Developmental Center.

PALMYRA

Palmyra, named for the Syrian city, is located at the intersection of routes 21 and 31. The first settlers were surveyors John Jenkins and John Swift who came from the Wyoming Valley of Pennsylvania in 1789. Swift built a log house on Ganargua Creek, at the eastern boundary of the present Village of Palmyra. In the Iroquois language, "Ganargua" means "a village, suddenly sprung up." Swift built mills at Canal and Main Streets; he became the first citizen of the village, which was known as Swift's Landing.

Swift trained militia during the War of 1812, attained the rank of general, and was killed at the Battle of Queenstown Heights.

A group of families from Rhode Island settled in Palmyra in 1791. They included the Durfee family, who planted the first apple orchards in the area. David Wilcox, Winston Churchill's great-grandfather, was one of the settlers from Rhode Island. Louis Philippe, later the "Citizen King" of France, stayed with the Durfees on a tour of the region in 1796. Swift's Landing was renamed Palmyra in 1797.

Joseph Smith, Sr., moved to Palmyra in 1816 from Royalton, Vermont with his wife, three daughters, and six sons. Joseph, Jr., was the third-oldest son. The family moved to a farm about four miles south of Palmyra in 1818, where Joseph, Jr., was visited by the angel Moroni, and founded the Mormon religion in 1827. The Book of Mormon was printed in the Grandin Building in Palmyra in 1830.

The completion of the Erie Canal in 1825 brought an economic boom to the village. The boatyard at Palmyra built the packet boats *Myron Holley* and the *Twin Brothers,* owned by John and Levi Thayer. Henry Wells of Wells-Fargo is a favorite son of Palmyra. He began his career by delivering packages around the village on foot, and then by horse and wagon. He founded the Wells and Company express agency; later, he teamed up with Henry Fargo to run the pony express in the western United States.

The Alling Coverlet Museum is located at 122 William Street in Palmyra, and the "corner of four churches" is located at the intersection of routes 21 and 31 in the village. A church occupies each of the four corners of the intersection. The First United Methodist Church, the Western Presbyterian Church, the Zion Episcopal Church, and the First Baptist Church each occupies one of the corners. The Palmyra Macedon Aqueduct County Park is located at Erie Canal Lock 29, which is at the western edge of Palmyra on Route 31 in Town of Macedon. Swift's Landing County Park is located on Hogsback Road, off Route 223 in the Town of Palmyra.

MUSEUMS

ALLING COVERLET MUSEUM

The Alling Coverlet Musuem, located at 122 William Street in Palmyra, houses the largest collection of coverlets in the United States. The museum, which is administered by Historic Palmyra, Inc., contains coverlets collected by Mrs. Harold Alling for over thirty years. The museum is located in a two-story brick building donated by Mrs. Henry Griffith.

One of the coverlets on display is the woven coverlet "American Tapestry," an approximately eighty inches by ninety inches bed cover woven of homespun wool and linen. Coverlets were made to be used, but they were also heirlooms. The flax and wool were raised by the early pioneers, cleaned, sorted by quality, and spun prior to weaving the coverlet. Dyes were made from local flowers, roots, and weeds.

Most coverlets were made by professional weavers. Two of the best in the mid-1800s were Ira Hadsell and James Van Ness. Professional weavers wove in geometric patterns; they sometimes used as many as twenty-four harnesses. Later, they used the French Jacquard loom controlled by punched cards to make more complicated patterns. Coverlets made by housewives were usually made on four-harness looms, using the overshot weave.

Historic Palmyra, Inc., operates a gift shop in the coverlet museum that offers hand-crafted items and books about textiles. The Alling Coverlet Museum is open afternoons from June through September. It is open at other times by appointment.

Historic Palmyra, Inc. is a tax exempt, non-profit organization dedicated to community service, historic preservation, and the operation of the Alling Coverlet Museum, the Palmyra Historical Museum, and the William Phelps General Store Museum. The Historical Museum, located at 132 Market Street, houses antiques, Palmyra memorabilia, and Victorian period rooms. The main floor and the Phelps' home on the upper floors of the General Store Museum, located at 140 Market Street, are furnished with original Phelps family artifacts and furniture.

DIRT MOTORSPORTS HALL OF FAME & CLASSIC CAR MUSEUM

The Drivers Independent Race Tracks (DIRT) Motorsport Hall of Fame and Classic Car Museum is located at the Cayuga County Fairgrounds on Route 31, one mile from New York State Thruway Exit 40. It displays over thirty modified racing cars and more than fifty classic cars. The Hall of Fame and Museum, which opened in 1992 to preserve the history of modified dirt racing and to display classic cars, is the filming site of a weekly show that is nationally-televised, "This week on DIRT."

The Jack Burgess National Parts Peddler Theatre Room shows films of old-time races. A world-wide finders' network provides classic car enthusiasts with a way of finding rare and collectible classic cars. An on-site gift shop offers apparel, collector's items, and souvenirs. The museum is open all year; a nominal admission fee is charged.

HOFFMAN CLOCK MUSEUM

The Hoffman Clock Museum, which is located in the Newark Public Library at the corner of Mason and High Streets in Newark, has over 100 horological items on display--

mainly nineteenth-century American clocks. The collection has fifteen clocks made in New York State, and includes Dutch, English, French, German, and early Japanese clocks.

The museum's exhibits introduce visitors to the development of timekeeping technology and clock styles. They provide an opportunity to learn about the history of timekeeping; the unique collection of timepieces has something for everyone--young and old, novice and expert. Each travel season, a particular facet of timekeeping is highlighted in a special display.

The core collection was assembled by Augustus and Jennie Hoffman of Newark. The Hoffman Foundation, established in 1950, was organized to preserve the Hoffman's collection for the education and enjoyment of the community. The museum is open daily during regular library hours, Monday through Saturday. However, the library and the museum are closed Saturdays during July and August. Arrangements for group tours of the museum may be made with the curator. Admission to the museum is free.

RADIO MUSEUM

The Antique Wireless Association Radio and Communications Museum is housed in the restored 150-year-old Academy Building on Routes 5 and 20 in East Bloomfield. The museum contains one of the largest collections of radio apparatus associated with the early pioneers, such as DeForest, Edison, and Marconi. Displays in the museum include:

o A "cat's whisker" radio

o Marconi wireless apparatus

o Nineteenth century telephones

o Working model of world's first wireless apparatus

o Shipboard wireless transmitters

o A fully-stocked 1925 radio store

o Western Union Telegraph Office

o An early Telsa spark coil in operation

o First radio and television tubes

o Atwater Kent and Stromberg Carlson radios

o A two-inch television screen

o An early broadcast studio

In addition, the museum has a modern amateur radio station, W2AN.

The Antique Wireless Association, founded in 1952, was chartered as a non-profit corporation by the State of New York. The association, a member of the American Association of Museums and the Regional Conference of Historical Agencies, is devoted to research and documentation of the history of wireless communications. The museum is open Sunday afternoons from May through October, and Saturday afternoons and Wednesday evenings from June through August. It is closed on holidays. Admission is free.

SODUS BAY LIGHTHOUSE MUSEUM

The Sodus Bay Lighthouse Museum, operated by the Sodus Bay Historical Society, is located on Lake Street in Sodus Point. The state-chartered non-profit institution, which received its charter in 1979, is supported by contributions and memberships.

The Sodus Bay region has been known for its commercial fishing, ice industry, grain exports, lumber trade, and shipbuilding. The first settlers entered the area in the late 1700s, and Sodus Bay became a busy harbor for exporting farm products and other commodities. Congress appropriated $4,500 for the construction of a lighthouse and keeper's house on the site in 1824; Ishmael Hill was the first lighthouse keeper.

Congress appropriated $14,000 in 1869 to replace the original structures, since they had deteriorated beyond mere maintenance. That lighthouse was used from 1871 until 1901. West pier, constructed in 1834 at the new entrance to the bay, was a more favorable location for the beacon and light that were installed in 1901. The lighthouse on West Pier was used as a residence for maintenance personnel until 1984.

The lighthouse served an area with heavy boat traffic of both commercial and pleasure boats. A railroad connecting Sodus Point with the coal fields of Pennsylvania was completed in 1872, along with a small coal loading trestle at the west end of the bay. The trestle was expanded considerably in 1927; in the five-year period from 1861-1865, seven and a half million tons of coal were shipped using the trestle. While the wooden trestle was being dismantled in 1971, due to the reduced market for coal, it caught fire and was destroyed.

The area served by the lighthouse has been a popular summertime recreation spot since the 1850s. It is used by boaters, campers, fisherman, and picnickers. It is also a center for winter activities such as ice boating, ice fishing, and snowmobiling. The Sodus Bay Lighthouse Museum, which is open from May 1st through October 31st, contains many nautical artifacts and items of local history. Its D. Russell Chamberlain Memorial Library is open during museum hours. The museum is also open by appointment for adult group tours, bus tours, and school group tours.

VALENTOWN MUSEUM OF LOCAL HISTORY

The Valentown Museum of Local History, located on Route 96 opposite Eastview Mall, was built in 1879 as a community center and shopping plaza. The Pittsburgh, Shawmut, and Northern Railroad planned a line from Pittsburgh to link up with the New York Central Railroad at Macedon; it was to compete with the Pennsylvania Railroad in carrying coal to the Great Lakes. The preliminary railroad survey showed that the new line would pass through Levi Valentine's farm, which was located just north of Victor.

Valentine laid out a new village with streets and building lots. He constructed a four-story frame building that was to be the center of the village. He named his village Valentown, a combination of his last name and the last name of his grandfather, Ichabod Town. Unfortunately, the raiload went bankrupt after reaching Wayland, and did not extend as far north as Valentine's farm. However, the Valentown building became a center of business and rural social life in the area. Its use declined early in the 1900s, and, after the Grand Military Balls of the hamlet of Fishers' Home Defense were held there in 1917-18, it was closed.

The building was vacant for over twenty years. Historian Sheldon Fisher, whose great-grandfather founded the nearby hamlet of Fishers in 1811, purchased the property in 1940 to restore it. The Valentown Musem has been restored to look as it did over 100 years ago. Many of the displayed artifacts were originally used there. Museum exhibits include:

- o Displays of Indian artifacts from Ganondagan, Seneca capital in Victor from 1650-87
- o Items from the 1687 battle between Denonville's French Army and the Senecas
- o Artifacts and documents of the Phelps-Gorham Purchase of western New York in 1788
- o Original interior of the Auburn and Rochester Railroad station in Fishers
- o Civil War memorabilia from area soldiers
- o Haberdashery and millinery shops with a display of many hats and molds
- o Artifacts from the Mormon leader Brigham Young's local 1829 home and mill site
- o The original country store as it was in the 1800s
- o Early musical instruments and sheet music
- o Pioneer hand tools and farm implements

The basement of the building was used as stabling for visitor's horses. The first floor included a grocery store, meat market, harness maker's shop, cobbler's shop, bakery, and the community room, which provided a meeting place for church and social groups. The second floor housed the grange room, art school, theatrical school, business school, and the school of music for members of the 54-piece Valentown band. The most well-known graduate of the theatrical school was Jessie Bonesteele in 1882. She trained Melvin Douglas and Catherine Cornell for her traveling stock company.

The third floor has an 18-foot ceiling with four chandeliers and a full stage at one end. It was used for concerts, dances, church services, and plays. The Valentown Museum is open from Wednesday through Sunday, May 1st through October 31st. There is a nominal admission fee.

PLACES OF INTEREST

HILL CUMORAH AND MORONI MONUMENT

The brochure,*Welcome to Historic Mormon Country*, contains the following explanation of Hill Cumorah, four miles south of Palmyra:

> In A.D. 421, Moroni, the last survivor of a great civilization that inhabited the Americas from 600 B.C. to A.D. 420, buried in this hill a set of gold plates on which was recorded the history of his people. By commandment of God, Moroni returned as an angel and delivered the plates to Joseph Smith in 1827. Joseph Smith translated the plates as the Book of Mormon, a companion scripture to the Bible. The Book of Mormon tells of the visit of Jesus Christ to the ancient Americans.

Hill Cumorah is a notable drumlin, formed by glacial activity, in the region north of the lakes. It is the site of a spectacular outdoor religious pageant, *America's Witness for Christ*, performed each summer by a cast of over 600 for audiences of 100,000 people. The significance of Hill Cumorah is explained in the Visitor's Center through exhibits, paintings, and video presentations. Free guided tours are conducted daily.

HISTORIC GRANDIN BUILDING

The Historic Grandin Building in Palmyra was constructed in 1828, three years after the completion of the Erie Canal. E. B. Grandin supervised the printing of the first edition of the Book of Mormon in 1830. This first edition of the companion scripture to the Bible consisted of 5,000 leather-bound 590-page copies. The Visitor Center is open year-round; it has free displays, films, and guided tours.

JOSEPH SMITH HOME

Joseph Smith, the first president of The Church of Jesus Christ of Latter-Day Saints, and his father and brothers built this frame house in Palmyra in 1820. He lived in the house between the ages of nineteen and twenty-two. The homestead, located south of Route 31 and west of Route 21, has been restored to its original condition. It is furnished with period furnishings. The Visitor's Center is open year-round; it has free displays, films, and guided tours.

MARTIN HARRIS FARM

Martin Harris was an early follower of Joseph Smith, and a strong believer in the book of Mormon. He mortgaged his farm to finance the first printing of the Book of Mormon, a companion scripture to the Bible. The 5,000 copies of the first edition of the Book of Mormon were printed at the historic E. B. Grandin Building in Palmyra in 1830.

An 1850 Erie Canal cobblestone house is now located on the former Harris farm in Palmyra. The Visitor's Center is open year-round; it has displays, films, and free guided tours.

THE SACRED GROVE

The Sacred Grove, located south of Route 31 and west of the Joseph Smith Home in Palmyra, was the site of a visitation at which Joseph Smith learned from Heavenly Beings that he should join no established church.

When Joseph Smith was fourteen, he wondered which of the local churches he should join. He noted a passage in the Bible, James 1:5, "If any lack wisdom, let him ask of God ..." He walked westward from his home on a beautiful spring morning into a grove of trees nearby. He knelt in prayer in the grove, and had a vision: "I saw a pillar of light. When the light rested upon me, I saw two personages, whose brightness and glory defy all description, standing above me in the air. One of them spoke unto me, calling me by name and said, pointing to the other, 'This is my Beloved Son; hear him!'"

Seven years later he was directed to the gold plates, buried in Hill Cumorah, from which he translated the book of Mormon.

HISTORIC SITES

GANONDAGAN STATE HISTORIC SITE

The Ganondagan State Historic Site, which is located at 1488 Victor-Holcomb Road in Victor, is the location of a major Seneca Indian town and palisaded granary. The Senecas stored hundreds of thousands of bushels of corn in the granary, which was built on a mesa; they used it as a fort when they were attacked. The town and its Boughton Hill burial grounds were designated a National Historic Landmark in 1964. The granary at Fort Hill, which was in the path of destruction of the Marquis de Denonville in 1687, was placed in the National Register of Historic Places in 1966. Denonville, the Governor General of New France, led a campaign against the Iroquois in July, 1687, to destroy the Seneca Nation and to eliminate their competition in the fur trade.

The historic site has three trails marked with illustrated signs: Earth is our Mother Trail, Trail of Peace on Boughton Hill, and Granary Trail on Fort Hill. The Visitor Center has an audiovisual program, research archives, and special seasonal events. It is open daily from mid-May through Labor Day and Wednesday through Sunday between Labor

Day and the end of October. The trails are open year round during daylight hours. Admission is free; reservations may be made for group tours. The Visitor Center and some of the trails are accessible to the handicapped.

RESTAURANTS--HISTORIC

THE HOLLOWAY HOUSE

The Holloway House is located on Routes 5 and 20, eight miles west of Canandaigua. The colonial house was built by Peter Holloway in 1808. It was a tavern and a stagecoach stop on the post road that became Routes 5 and 20. The restaurant has a relaxed atmosphere that is reminiscent of a Norman Rockwell painting.

The Holloway House specializes in American food such as fried chicken, baked ham, lamb chops, roast turkey, and seafood. The Saturday night special is prime ribs of beef. Bread and rolls are a specialty of the house, particularly the light Sally Lunn bread and the home-style orange rolls. The restaurant is also known for its desserts and its extensive wine cellar.

NORTH OF THE LAKES--PERSONS

ISAAC MERRITT SINGER

Isaac Merritt Singer, promoter of the sewing machine, was born near Troy, New York, on October 27, 1811, the eighth and youngest child of Adam and Ruth Singer. Adam, a cooper and millwright, moved his family to Oswego shortly after Isaac's birth. Isaac did not have a happy childhood. His parents were divorced when he was ten years old. Adam Singer remarried, and young Isaac did not get along with his stepmother. He left home at the age of twelve, in his words, "without money, without friends, without education, and possessed of nothing but a strong constitution and a prolific brain [and without humility, for that matter]."

In 1822, Singer moved to Rochester, which was experiencing a boom due to the construction of the Erie Canal, to live with an older brother. He worked part of the year as a laborer, and went to school the remainder of the year. In 1830, he moved to Auburn, where he accepted a job manufacturing lathe-making equipment. He established a nomadic pattern early; it was to become a way of life.

Singer's goal in life was to be an actor. In fact, he was one of those people who was, inherently, an actor. Throughout his life, he frequently talked about his ambition to be on the stage. He was good-looking, over six-feet tall, blond-haired, and outgoing. He possessed considerable assertiveness and charisma; he had a knack of winning people over to his viewpoint. These personal qualities served him well in promoting the sewing machine in later years. Women were charmed by him; he instilled trust in people, which a number of his partners lived to regret.

Singer joined a troupe of players in Rochester in 1830. His Shakespearean roles with this troupe were his first acting experience. He married Catherine Haley of Palmyra, New York, in December, 1830. Catherine was fifteen when they married, and initially they lived with her parents. Singer continued to act, but he worked as a woodworker and drygoods clerk in Port Gibson when he wasn't on the stage. Their first son, William, was born while the Singers lived in Port Gibson. They moved to New York City in 1835, where Singer accepted a position at Hoe's press. He left Hoe's in the spring of 1836, and joined a troupe of traveling players as their advance man.

Singer traveled, and did odd jobs over the next two years. He devised his first invention in 1839, a rock-drilling machine that was powered by horses walking in a circle to turn a crank supported by wooden framework. He patented the invention, sold the patent for $2,000, and returned to his first love, acting. He founded the Merritt Players in Chicago; they stayed together until 1844, when they disbanded in Fredericksburg, Ohio.

Singer worked for a press in Fredericksburg, where he developed a machine for carving wooden type for printers. He moved to Pittsburgh, and then to New York City to take advantage of larger markets for his invention that he patented on April 19, 1849.

The design of the machine was ingenious. A parallelogram device, or pantograph, was used to move the cutter and follow the letter or number being drawn or traced. However, Singer's timing was off; the use of wooden type was being replaced with lead type, which could be melted down and reused. At this time, Singer was thirty-eight years old, and, by any criteria, could not be considered a success. His personal qualities of motivation and boundless optimism would not allow him to settle into quiet but secure existence. He was a driven man.

George Zeiber, a Philadelphia book publisher and jobber, financed a prototype of Singer's machine in June, 1850, which they took to Boston in search of customers. They rented a room in Orson Phelps' shop at 19 Harvard Place, Boston. Phelps manufactured sewing machines that did not work well, and required frequent maintenance. Phelps asked Singer to redesign the machine, to make it more reliable, and to fund the development effort. Phelps convinced Singer that there was more money to be made from sewing machines than typecarving machines.

Singer formed a way of thinking that became his credo in establishing his fortune: "I don't give a damn for the invention, the dimes are what I'm after." Singer redesigned the machine, and he and Phelps applied for a patent. Singer and Zeiber encountered considerable resistance to their machine from customers who had tried earlier machines and were dissatisfied with them. Singer was in his element while promoting the new machine. He may have been an actor and an inventor, but he demonstrated clearly in this phase of his life that his real strength lay in promoting.

Singer realized that neither he nor Zeiber had the necessary financial or legal background to deal with the business as it grew. Singer offered Edward Clark, a partner in the firm of Jordan, Clark and Company, a one-third share of the business for his services. Clark was a vital addition to the business, and the source of many of the innovations that generated profits for the enterprise. Clark was effective in dealing with patent suits for the sewing machine, but even he couldn't prevent Elias Howe from winning a suit against them. The design of the sewing machine had evolved from the contributions of many inventors, including Howe. In July, 1854, Singer was directed to pay Howe $15,000 and a royalty of twenty-five dollars per machine.

One of Clark's innovations was to lease sewing machines, with an option to buy; this opened the market to housewives who couldn't afford the purchase price. The I. M. Singer Company expanded its manufacturing and sales to Europe, and by 1861, it sold more machines in Europe than in the United States. Singer was one of the earliest multi-national corporations. The manufacture of sewing machines expanded rapidly by 1870, because of the use of interchangeable parts-- a concept devised by Eli Whitney.

Clark and Singer dissolved their partnership in 1863, and Singer retired a wealthy man. Singer and his wife moved to England, and built a mansion called The Wigwam near Torquay, on the South Devon coast. The Wigwam had a private theatre; Singer never outgrew being an actor. However, he didn't live to see The Wigwam completed. He developed a heart condition, and the combination of a chill and heart problems caused his death on July 23, 1875. He was buried in Torquay cemetery.

JOSEPH SMITH

Joseph Smith, founder of the Mormon church, was born in Sharon, Vermont, on December 23, 1805, the fourth child and third son of Joseph Smith, Sr., and Lucy Mack Smith. Smith, Sr., had difficulty making ends meet by farming the rocky soil of Vermont. He tried farming in several New England locations without success. During the winter of 1812-13, young Smith contracted typhoid fever, and developed an abscess on his leg. The doctors decided to amputate the leg, but he was strong-willed even at the age of nine. He refused to let the doctors amputate it, and subjected himself to an operation in which the diseased bone was removed without the benefit of anesthesia. The leg was saved, but he walked with a limp for the rest of his life.

In 1816, the family moved to Palmyra, New York. The family was penniless upon their arrival in the small frontier village, but they were willing to work hard. Joseph, Sr., and his two oldest sons, Alvin and Hyrum, did odd jobs such as harvesting, well-digging, and making maple syrup. In 1820, Smith thought that he should join a church, but he could not find a denomination that was aligned with his understanding of the gospel of Jesus Christ as set forth in the new testament.

Smith went into the woods by himself in response to the Epistle of James, Chapter 1, verse 5, which reads, "if any of you lack wisdom, let him ask God," and said that a pillar of light fell upon him:

> ... immediately I was seized by some power which entirely overcame me, and had such astonishing influence over me as to bind my tongue so that I could not speak. Thick darkness gathered around me, and it seemed to me for a time that I were doomed to sudden destruction ... just at this moment of great alarm, I saw a pillar of light exactly over my head, above the brightness of the sun, which gradually descended until it fell upon me.
> It no sooner appeared than I found myself delivered from the enemy which held me bound. When the light rested upon me I saw two personages, whose brightness and glory defy all description, standing

above me in the air. One of them spake unto me calling me by name and said--pointing to the other--"This is my beloved Son, hear him."

My object in going to inquire of the Lord was to know which of all the sects was right ... I was answered that I must join none of them, for they were all wrong, and the personage who addressed me said that all their creed were an abomination in His sight; that those professors were all corrupt, that "they draw near to me with their lips but their hearts are far from me; they teach for doctrines the commandments of men: having a form of godliness but they deny the power thereof.

A second visitation occurred to Smith on September 21, 1823, in his room at home late on a Sunday evening:

... a personage appeared at my bedside, standing in the air, for his feet did not touch the floor. He had on a loose robe of most exquisite whiteness ... his whole person was glorious beyond description ...

I was afraid; but the fear soon left me. He called me by name, and said that his name was Moroni; that God had work for me to do; and that my name should be had for good and evil among all nations, kindreds, and tongues ... He said there was a book deposited, written upon gold plates, giving an account of the former inhabitants on this continent, and the sources from whence they sprang. He also said that the fullness of the everlasting Gospel was contained in it, as delivered by the Saviour to the ancient inhabitants; also that there were two stones in silver bows--and these stones, fastened to a breastplate, constituted what is called the Urim and Thummin--deposited with the plates; and the possession and use of these stones were what constituted "Seers" in ancient and former times; and that God had prepared them for the purpose of translating the book.

Smith went to the hill described in the vision, several miles south of Palmyra and east of the Palmyra-Canandaigua mail road. He found the plates and the breastplate with the Urim and Thummin under a large stone near the top of the hill on the west side. They were in a box made of stones cemented together. However, the messenger would not allow him to take the objects with him; he was not to have them for four more years. He was asked to meet the messenger at Hill Cumorah each year at the same time.

In October, 1825, Smith was hired to search for a silver mine in the Susquehanna Valley by Josiah Stowell of South Bainbridge, New York. Treasure hunting or "money-digging" was a fad at the time. He roomed with the Hale family in Harmony, Pennsylvania, near the perceived site of the mine. Smith became attracted to Emma Hale, a twenty-one-year-old schoolteacher. When the search for the mine was concluded, unsuccessfully, Smith worked for Stowell at South Bainbridge. He frequently visited Emma at Harmony. Smith and Emma were married on January 18, 1827, and they moved in with his parents in Palmyra.

On September 21, 1827, Smith went to Hill Cumorah, where the messenger Moroni gave him the plates, the Urim and Thummin, and the breastplate. He began the laborious task of translating the plates with one of the "Seer" stones. Smith entrusted a loyal neighbor, Martin Harris, to take the transcript of the translation to New York City for evaluation; Charles Anthon of Columbia College said they were "Egyptian, Chaldaic, Assyric, and Arabic."

In 1829, Smith chose Egbert B. Grandin of Palmyra, publisher of the *Wayne Sentinel,* to publish the *Book of Mormon.* Martin Harris mortgaged his farm for $3,000 to pay Grandin for 5,000 leather-bound copies of the 590-page book. On April 6, 1830, Smith and six witnesses formally signed the papers to organize the Church of Jesus Christ at Peter Whitmer's farm in Fayette. Now known as the Church of Jesus Christ of Latter-Day Saints, they were called "Mormons" because the messenger Moroni's father, Mormon, was the major compiler of the ancient records.

On January 2, 1831, Smith had a revelation to move the church, which consisted of sixty members, from Palmyra to Kirkland, Ohio. The church in Kirkland, which had been founded by missionaries, had grown to 100 members. There was resistance to the new church in Ohio, and on March 24, 1832, Smith was dragged from his home and tarred and feathered. Another Mormon, Sidney Rigdon, was beaten severely. Some of the church members moved to Missouri, but there was more antagonism towards them in Missouri than in Ohio.

In May, 1839, many of the Kirkland members of the church moved to Commerce, Illinois, which they renamed Nauvoo. The City of Nauvoo received a charter from the State of Illinois that gave it considerable autonomy. Between 1841 and 1844, Nauvoo grew so rapidly that it became the largest city in Illinois, even larger than Chicago. The practice of plural marriage, polygamy, was inaugurated by the church in 1842, a practice that caused dissension within the church and outrage outside of it.

One June 7, 1844, the *Nauvoo Expositor* published its first issue openly criticizing Smith's leadership of the church. Smith and the city council authorized the destruction of the *Nauvoo Expositor's* press. Smith and his brother, Hyrum, were jailed in Carthage, Illinois, for the suppression of the *Navoo Expositor.* A mob stormed the jail and Smith and Hyrum were murdered on June 27, 1844. The Council of Twelve announced in 1845 that the church in Nauvoo would leave Illinois. A site was selected for a temple in Salt Lake City in July, 1847. On December 27, 1847, Brigham Young was sustained as the President of the Church of Jesus Christ of Latter-Day Saints to carry on the work of Joseph Smith.

Syracuse University crew, Onondaga outlet

TABLE OF CONTENTS

CHAPTER 4

SYRACUSE: THE EASTERN GATEWAY

PAGE NO.

CHAPTER 4

SYRACUSE: THE EASTERN GATEWAY

```
-------------------------------------
Ye whose hearts are fresh and simple,
Who have faith in God and Nature,
Who believe, that in all ages
Every human heart is human,
That in even savage bosoms
There are longings, yearnings, strivings
For the good they comprehend not,
That the feeble hands and helpless,
Groping blindly in the darkness,
Touch God's right hand in that darkness
And are lifted up and strengthened;--
Listen to this simple story,
To this song of Hiawatha!
-------------------------------
```

From *The Song of Hiawatha* by Henry Wadsworth Longfellow

SYRACUSE: THE EASTERN GATEWAY--INTRODUCTION

SYRACUSE: THE EASTERN GATEWAY--DESCRIPTION

Syracuse, located halfway between Buffalo and Albany, is the geographic center of upstate New York. Because of its location, it is frequently chosen as the site for the regional headquarters for organizations that serve the entire state. Syracuse is at the intersection of two major expressways, the east-west New York State Thruway and the north-south I-81 Expressway. It is known as "Salt City" because of its founding in a salt marsh, and its salt production in the nineteenth century.

According to the 1990 census, the population of the City of Syracuse is 163,860 people, the 107th largest city in the United States. The population of the Syracuse metropolitan area is 742,177 people, the fifty-seventh largest in the country. Two of the notable topological features of the Syracuse area are Onondaga Lake, whose southern shore is within the city limits, and the much larger Oneida Lake eleven miles northeast of the city. The Onondaga Lake inlet is Onondaga Creek, which flows through the City of Syracuse. Oneida Lake is twenty-one miles long, and five and a half miles wide at its widest point; it has an area of eighty square miles, and a maximum depth of fifty-five feet.

Syracuse has three exits, Exits 35, 36, and 37, on the New York State Thruway, which passes just north of the city. The I-690 Expressway traverses east-west through the city.

153

Syracuse is the home of a major university, Syracuse University, as well as the State University of New York--College of Environmental Science and Forestry, LeMoyne College, and the Onondaga Community College. Syracuse has many fine hospitals, including The State University of New York--Health Science Center at Syracuse (formerly the Upstate Medical Center).

Syracuse has an outstanding orchestra, the Syracuse Symphony Orchestra, and the Syracuse Opera Company opera has a national reputation. Also, the City of Syracuse and Onondaga County have excellent park systems. Among Syracuse's many activities and places of interest are Armory Square, the Erie Canal Museum, The Everson Museum of Art, the Museum of Science and Industry, and the New York State Fair. In addition, Syracuse is an excellent sports town. It has the International League Syracuse Chiefs, a Triple-A farm team for the Toronto Blue Jays, and outstanding athletic teams at Syracuse University, including those in basketball, football, and lacrosse.

SYRACUSE: THE EASTERN GATEWAY--BRIEF HISTORY

Father Simon LeMoyne, a French missionary, recorded in his journal of August 16, 1654 that he had found a salt spring near the head of Onondaga Lake. Indians and fur traders took salt from the springs to both Albany and Montreal. The source of the name Onondaga was the Indian word On-on-dah-ka, which meant "swamp at the foot of a hill."

In 1751, Sir William Johnson, who was instrumental in settling the Mohawk Valley for the British, persuaded the Indian tribes allied with France to sign a treaty with Britain. This prevented the French from establishing a significant military fort in the area of Onondaga Lake as they had planned. Recognizing the importance of the salt springs, Johnson purchased Onondaga Lake and a two-mile wide band of land around it for 350 pounds sterling. However, Sir William Johnson died before the Revolutionary War began, and his Royalist heirs fled to Canada. The land claims reverted to the Onondaga Indian nation.

Ephraim Webster, who was born in 1762 in New Hampshire, served in the Revolutionary War. He became a fur trader after the war, and traded with the Onondaga Indians. In 1786, he built a log cabin on the east bank of Onondaga Creek, where it enters Onondaga Lake. Later, this site became known as Webster's Landing. Webster was the first permanent settler in the region. Soon afterward, Asa Danforth, born in 1746 in Massachusetts, moved to the area. He built a cabin on the west bank of Onondaga Creek, near the great Iroquois Trail. His building site was later known as Danforth's Landing. When Onondaga became a village, Danforth became a commander of militia, a judge, and a State Senator. He was known as the "Father of the County."

Comfort Tyler was another early settler. He cleared the first land, and built the first turnpike road in the region. Tyler was one of the earliest to become involved in the manufacture of salt. The Onondaga Indians called him To-whan-ta-qua, the man who can do two things at once. James Geddes was another early settler who became involved early in the salt industry. He set up his evaporating kettles on the southwest corner of Onondaga Lake. Abraham Walton of Albany built a grist mill on Onondaga Creek that was called the "old red mill." Syracuse grew around this early mill.

As the demand for salt grew and the surface brine was used up, wells were sunk 1,200 feet into the salt strata. Beginning in 1821, a solar evaporation method was used to reclaim the salt. In poor weather, sliding roofs covered the vats. Eventually, there were over 10,000 shed structures. Salt production peaked in 1862, when nine million bushels of salt were shipped. More readily accessible salt was discovered in the West, and the salt industry in Syracuse waned. The salt springs were sold to the state in 1908 for $15,000.

James Geddes of Syracuse did a preliminary survey for the Erie Canal in 1808. In 1816, Geddes and Benjamin Wright surveyed the route of the canal, from the Hudson River to Lake Erie. Construction of the Erie Canal from the Mohawk River through Syracuse to the Seneca River was authorized in 1817. The eastern section of the canal was opened in 1823; the entire length of the Erie Canal was formally opened by Governor DeWitt Clinton in 1825. The economy of the Syracuse region boomed with the opening of the canal.

Early names for Syracuse were Borgardus' Corners, Milan, South Salina, and Cossitt's Corners. John Wilkinson, a young lawer, and Joshua Forman, one of the town fathers, thought that the name should be changed from Cossitt's Corners; Forman thought that Corinth had a nice ring to it. However, when Wilkinson applied to the federal government for a post office for Corinth, he was told that another New York State village had already chosen that name.

During a visit to New York City, Wilkinson came across a poem in a periodical. The poem, entitled "Syracuse," described a city in Sicily that had a lake nearby where fresh water and salt water mingled. The city was near a town named Salina. Cicero, the Roman statesman, and Marcellus, the Roman general, were mentioned in the poem. Then Wilkinson discovered that the areas of Syracuse in Sicily, and Cossitt's Corners, New York, both were one mile long and a half mile wide. In 1820, Syracuse became the new name for Cossitt's Corners; Wilkinson couldn't ignore the coincidences, including the fact that the three nearby towns of Cicero, Marcellus, and Salina were mentioned in the poem. Wilkinson went on to become president of the Bank of Syracuse, president of the Syracuse and Utica Railroad Company, and a State Senator.

The first railroad in Syracuse, the Syracuse and Utica Railroad Company, opened in July, 1839. The track was laid along Washington Street, through the middle of the city. The railroad to the west of Syracuse was the Auburn and Syracuse Railroad. It was incorporated in 1834, but had early financial difficulties. The next railroad was the Syracuse, Cortland, and Binghamton Railroad. In 1853, Syracuse and Rochester were joined by rail. Eventually, these railroads became part of the New York Central Railroad.

In 1871, Syracuse University began its first academic year in a downtown office building. The university completed its second year in the Hall of Languages, the first building constructed on fifty acres of farmland purchased for a campus. Syracuse University is a successor of Genesee College founded in Lima, New York, in 1849. Genesee College was incorporated into Syracuse University in 1871.

In 1879, W.B. Cogswell, a local engineer, learned about the manufacture of soda ash and alkalies. Alkalies are used in products such as glass, paint, and soap. The process requires quantities of limestone and salt, both of which are available in the Syracuse area. Cogswell went to Belgium to convince Ernest Solvay, inventor of the Solvay process, to build a plant in the area. The Solvay Process Company became a major industry in Syracuse, and eventually became part of the Allied Chemical and Dye Corporation.

SYRACUSE: THE EASTERN GATEWAY--THINGS

ITEMS OF INTEREST

CARPENTER'S BROOK FISH HATCHERY

Carpenter's Brook Fish Hatchery, located five miles west of Camillus on Route 321, is a hatchery for brook, brown, and rainbow trout. The hatchery is responsible for stocking Green Lakes, Otisco Lake, and Skaneateles Lake, as well as Onondaga County streams. Visitors can tour the indoor hatching areas and ponds, and view 90,000 fingerlings and trout. They can also feed the fish as they learn about the hatchery process. The hatchery is open year-round; guided tours can be scheduled Monday through Friday. The park and picnic areas are open during the summer months. Admission is free.

CARRIER DOME

The Carrier Dome, located on the campus of Syracuse University, is the arena for Syracuse University football games, basketball games, and other sports events, as well as concerts and special events. The 50,426-seat dome, which sits on 7.7 acres on University Hill, cost $28 million to build.

It replaced Archbold Stadium, which had been the home of Syracuse University football since 1907. Basketball games were shifted from the Manley Field House. For basketball games, the dome is split in half by a large curtain that converts it into a demi-dome, with seats for about 33,000. Behind the curtain is a wide-screen television for "long-range viewing" of the game. Syracuse University's indoor track, lacrosse, and soccer teams also utilize the dome. The capacity for concerts is about 45,000.

The dome is 570 feet long, 497 feet wide, and has 527,320 feet of floor space. The fiberglass fabric roof is 160 feet above the playing surface. The teflon-coated roof of the dome has an area of 287,000 square feet with sixty-four roof panels; it weighs 220 tons. Sixteen fans, each five feet in diameter, produce the necessary air pressure to inflate the roof. Once the roof is inflated, two fans provide the required air pressure to keep it aloft.

The Carrier Dome has five separate locker rooms, including one for referees. The facility has fourteen concession stands, and the Backcourt restaurant.

THE GREAT NEW YORK STATE FAIR

The Great New York State Fair, held at the New York State Fairgrounds on State Fair Boulevard in Syracuse, is attended by over 850,000 people each year. The fair, which runs for twelve days and ends on Labor Day, has agriculture and livestock competition,

Grand National Tractor Pull events, an International Horse Show, an amusement midway, and stock car racing. The state fair, a tradition that began in 1841, also has business and industrial exhibits, big-name entertainment, talent competitions, and diverse ethnic displays in the International Bazaar. The competitions at the fair are varied; they include art and home fine art shows, cooking contests, flower shows, photographic shows, and rose shows. The fair also has 4-H sheep showmanship contests, 4-H welding tests, dairy cattle shows, and horse shows.

SYRACUSE AREA LANDMARK THEATRE

The Syracuse Landmark Theatre, located at 362 South Salina Street, opened in 1928 as a movie / vaudeville theatre. The 2,922-seat theatre was listed in the National Register of Historic Places in 1977. The Syracuse Landmark Theatre, with the interior decor of an Indo-Persian palace, is filled with carvings, gold-leaf, and ornate decorations. The theatre is home to classic movies, community theatre, concerts, dances, and receptions. It is open Monday through Friday. Tours are available by appointment.

SYRACUSE CHIEFS BASEBALL TEAM

The Syracuse Chiefs baseball team, the Triple-A International League farm team of the Toronto Blue Jays, plays at McArthur Stadium. McArthur Stadium, located at Hiawatha Boulevard and Second North Street in Syracuse, has a seating capacity of 10,000 seats. The ballpark has general admission, reserved seats, and box seats; group rates are available. MacArthur Stadium is handicapped accessible. The stadium also hosts a range of special events such as collegiate sporting events, concerts, and fireworks.

SYRACUSE OPERA

The Syracuse Opera, the third largest professional opera company in New York State, performs at the John H. Mulroy Civic Center, located at 411 Montgomery street. Three or four main stage productions are presented from October through May each year. International and national artists are featured. The Syracuse Opera Ensemble performs over 100 concerts each year for area community centers, nursing homes, and schools.

The John H. Mulroy Civic Center is also the home of the Syracuse Symphony Orchestra. The center is open Monday through Friday. Group tours are available.

SYRACUSE SYMPHONY ORCHESTRA

The Syracuse Symphony Orchestra, the 28th largest orchestra in the United States, performs at the John H. Mulroy Civic Center, located at 411 Montgomery Street. The orchestra has sixty-six full time musicians who perform during a forty-four week season. The Syracuse Symphony Orchestra offers classical music concerts, educational activities, ensemble programs, family series, and popular music concerts, including a "Summer Cooler" series of concerts in the city and in county parks in July.

The John H. Mulroy Civic Center is also the home of the Syracuse Opera Company. The Center is open Monday through Friday. Group tours are available.

LEGENDS AND STORIES

THE AIR-COOLED FRANKLIN AUTOMOBILE

Herbert Henry Franklin, owner of a die-casting company, and John Wilkinson, designer of a "horseless carriage," met in 1901. In 1903, Franklin opened an automobile plant on South Geddes Street in Syracuse to produce automobiles to Wilkinson's design. The first model was a two-passenger car with a valve-in-head four-cylinder air-cooled engine. The first car off the line cost $1,000, and had a top speed of thirty miles per hour. The advantages of the air-cooled engine were the elimination of the radiator and a reduction in the weight of the car.

In 1906, the Franklin automobile ranked third in sales of all cars manufactured in the United States. By 1916, the H. H. Franklin Manufacturing Company had 2,300 employees, and produced 15,000 cars per year. In the late 1920s, the company had eighteen buildings with thirty-four acres of floor space on sixteen acres of land. Franklin automobiles were known for their quality engineering and their dependability. Included in their innovations were:

- o first six-cylinder engine (1905)
- o first drive-through springs and transmission service brakes (1906)
- o first use of automatic spark advance (1907)
- o first use of aluminum pistons (1911)
- o first exhaust jackets for heating intake gases
- o first closed bodies and sedans

Franklin designed a transmission for U. S. Army tanks in World War I. The company also produced parts for airplane motors, depth charges, and for the Curtiss biplane during the First World War. By 1929, the H. H. Franklin Manufacturing Company had 3,200 employees, and was the largest employer of skilled labor in the Syracuse area. However, as the Great Depression progressed, the company encountered continuing financial difficulties. No one could afford to buy their fine cars. The company filed for bankruptcy and closed in 1934, after experiencing significant annual losses, and many overdue notes.

However, the facilities of the Franklin Manufacturing Company were one of the attactions that drew the Carrier Corporation to Syracuse in 1937. After twelve years at the old Franklin site, Carrier moved to its Thompson Road facility in 1949. The Franklin plant was demolished, and the Fowler High School and athletic fields were constructed on the site. However, the two-story brick building at 218 South Geddes Street that housed the Lipe Machine Shop still stands. This shop was the site of the meeting between Herbert Franklin and John Wilkinson, and of the assembly of the first Franklin protype.

THE "FLASH OF GENIUS" IN THE RAILROAD STATION

Willis Carrier, founder of the Carrier Air Conditioning Company of Syracuse, stood on a railway platform in Pittsburgh in the late fall of 1902. The temperature was in the low thirties that evening, and the railway platform was shrouded in fog. As he paced back and forth on the platform, Carrier realized that the fog was made up of tiny drops of water that had been condensed out of completely saturated air because of the low air temperature.

He knew that warm air holds more moisture than cool air. He concluded that the moisture content of air could be lowered by cooling a water spray using mechanical refrigeration. The temperature of the water spray could be raised when it was desirable for the air to hold more water. Carrier designed an apparatus that manipulated the moisture content of air, and submitted a patent on September 16, 1904 for "an apparatus for treating air." His mechanism had a water spray device through which air was drawn to humidify it by heating the water or to dehumidify it by cooling the water. Dehumidifying air by using water was questioned--drying air with water--but Carrier proved that it worked.

The kernel of an idea on the railway platform led to the development of the concept of "dew point control" for maintaining specified amounts of water in air that, in turn, led to the founding of the air conditioning industry. The earliest users were textile mills; they had a requirement for constant high humidity. The film industry was another user of the equipment; they used it to address the temperature / humidity control needs of film. Next, the equipment was used in tobacco factories; it also helped to reduce the quantity of dust particles in the air. The use of air conditioning expanded rapidly. In addition to the comfort applications, it was used in many health applications.

HOW THE LAND OF OZ WAS NAMED

Frank Baum, the author of the book, *The Wonderful Wizard of Oz*, and many other books, was born in Chittenango, which is located east of Syracuse. When he was five, his family moved to Rose Lawn Farm, in what is now the Syracuse suburb of Mattydale. Later in life, the story of the land of Oz evolved in his mind long before he wrote the story.

Baum was a natural storyteller; while living in Chicago, he frequently invited the neighborhood children in for a story.

One evening, he told the children about Dorothy's travels and her new friends, the Scarecrow and the Tin Woodman. When Baum paused in telling his story, a young neighbor girl asked: "Oh please, Mr. Baum! Where did the Scarecrow and the Tin Woodman live?"

Baum had not given any thought to the name of the land where Dorothy's new friends lived, until then. He looked around the room, hoping to see something that would inspire a name. He looked at the piano, the worn rug, the pot-bellied stove, the oak dining table, the picture with the gilt frame, his wife's chair, and the kerosene lamp; he saw nothing that helped him find a name. Next, he scanned the headline of that day's *Chicago Journal* announcing Admiral Dewey's victory at Manila Bay; the May 7, 1898 issue of the local paper was no help to him either.

Finally, his gaze focused on an old two-drawer filing cabinet in the corner of the room. The top drawer was marked with the letters A-N. The bottom drawer was labeled O-Z. Baum knew that he had found the name for the land of the wizard. He could think of no better name for a magical country than the land of Oz.

THE STORY OF THE BRANNOCK DEVICE

Customers who enter a shoe store to buy a pair of shoes take for granted the foot measuring device used to ensure a good fit. Prior to the 1930s, a customer's foot was measured with a set of sticks that measured only the heel-to-toe dimension. Charles F. Brannock, president of the Park-Brannock Shoe Store in Syracuse, wanted an improved method for accurately measuring feet. He worked for two years to develop a device with design criteria that included:

- o The requirement to measure the arch of the foot, from ball to heel
- o The requirement to measure the length of the foot, from toe to heel
- o The requirement to measure the width of the foot
- o The need for all three measurements in relationship to one another
- o The need to take all three measurements at the same time
- o The need for a measuring device that was accurate and practical
- o The need for a device that was easy to operate.

Desirable characteristics, but not requirements, were portability and the ability to use the device without requiring customers to stand while their feet were being measured.

Brannock began to use the foot measuring device at his store, and was deluged with requests to make the device for other shoe stores. He began the manufacture of the devices on the top floor of his shoe store at 427 South Salina Street. He moved to larger quarters on Oneida Street, and then moved again to even larger quarters at 509 East Fayette Street. Brannock also designed and manufactured a Junior Brannock Device for measuring infant's and children's feet. Soon, the Brannock Device was in use all over the world.

THE LEGEND OF HIAWATHA

Hiawatha, the great Onondaga chief and hunter, lived on the south shore of Cross Lake, west of Syracuse. In his *Song of Hiawatha*, Henry Wadsworth Longfellow transported Hiawatha to the shores of a lake in Minnesota, and made him an Ojibway Indian via poetic license.

Hiawatha spoke to the chiefs of the Cayuga, Mohawk, Oneida, Onondaga, and Seneca Nations one day near present-day Liverpool, on Onondaga Lake. The chiefs counted on Hiawatha to lead them to a more peaceful way of life. He held a single arrow in his outstretched hand and, facing the chiefs, broke the arrow over his knee. Next his took from his quiver five arrows that had been bound together with deerskin thongs. The five arrows represented the five Nations of the Iroquois, and, when he tried to break them over his knee, he couldn't.

Hiawatha's demonstration of strength in unity was the underlying principle of the Iroquois Confederacy. The Iroquois maintained a strong confederacy for over two hundred years, and hostile tribes, such as the Hurons, provided a lesser threat than before the confederacy was formed.

SYRACUSE'S FIRST WOMAN VOTER

Matilda Joslyn Gage, born in 1826, was active in both the Anti-slavery and Women's Rights Movements. She was the daughter of a physician from Cicero and the wife of Henry Hill Gage, a wealthy Fayetteville dry goods merchant. Gage first attracted the attention of the leaders of the Women's Rights Movement when she asked permission to speak at the Women's Rights Convention in Syracuse in 1852. Her forceful personality allowed her to make a significant contribution to the movement. The activist, who lived at 210 East Genesee Street in Fayetteville, was elected to the executive committee of the National Woman Suffrage Association upon its founding on May 11, 1869. Elizabeth Cady Stanton was elected president and Susan B. Anthony led the executive committee.

Gage, the mother of four children, was a strong-willed individual, and everyone knew her opinions on women's rights. She once wrote: "Women, if you will not be crushed, arise and fight your own battles. Man, your so-called protector, is your worst foe. Experience shows you cannot trust father, nor husband, nor brother, nor son ..." She was prominent in the Women's Rights Movement, but she spoke too softly to be an effective speaker. However, she was an effective organizer and writer.

Stanton's mentor in the Women's Rights Movement, Lucretia Mott, urged her to write a history of the movement. In 1876, Gage joined in a partnership with Anthony and Stanton "for the purpose of preparing and editing a history of the woman suffrage movement." Gage's and Stanton's tasks were to "write, collect, and arrange material;" Anthony's task was to "secure publication." In November, 1880, they began writing the history at Stanton's home in Teaneck, New Jersey. The first volume of *The History of Woman Suffrage* was published in May, 1881; the second volume followed in May, 1882. Gage's work on the history was cut short in 1884, when her husband died. Ida Husted Harper wrote a later volume of the work.

Gage attempted unsuccessfully to vote in 1872. She was the first woman to vote in the school board elections in Fayetteville in 1880, which was forty years before women were granted the right to vote in national elections. This breakthrough came when women property owners convinced a majority of the New York State Legislature that women should have a voice in the activities of the school districts in which they paid taxes.

Gage left the National Woman Suffrage Association in 1890; she formed a more progressive organization, the Woman's National Liberal Union. In 1893, she wrote a book stating her view on women's rights entitled *Woman, Church and State*. Count Leo Tolstoy wrote her a letter praising the book, and commenting that it proved that a woman could think logically. Poor health prevented her from becoming more of a national figure in the women's rights movement.

Gage's youngest daughter, Maud, married L. Frank Baum, the author of *The Wizard of Oz* and many other books. Maud had to overcome her mother's objections to marry the author. Gage died in 1898 while visiting the Baums. She wrote her own epitaph: "There is a word sweeter than mother, home, or heaven--that word is liberty."

PARKS, FORESTS AND TRAILS

BEAVER LAKE NATURE CENTER

Beaver Lake Nature Center, located two miles west of Route 370 on East Mud Lake Road, is a major resting place for thousands of Canada geese in the spring and the fall. The nature center has a 200-acre lake, which can be viewed from a floating boardwalk, and miles of woodland trails for cross-county skiing and hiking. The center provides interpretive programs presented by professional naturalists to aid in exploring the natural world. Visitors can also learn from state-of-the-art exhibits in the modern Visitor Center.

CAMILLUS ERIE CANAL PARK

Camillus Erie Canal Park, located on Devoe Road in Camillus, is a 300-acre park with seven miles of navigable canal and towpath trails. The Lock Tender's Shanty Museum and the Sims Store Museum, located at "Camillus Landing," are authentic replicas of actual buildings; they contain artifacts, memorabilia, and photographs of the Erie Canal. The Nine Mile Creek Aqueduct is within the park, along with flower gardens, nature trails, and picnic areas.

The Sims Store Museum is the point of departure for boat rides on the canal, which are offered on Sunday afternoons from May through October. The park is open daily year-round. Tours of the park are given by appointment.

CLARK RESERVATION STATE PARK

Clark Reservation State Park, located south of Syracuse and east of the I-81 Expressway on Route 173, is a 310-acre park that includes meadows, rugged cliffs, rocky outcrops, wetlands, woodlands, and a glacial plunge basin lake. The park is near the edge of the Appalachian Plateau; it is located east of Onondaga Valley and west of Butternut Valley. Elevation in the park ranges from 583 feet to 770 feet above sea level. Clark Reservation State Park has two pavilions, picnic areas with tables and fireplaces, playing fields, and a playground.

About 10,000 years ago, the melt-water of the glacier of the most recent ice age formed the features of the park, including natural amphitheaters, the glacial plunge pool with Glacier Lake, and ravines. Glacier Lake is a glacier cataract lake, one of the finest examples of its kind in the eastern United States. The melting waters of the glacier plunged over the edge of the escarpment from the 740 foot level to the 420 foot level into the drainage basin of the Mohawk River. The 320-foot waterfall was over twice the height of the present-day Niagara Falls.

Glacier Lake is a meromictic lake, one in which the bottom waters and the surface waters do not mix; the lake has no fall and spring turnover as most lakes do. The 10-acre lake is sixty-two feet deep at its deepest point. Fishing is permitted in the lake; it contains bullheads, pickerel, and sunfish.

The lake's swampy south shore is a good spot for birdwatching--for cedar waxwings, kingfishers, and woodpeckers. Also included in the 140 bird species that inhabit the park are the pileated woodpecker, scarlet tanager, rose-breasted grosbeak, ruffed grouse, winter wren, and many species of warblers. In addition, the Clark Reservation State Park has over 300 species of ferns and flowering plants.

Wildlife in the park includes a wide range of mammals, such as chipmunks, red and gray foxes, rabbits, mink, muskrats, raccoons, squirrels, deer, and woodchucks. Amphibians, such as frogs and salamanders, are found in the park; snakes and turtles also inhabit the park.

The Nature Center has a library of field guides and detailed information about the fauna, flora, and geology of the park, as well as exhibits of birds, fossils, insects, and mammals. All guided nature walks begin at the Nature Center.

Clark Reservation had its beginning as a public park in 1915, when 108 acres around Glacier Lake were purchased by Mary Clark Thompson of Canandaigua. She was a conservation-minded individual who wanted to preserve the area because of its unique geology and natural beauty. She deeded the land to the people of New York State in memory of her father, Myron Clark, who was Governor of the state from 1855 to 1857. Clark Reservation became a state park in 1926.

CLAY MARSH WILDLIFE MANAGEMENT AREA

Clay Marsh Wildife Management Area, located in the Town of Clay, northwest of North Syracuse, provides breeding, feeding, nesting, and resting opportunities for almost 200 species of birds. Access to the area is from Route 481 via Henry Clay Boulevard. Other accesses are via Wetzel Road in the west and via Bear Road and Davis Road in the east. The Wildlife Management Area, a 1,450-acre wetland about four miles long and from one-quarter mile to one mile wide, is located on gentle rolling land with an average elevation above sea level of 400 feet. Clay Marsh is drained by Mud Creek, which winds through the area.

Clay Marsh contains the largest stand of cattails in Onondaga County, as well as trees such as ash, hickory, oak, red maple, tulip tree, and willow. Other vegetation is typical marshgrowth: alder, arrowhead, button bush, smart weed, and water lilies. Mammals using Clay Marsh as a habitat include beavers, foxes, moles, muskrats, raccoons, and deer. The area is also home to frogs, toads, turtles, and warm-water fish.

In the early 1800s, peat was harvested from the south central section of the marsh for use as heating fuel. Mining of the peat bog was discontinued in the early 1900s, but the four-acre, fifteen- to twenty-foot deep hole is still there. New York State purchased Clay Marsh for a wildlife management area in 1975.

A periphery trail is available for use in bird watching, cross-country skiing, hiking, and photography. Fishing, hunting, and trapping are permitted under New York State Fish and Wildlife Laws and special regulations. Prohibited activities include boats with motors, camping, off-road vehicular travel (all-terrain vehicles, cars, motorcycles, and snowmobiles), and swimming. Overnight mooring and storage of boats is not permitted.

GREEN LAKES STATE PARK

Green Lakes State Park, located at 7000 Green Lakes Road in Fayetteville, is a 1,700-acre park with meadows, rolling wooded hills, and two glacially-formed lakes with 13,200 feet of shoreline. Both Green Lake and Round Lake are meromictic lakes in which the bottom water and the surface water do not mix. There is no fall and spring turnover as there is in most lakes. Wind is the main cause of turnover of water in a lake. The hilly, forested watershed around Green Lake and Round Lake acts as a windbreak.

Round Lake is set in a steep circular basin of limestone. Green Lake is 195 feet deep and Round Lake is 180 feet deep. Round Lake was designated a National Natural Landmark in 1975 by the Department of the Interior. The shorelines of the lakes have deposits of marl, which is a mixture of clay, calcium carbonate, and fossil remnants. The unique green color of the water is due to a number of factors: very deep and clear water, little aquatic plant life, minimal suspended material in the water, and a calcium carbonate level that reduces the filtering effect of dissolved organic material.

The wildlife of Green Lakes State Park provides a habitat for a variety of mammals, including chipmunks, rabbits, mink, raccoons, red and gray foxes, red and gray squirrels, skunks, deer, and woodchucks. Over 100 species of birds can be observed in the park. In addition, the park is home to over 200 species of plants, including twenty-five species of ferns, over one hundred types of herbaceous flowering plants, and sixty kinds of trees and shrubs. Tree species include basswood, beech, hemlock, and maple.

The park has over seventeen miles of cross-country and hiking trails. Both lakes are encircled by trails; it takes one hour to walk around Green Lake and two hours to walk around both lakes. Elevation in the park ranges from 418 feet to 1,400 feet above sea level. Other activities include fishing, golfing on an 18-hole golf course, and swimming along the sandy lakeshore. There is a concession stand at the beach, and the park has rowboat and paddleboat rentals. The golf course has a clubhouse with a bar and a snack bar, hand carts, a practice putting green, power cart rentals, and a pro shop.

Green Lakes State Park has seven cabins, 137 campsites (42 electric), flush toilets, hot showers, two pavilions, and picnic areas with tables and fireplaces. The park also has playing fields, a playground, and a trailer dumping station.

Green Lakes became a state park when the state purchased 500 acres surrounding Green and Round Lakes in 1928. The park has been increased to its present size by the purchase of an additional 1,200 acres. The state acquired 188 acres at the southern boundary of the park, including the drainage basin of Round Lake, in 1975 to protect the unique characteristics of the lake.

HIGHLAND FOREST

Highland Forest, located on Route 80, twelve miles east of Exit 14 of the I-81 Expressway at Tully, contains 3,000 acres of hilltop vistas, rugged terrain, and woodlands. Highland Forest offers trails for cross-country, hiking, and horseback riding. Twenty miles of multi-level cross-country ski trails provide some of the premier skiing in the region. A rustic lodge offers a place for after-ski eating and resting.

Highland Forest has several reservable picnic shelters and a hilltop Skyline facility with a commanding view of the area's countryside. Hayrides are offered in the fall and sleighrides are provided in the winter. The Pioneer Museum in Highland Forest provides a vision of the 1800s as seen by the early settlers of Onondaga County.

HOPKINS ROAD PARK

Hopkins Road Park, located on Hopkins Road between Electronics Parkway and Buckley Road, is a softball field complex with four high-quality playing fields. The park has an electronic scoreboard, a food concession area, and modern facilities. This premier Onondaga County softball complex attracts local teams and regional tournaments.

JAMESVILE BEACH PARK

Jamesville Beach Park, located along the Jamesville Reservoir on Apulia Road, provides a lakeside setting among scenic hills. The park offers picnicking, sailboarding, and swimming, as well as cross-country ski trails. Over fifty balloons participate in the Hot Air Balloon Festival each June, which is accompanied by live entertainment and refreshments. The festival also includes parachute demonstrations, aerobatics, and radio-controlled aircraft demonstrations.

MARCELLUS PARK

Marcellus Park, located on Platt Road in Marcellus, is an idyllic woodland setting for picnics; there are four reservable shelters and many tables interspersed throughout the park. The park has basketball courts, softball fields, and tennis courts. Marcellus Park also offers fishing in Nine Mile Creek, and winter activities supported by year-round staffing.

OLD ERIE CANAL STATE PARK

Old Erie Canal State Park consists of thirty-five miles of the Old Erie Canal; it runs from Syracuse to Rome, and has canoe launch facilities, picnic areas, and trails for biking and hiking. The Erie Canal Center, off Cedar Bay Road in DeWitt, has an interpretive building with maps of the canal park region and numerous exhibits. The interpretive building is open Tuesday through Sunday afternoons during June, July, and August, and weekends only during May and September. Admission is free; donations are accepted.

ONEIDA SHORES PARK

Oneida Shores Park, located along Oneida Lake on Bartell Road, offers sandy beaches, sailboarding, and swimming. The park has a boat launch, modern facilities, and picnic areas. Arrowhead Lodge, a contemporary year-round facility, can be reserved for conferences, group receptions, and large gatherings. The lodge has a fireplace, an indoor hall, a kitchen, and outdoor recreational activities.

ONONDAGA LAKE PARK

Onondaga Lake Park, located on Onondaga Lake Parkway near the northern end of the lake, is the home of "Sainte Marie Among the Iroquois" (The French Fort) and the Salt Museum. The shoreline of Onondaga Lake has been the site of many historic events, including the founding of the Iroquois Confederacy, settlement by French missionaries, invasions by colonial armies, and the development of Victorian resorts.

The park can be toured by horse-drawn carriages and by motorized trams. Onondaga Lake Park has picnic areas along eight miles of shoreline. The park also has hydroplane races, jazz fests, regattas such as the inter-collegiate rowing regatta each June, and a Waterfront Extravaganza.

ONONDAGA PARK

Onondaga Park, located southeast of downtown Syracuse on Roberts Avenue, is a neighborhood park designed by Frederick Law Olmstead. Onondaga Park is the only historic landscape in Onondaga County registered with the New York State Historical Association. From the Hiawatha Lake gazebo to Bissell Wood, Olmstead's design incorporated landscape and architecture.

PRATT'S FALLS PARK

The focal point of Pratt's Falls Park, located northeast of the Village of Pompey, is the 137-foot Pratt's Falls. The waterfall can be viewed from the top, or visitors can walk down a pathway to the base of the falls. Pratt's Falls Park has picnic areas and a peaceful pond. The park offers excellent cross-country skiing trails and hiking trails along the edge of a steep gorge.

THORNDEN PARK

Thornden Park, located on Ostrum Avenue in Syracuse, became a city park in 1921. The park is the home of the E. M. Mill Rose Garden, which was initially planted in 1914. It is one of the oldest rose gardens in the United States. The rose garden was honored in 1951 when it was selected as one of six accredited New York State public gardens to receive yearly plantings of the All-American Rose selection. Thornden Park is also the home of Thornden Park Amphitheatre, a site for open air concerts and summer festivals.

THREE RIVERS WILDLIFE MANAGEMENT AREA

Three Rivers Wildlife Management Area, located north of Syracuse between Baldwinsville and Phoenix, is a 3,497-acre tract that provides a habitat for over 118 species of birds, including bald eagles, blue herons, Canada geese, and osprey. Access is from Route 48; Kellogg Road and Potter Road traverse the Wildlife Management Area. Three Rivers Wildlife Management Area was named "Three Rivers" because it is near the site where the the Oneida and Seneca Rivers form the Oswego River. The Wildlife Management Area is flat and poorly drained.

The area has brushlands, open areas, wetlands, and woodlands that provide a habitat for eight species of amphibians, eleven species of fish, twenty-five species of mammals, and six species of reptiles. Aspen, beech, birch and sugar maple trees grow in the drier areas and ash, hemlock, red maple, and white pine in the lowlands. Plantation conifers such as larch, Norway spruce, white spruce and red, white, and Scots pine are also found in the area. Over 50,000 evergreens and shrubs have been planted to provide cover and food for wildlife.

Since 1950, pheasant retriever trial areas have been maintained for training bird dogs. National and local events are held each year, with dogs, owners, and trainers attending from across North America and from several foreign countries. Field trials are open to the public.

Fishing, hunting, and trapping are allowed in the Wildlife Management Area. Hunting, which is controlled under statewide regulations, is for deer, pheasants, rabbits, ruffed grouse, squirrels, and waterfowl. Fishing access to the Oswego River is provided on an undeveloped site. Maintenance roads and town roads provide access to the area for birding, bicycling, cross-country skiing, horseback riding, and nature study and observation.

Educational, school, and scout outings are allowed by permit. Individual camping is prohibited in the Three Rivers Wildlife Management Area. Boating, swimming, and overnight mooring and storage of boats is not permitted. Off-road vehicular travel is prohibited except on town and county roads.

SHOWS AND FESTIVALS

CIVIC CENTER SUMMERFEST

The Civic Center Summerfest, held at the John H. Mulroy Civic Center at 411 Montgomery Street in Syracuse, is a six-week summer theater festival sponsored by the Cultural Resources Center. The Summerfest brings together six of the area's best professional and community theater companies in the Civic Center's Carrier Theater. A variety of comedies, musicals, and dramas are offered in addition to classic and contemporary stage performances. Each production runs for five performances from Wednesday evening through Sunday afternoon during July and August.

ONONDAGA LAKE WATERFRONT EXTRAVAGANZA

The Onondaga Lake Waterfront Extravaganza, held at the Onondaga Lake Park Marina in July, provides four days of on-shore and off-shore entertainment at the park. It features concerts, mimes, a showplace of foods, theater, and a water circus ski show. The Waterfront Extravaganza's fireworks display is launched from barges in the middle of the lake.

SYRACUSE ARTS & CRAFTS FESTIVAL

The Syracuse Arts and Crafts Festival is held every July at Columbus Circle in downtown Syracuse. Over 150 exhibitors from across the country participate in a juried show that showcases demonstrations of craft techniques, fine arts and crafts, and special children's activities. The festival features continuous entertainment by local performing arts groups, including ethnic dancers, classical music, jazz, and popular music.

TOUR BOATS

MID-LAKES NAVIGATION CO., LTD.

Mid-Lakes Navigation Co., Ltd., located at 11 Jordan Street in Skaneateles, offers cruises on Skaneateles Lake, Onondaga Lake, and the Erie Canal. Erie Canal cruises are offered on the *Emita II*, a 65-foot passenger boat. Onondaga Lake cruises are on the *City of Syracuse*. Three Onondaga Lake cruises are offered: a luncheon cruise, a prime rib and champagne dinner cruise, and an old fashioned Sunday excursion.

The luncheon cruise is a two-hour cruise west to lock #24 at Baldwinsville and return. The dinner cruise is a three-hour cruise through lock #24 at Baldwinsville to Seneca Estates with return via Onondaga Lake. The Sunday excursion is a four-hour trip that begins with a continental breakfast, locking through at Caughdenoy, and returning via Three Rivers where the Seneca and Oneida Rivers meet. The Onondaga Lake cruises leave from the Mid-Lakes Navigation terminal at Dutchman's Landing at the end of Hillside Road in Cold Springs.

Mid-Lakes Navigation also offers charters of Lockmaster hireboats from May 1st to October on the Erie Canal between Buffalo and Syracuse, the Cayuga-Seneca Canal, and the Oswego Canal. The Lockmaster hireboats are 41-foot steel-hulled, diesel-powered packetboats that are designed for comfort and ease of handling. The boats sleep six, and have knotty pine paneling and fully-equipped galleys.

WATERFALLS

EDWARDS FALLS

Edwards Falls is a 70-foot waterfall on Limestone Creek. It is located off Broadfield Road in the Town of Manlius.

PRATT'S FALLS

Pratt's Falls is a 137-foot waterfall in Pratt's Falls Park that can be viewed either from the top or from the base. Pratt's Falls Park is northeast of the Village of Pompey off Pratt's Falls Road.

SYRACUSE: THE EASTERN GATEWAY--PLACES

COLLEGES AND UNIVERSITIES

LEMOYNE COLLEGE

LeMoyne College, located in eastern Syracuse near the intersection of Salt Springs and Springfield Roads, was founded by the Jesuits in 1946. The College, established on LeMoyne Heights at the invitation of the Bishop of Syracuse, was the first coeducatinal college in the 400-year history of the Society of Jesus. From its early days, the administrators of LeMoyne College understood that the study of subjects such as business and industrial relations were not in opposition to a liberal arts education. The college continues to be a community of scholars in the liberal arts tradition.

LeMoyne College recognizes that the pursuit of truth and the achievement of academic excellence is important in and of itself. However, the college also affirms that no important truth is without significance in practical deliberations. Therefore, LeMoyne College, as a modern college of liberal arts, science, and business, has a goal to prepare its students to make sound decisions, including those that affect both personal lives and social policy, as well as those that require a synthesis of foresight, discriminating sensitivity, and scientific and speculative knowledge.

The college provides superior programs in the natural and social sciences and in business for their inherent value as well as to assure an understanding of the natural and human world. LeMoyne College offers studies in fine arts, history, language, literature, mathematics, and computer science.

ONONDAGA COMMUNITY COLLEGE

Onondaga Community College, located in southwest Syracuse near the intersection of Routes 173 and 175, is one of the thirty two-year colleges of the State University of New York system. The college was established by Onondaga County in 1961; it opened in 1962. By 1991, Onondaga Community College had 8,406 students: 4,027 full-time and 4,379 part-time.

Onondaga Community College offers two-year programs leading to Associate degrees in Art, in Applied Science, and in Science. The college offers both transfer and career degree programs. Both programs include core requirements in liberal arts and sciences. Students who plan to complete a four-year degree enroll in a transfer program; students who plan to seek employment after earning a two-year degree enroll in a career program.

SUNY--COLLEGE OF ENVIRONMENTAL SCIENCE AND FORESTRY

The State University of New York College of Environmental Science and Forestry adjoins the Syracuse University campus and is closely associated with the university. The College of Environmental Science and Forestry is a specialized center of the State University of New York. The enrollment of the college is 1,880, including 650 graduate students. Off-campus facilities of the college, used for demonstration, instruction, and research, include 25,000 acres of forest land in seven locations.

The College of Environmental Science and Forestry and Syracuse University have a dual enrollment agreement in which students may enroll in the University's College of Arts and Sciences pre-environmental science and forestry program, and be guaranteed transfer to the College of Environmental Science and Forestry upon successful completion of the appropriate coursework. College of Environmental Science and Forestry students have the same privileges as Syracuse University students with regard to health services and the use of athletic facilities, dining halls, library facilities, recreational facilities, residence halls, and testing services. In addition, they share a variety of cultural and social resources available at the university.

The administrative office of the College of Environmental Science and Forestry is located in Bray Hall, adjacent to the campus of Syracuse University. The college also offers a two-year forestry technician program at the Ranger School at Wanakena, New York.

SYRACUSE UNIVERSITY

Syracuse University, located south of downtown Syracuse and east of the I-81 Expressway, is a private, coeducational, residential university. The university has over 12,000 undergraduate students and more than 4,500 graduate students, who represent all fifty states and about 100 foreign countries. The small coeducational liberal arts college founded by the Methodist Church in 1871 has grown to a nonsectarian university of fifteen colleges and schools on a 200-acre main campus. The university offers more than 200 different subjects. Syracuse University is one of fifty-nine American and Canadian Universities chosen for membership in the prestigious Association of American Universities.

The university has a total of 900 acres on its campuses with 324 buildings. The colleges and schools of the university include:

o College of Arts & Sciences
o College of Visual and Performing Arts
o School of Computer & Information Science

o School of Architecture
o School of Education
o College of Nursing

o School of Management   o School of Social Work

o Newhouse School of Public Communications

Syracuse University owns and operates Minnowbrook Lodge, a conference center in the Adirondack Mountains at Blue Lake. The university-owned Joseph I. Lubin House in New York City is used by the Office of Admissions, Office of Development, the Financial Aid Office, New York area alumni functions, and some academic programs. The Greenburg House in Washington, D.C. provides space for academic programs and continuing education programs.

MUSEUMS

ERIE CANAL MUSEUM

The Erie Canal Museum, located at 318 Erie Boulevard in Syracuse, is the leading maritime museum specializing in Erie Canal History in the United States. The museum is housed in the 1850 Weighlock Building. It has been restored to its appearance of the 1850s, when it was a canal boat weighing station. The Weighlock Building, the only surviving canal boat weighing station on the Erie Canal, was designed to weigh boats of up to 100 feet in length. It is a National Historic Landmark.

Visitors to the museum can explore the history of Syracuse as it grew from a salt marsh to a city. They can also board a 65-foot canal boat, the *Frank Thomson*, to experience life and work on the Erie Canal. The Education Gallery has historic stereoviews of the Erie Canal, live demonstrations, period room settings, and participatory exhibits that allow the visitor to operate a bilge pump and to try on a diving helmet. Special exhibitions showcase the museum's collections of canal boat models, china, costumes, and patent models. The orientation theatre provides an overview of the history of the world's most successful canal.

The Erie Canal was the only water route through the Appalachian Mountains. It provided the capability to ship coal, grain, and lumber from America's western frontier to eastern seaboard cities. The Erie Canal also provided a means of transportation for European immigrants from eastern port cities to travel to the expanding West.

The museum's research library is open to the public by appointment. The Erie Canal Museum offers a gift shop, group tours, a speaker's bureau, and videotape rentals. The museum also provides current information on the cultural and educational activities available throughout the New York State Canal System. The museum is open Tuesday through Sunday year-round; it is closed Mondays, Thanksgiving Day, Christmas Day, and New Year's Day.

EVERSON MUSEUM OF ART

The Everson Museum of Art, located at 401 Harrison Street in Syracuse, has one of the most comprehensive collections of ceramics in the world. The museum, the first museum designed by I. M. Pei, is recognized internationally for its unique architecture. It was built in 1968. Ten galleries on three levels showcase a range of art, including:

- o African folk art
- o the art of photography
- o Asian art
- o avante-garde sculpture
- o ceramics, from ancient to modern
- o eighteenth-century American portraits
- o Latin American folk art

The Everson Museum of Art is the home of the Syracuse China Center for the Study of Ceramics. The museum's collection of 3,000 ceramic items, which is displayed in open-storage galleries, includes American pottery, early American salt-glazed stoneware, ancient Asian pottery, and European porcelain. Art pottery, contemporary clay sculpture, and vessel forms from around the world are also exhibited. Temporary exhibitions present works by the world's great artists, including Ansel Adams, Henry Moore, and Jackson Pollack. The Everson Museum places emphasis on American art such as works by Helen Frankenthaler, Winslow Homer, Barbara Kruger, Gustav Stickley, and Andrew Wyeth.

The museum has an active education program for both adults and children, and guided tours are offered for both civic and school groups. Guest lectures, slide and video presentations, and special community events are held in the galleries and in the 275-seat Hosmer Auditorium.

The Museum Cafe is a popular spot for lunch, and the Everson Museum Shop offers art books, cards, children's items, distinctive ceramics, handcrafted jewelry, and postcards. The museum is open Tuesday through Saturday and Sunday afternoons. The museum is closed on Monday. The suggested donation is nominal.

THE MUSEUM OF SCIENCE AND TECHNOLOGY

The Museum of Science and Technology, located at Franklin and Jefferson Streets in Armory Square, is a "hands-on" museum with exhibits that explain scientific and technological phenomena. The museum contains displays on subjects such as color, computers, gravity, light, sound, and the stars. Demonstrations are conducted daily. The planetarium, a 24-foot domed star theatre, offers shows Tuesday through Saturday that highlight the constellations, planets, and stars. The museum is open Tuesday through Saturday and Monday holidays. A nominal admission fee is charged to the museum and to the planetarium.

ONONDAGA HISTORICAL ASSOCIATION MUSEUM

The Onondaga Historical Association Museum, located at 321 Montgomery Street, provides an overview of the area's cultural, industrial, and natural history through artifacts and paintings. The Research Center, located at 311 Montgomery Street, provides material for genealogical and historical researchers. The museum is open Tuesday through Saturday afternoons. Reservations are required for group tours. The Research Center is open Monday through Saturday afternoons and mornings by appointment. Admission is free to both the museum and the research center.

SALT MUSEUM

The Salt Museum, located in Onondaga Lake Park on Onondaga Lake Parkway, depicts the Onondaga County salt industry during the period of 1788-1926 when Syracuse earned its name as "Salt City," and was the leading salt producer in the United States. Production of salt peaked at nine million bushels per year during the Civil War. Discovery of easily-mined rock salt in the western United States and the completion of railroads across the continent to transport it, caused the evaporation process used in Syracuse to be less economical. This forced the shutting down of hundreds of boiling blocks and thousands of evaporating sheds utilized to produce salt from brine.

Salt Museum exhibits include the full size reconstruction of an 1856 boiling block, re-created craft shops, and a "sights and sounds" tour of an 1800s salt workers' neighborhood. A gift shop is located on the site of the museum. The museum is open from Monday through Saturday and Sunday afternoon from May to October. A nominal admission fee is charged.

PLACES OF INTEREST

ARMORY SQUARE

Armory Square, originally settled in 1804, is bounded by West Fayette Street, South Clinton Street, South Salina Street, and Onondaga Creek. Most of Armory Square's historic buildings were built between 1860 and 1890 as factories or warehouses. The Jefferson Street Armory, constructed in the early 1900s, was used to quarter the cavalry and infantry. Armory Square was designated a National Historic Landmark in 1984.

Dozens of historic buildings have been restored, creating office, residential, restaurant, and retail space, while retaining the original character of the buildings. Armory Square is an outstanding example of urban renaissance, and is a popular place for dining, employment, entertainment, shopping, and urban living. The area has become Syracuse's liveliest night spot. It has fine dining establishments, friendly neighborhood taverns, and live entertainment.

Armory Square is also the home of galleries that exhibit original art work. Activities in the area include a contemporary craft show, evenings of candlelight ballet, free lunchtime concerts, and festivals, including a winter festival. Both the Museum of Science and Technology and the Syracuse Area Landmark Theatre are within the Armory Square District.

BURNET PARK ZOO

Burnet Park Zoo, located off South Wilbur Avenue in the southwest section of Syracuse, provides a habitat for over 1,000 animals. Visitors can trace the origins of life from 600 million years ago, learn about the unique adaptations that help animals survive, and hike the "Wild North." They can also walk though a prehistoric cave, view a rainstorm in a tropical forest, walk along a treetop boardwalk, and explore the wildlife of North America. Other exhibits address how animals and people benefit each other, and the future of wildlife on this planet Earth.

The Burnet Park Zoo has a restaurant, outside snack areas, and a gift shop. Special group tours and school tours can be arranged. The zoo is open year-round; it is closed on Christmas Day and New Year's Day. Burnet Park Zoo is wheelchair accessible.

HISTORIC SITES

PARKE AVERY HOUSE

Parke Avery House, located at 1509 Park Street in Syracuse, is a mid-1800s residence built by salt baron Parke Avery. It is operated by the Preservation Association of Central New York, a non-profit organization dedicated to historic preservation. Exhibitions and special events are shown at the house throughout the year. Parke Avery House is open Sunday and Wednesday afternoons for guided tours. Reservations are required for group tours on other weekdays. A nominal admission fee is charged.

SAINTE MARIE AMONG THE IROQUOIS

"Sainte Marie Among the Iroquois" (The French Fort), located in Onondaga Lake Park on Onondaga Lake Parkway, portrays the cultures of two 17th-century people--the Iroquois and the French missionaries. Visitors can walk through a series of interactive museum galleries that depict the culture and customs and the flora and fauna of the Native

American world. Visitors can also view the interior of a typical European ship used to transport immigrants to the New World. Family life among the Iroquois and life among the Europeans is depicted in the galleries. The original fort on the site was erected in 1656 by Father Simon LeMoyne.

Outside of the galleries, but inside the rough-hewn palisade walls of the mission, the life of the French occupants of the fort in 1657 is depicted. Catholic clerics and soldiers wear the clothing of middle-class Frenchmen, bake bread in beaverback ovens, and respond to the chapel bells calling them to daily vespers. Blacksmithing, carpentry , and farming are also portrayed at the fort.

The Museum Store offers locally hand-crafted items and a range of special mementos. The museum is open daily from April through December. It is closed on Monday and Tuesday from January through March. A nominal admission fee is charged.

WILCOX OCTAGONAL HOUSE

The Wilcox Octagonal House, located at 5420 Genesee Street in Camillus, is one of a dwindling number of octagon houses in the United States. The attractively furnished house is listed in the National Register of Historic Buildings. The house has been returned to its original red color; the historic herb gardens at the rear of the east lawn have been maintained. Visitors can take a guided tour up five floors of the circular stairway to the cupola. The Wilcox Octagon House is open Sunday and holiday afternoons. Admission is free.

RESTAURANTS-HISTORIC

GREEN GATE INN

The Green Gate Inn, located at 2 Main Street in Camillus, was built in 1861 as a private home. It became the Green Gate Inn in 1939. The dining room has the elegant atmosphere of a nineteenth-century country home, with bentwood chairs, a circular staircase, crystal chandeliers, and flowered wallpaper. Candles and floral arrangements accent the tables; the color scheme is subdued, with shades such as green and rose predominating.

The inn offers both Continental and traditional American cuisine. Continental entrees include beef, duck, and veal dishes. American main courses include New York Strip Steak and Surf and Turf, an eight-ounce lobster tail and a filet. The house speciality is chicken Carrington, a chicken breast stuffed with mushroom duxelles and spinach and covered with a special sauce.

The guest rooms, furnished with period furniture, all have private baths. Each guest room is different from the others, and each fits with the decor of a country home of the 1800s. The Green Gate offers dinner Tuesday through Sunday; it offers Sunday brunch, and the restaurant is closed on Monday. Reservations are recommended, particularly on weekends.

THE INN BETWEEN

The Inn Between, located at 2290 West Genesee Turnpike (Route 5 West) in Camillus, was built in 1880 as the manor house of the Munro family. The Munro family contributed significantly to the history of the Elbridge / Camillus area. Three dining rooms, located on the first floor, reflect the atmosphere of the manor house. They are a library, a formal dining room with a fireplace, and a wood-paneled porch that overlooks the garden and the rolling hills of Camillus. The decor utilizes the muted shades of cream and soft Wedgewood blue.

Continental entrees include Beef Wellington and Veal Oscar. Other main dishes include chicken Cape Cod, filet mignon, prime rib, rack of lamb, roast duckling, and a seafood platter. Seafood is shipped direct from Boston daily.

The second floor banquet and dining room is used for corporate events, special private parties, wedding receptions, and wedding rehearsal dinners. The restaurant also offers service for afternoon luncheons, catering, and showers. The Inn Between is open for dinner Tuesday through Sunday; it is closed Monday. Reservations are recommended.

SYRACUSE: THE EASTERN GATEWAY--PERSONS

FRANK BAUM

L. Frank Baum, the author of *The Wonderful Wizard of Oz*, was born in Chittenango, which is located fifteen miles east of Syracuse. Baum was the seventh child of Cynthia Stanton Baum and Benjamin Baum, a cooper who made his fortune in the oil fields of Pennsylvania in Titusville and Bradford. He was christened Lyman Frank Baum shortly after his birth on May 15, 1856, but he preferred to be called Frank.

The Baum family moved to Rose Lawn Farm, which was north of Syracuse in present-day Mattydale, when Frank was five years old. The fifteen-acre Rose Lawn Farm was adjacent to Spring Farm, the Baum's dairy farm. Young Frank developed a love for animals while living on the farm, and some of his farm memories stayed with him. He saw his first scarecrow on the farm, and had a recurring dream of being chased by one.

Baum's first choice of a vocation was acting. He began his acting career in Syracuse, and moved to New York City. He dabbled in writing plays in between his stage engagements. Upon his return home for the Christmas holidays in 1881, he met his cousin Josephine's Cornell University roommate, Maud Gage. Maud was the youngest daughter of Matilda Joslyn Gage, the women's rights activist. Frank and Maud fell in love, and he proposed to her during the summer of her sophomore year. Matilda Gage told Maud that she didn't want her to marry an actor. When Maud threatened to leave home, Matilda gave in, and consented to the marriage. Frank and Maud were married on November 9, 1882, in the Gage home in Fayetteville.

After the birth of their first child, Frank Joslyn Baum, on December 4, 1883, Baum became more active in his father's oil business, which allowed him to spend more time with his family. Baum's father, Benjamin, was injured in a horse and buggy accident, suffered a lengthy ilness, and died on February 14, 1887. The death of the financial mainstay of the family, coupled with the company's losses due to embezzlement by the accountant, left the family in reduced circumstances. They were forced to sell their farm.

Maud had two sisters and a brother living in Dakota Territory. They convinced the Baums to move to Aberdeen, a town of 3,000 residents in the territory. Maud's older sister, Helen, and her husband rented a store to them. The Baums went into the dry goods business. However, the population of the town wasn't sufficient to support the enterprise. Baum closed the store, and bought the local newspaper, the *Dakota Pioneer*, from a fellow Syracusan, John Drake. Lack of rain caused many crop failures in the Dakota Territory, and the circulation of the paper dwindled. Finally, Baum concluded that the sheriff wanted the paper more than he did, so he let him have the property.

The Baums moved to Chicago. He accepted a position as a reporter for the *Evening Post*, after being rejected by the *Tribune* and seven other newspapers. He supplemented his income with a second job as a salesman, since he now had a wife and four children to support. Baum had his first book published while living in Chicago, when the publishing firm of Way and Williams published his *Mother Goose in Prose* in October, 1897. After being an actor, merchant, newspaperman, and salesman, Baum had finally found his niche --making children happy. *Mother Goose in Prose* was followed by *Father Goose, His Book* in September, 1899, and *The Songs of Father Goose* in the summer of 1900.

The story of *TheWonderful Wizard of Oz* evolved in Baum's mind long before he wrote it down. It grew out of storytelling that he did regularly with the neighborhood children. His first title for the book was *Emerald City*; his second choice for a title was *The Fairyland of Oz*, followed by *The Land of Oz*. Finally, after discussing the title with his illustrator, William Denslow, and with Maud, he chose *The Wonderful Wizard of Oz*. The story had everything: travel to a strange land, friendly companions, suspense, a predicament that had to be overcome, and obstacles--the deadly poppy field, the fighting trees, the kalidahs, the winged monkeys, and wicked witches. Above all, it was an American fairy tale.

Hollywood had made four versions of *The Wonderful Wizard of Oz* prior to the immensely successful MGM Technicolor version that premiered at Grauman's Chinese Theater on August 15, 1939. The cast included:

- o Judy Garland as Dorothy
- o Ray Bolger as the Scarecrow
- o Jack Haley as the Tin Woodman
- o Bert Lahr as the Cowardly Lion
- o Frank Morgan as the Wizard
- o Billie Burke as Glinda, the Good Sorceress

With an outstanding cast and songs by Harold Arlen and E. Y. Harburg, the movie became a classic. The producer, Mervyn LeRoy, knew that the movie would have to appeal to adults as well as children, and realized that he would have to make this fairy tale a believable fantasy.

The Baums moved to Hollywood and built a home, Ozcot, which was located one block north of Hollywood Boulevard. Baum wrote more Oz books while they lived in Ozcot, including *Tik-Tok of Oz, The Scarecrow of Oz, The Lost Princess of Oz, The Tin Woodman of Oz,* and *The Magic of Oz*. L. Frank Baum died on May 6, 1919, at the age of sixty-two, after suffering from gall bladder problems that aggravated his heart condition. His life was occupied with doing what he wanted to do. He once said, "To please a child is a sweet and lovely thing that warms one's heart and brings its own reward."

WILLIS CARRIER

Willis Haviland Carrier, the father of air conditioning, was born in Angola, New York, on November 26, 1876. He was the only child of Duane Carrier, a farmer, and Elizabeth Haviland Carrier.

Carrier had difficulty learning the concept of fractions in school. His mother told him to go the cellar and bring a pan of apples up to the kitchen. She asked her son to cut the apples into halves, quarters, and eighths, and then to add and subtract the pieces. Suddenly, fractions became clear to him. In later years, he used this as an example of the power of illustration to clarify difficult concepts.

Upon his graduation from the Angola Academy in 1894, Carrier could not afford to go to college; instead, he taught school for two years. He attended Central High School in Buffalo during the 1896-97 school year to prepare himself to take competitive examinations for college scholarships. In the spring of 1897, he won a four-year state tuition scholarship to Cornell University, and a two-year H. B. Lord scholarship that helped pay for room, board, books, and expenses. He earned money by mowing lawns, waiting on tables, and by founding a cooperative student laundry in his senior year. He and his partner earned $1,000 each from the laundry.

Carrier graduated from Cornell University in 1901 with the degree of Mechanical Engineer in Electrical Engineering. He accepted a position with the Buffalo Forge Company in Buffalo, and began his job on July 1, 1901. His first assignment was designing a heating plant for the Erie City Boiler Company. He also worked on systems for drying coffee and lumber, and on forced draft systems for boilers. He soon realized that there was not sufficient empirical data to use in designing these systems. Seat-of-the-pants techniques were resulting in overdesigned systems in order to incorporate the necessary safety factors.

He assembled the empirical data needed to arrive at efficient designs. The value of his work was recognized, and he was asked to set up an industrial laboratory to continue his research. His next project was preparing data for use in testing and rating heaters.

Carrier met Irvine Lyle, manager of the New York Office of Buffalo Forge Company, on his first day of work with the company. Lyle forwarded a request to Carrier from the Sackett-Williams Lithographing and Publishing Company, who needed to solve a humidity problem. Using dew-point temperature data from Weather Bureau tables, Carrier designed the equipment to solve the Sackett-Williams humidity problem. His July 17, 1902 drawings represent the first scientific air conditioning system.

Air conditioning accomplishes multiple functions: control of temperature and humidity, control of air circulation and ventilation, and cleaning of the air. Years later, Carrier provided his definition of air conditioning: "Air conditioning is the control of the humidity of air by either increasing or decreasing its moisture content. Added to the control of humidity are the control of temperature by either heating or cooling the air, the purification of the air by washing or filtering the air, and the control of air motion and ventilation."

Carrier was not satisfied with the design of his first air conditioning system. He was particularly unhappy with the use of salts to control humidity. The salts had a corrosive effect on the metal parts of his equipment. He conceived the solution to this problem while waiting for a train in Pittsburgh in late fall, 1902. Temperature was in the low thirties, and Carrier was thinking about the dense fog as he paced the railroad platform. In later years, Carrier described how the concept of "dew point control" had come to him:

> Here is air approximately 100 percent saturated with moisture. The temperature is low so, even though saturated, there is not much actual moisture. There could not be at so low a temperature. Now, if I can saturate air and control its temperature at saturation, I can get air with any amount of moisture I want in it. I can do it, too, drawing the air through a fine spray of water to create actual fog. By controlling the water temperature, I can control the temperature at saturation. When very moist air is desired, I'll heat the water. When very dry air is required, that is, air with a small amount of moisture, I'll use cold water to get low temperature saturation. The cold spray water will actually be the condensing surface. I certainly will get rid of the rusting difficulties that occur when using steel coils for condensing vapor in air. Water won't rust.

Carrier applied for a patent on his invention, "Apparatus for Treating Air," on September 16, 1904; he was awarded patent no. 808897 on January 2, 1906.

The first sale of equipment with Carrier's new design was to the LaCrosse National Bank of LaCrosse, Wisconsin. However, it was only used to wash the air in the ventilating system. Carrier's next applications were in the textile industry. A textile engineer, Stuart Cramer of Charlotte, North Carolina, gave the industry its name when he used the words "air conditioning" in a patent application for a humidifying head in April, 1906.

Another early Buffalo Forge Company sale of air conditioning equipment was to Parke, Davis & Company for use in the room in which the pharmaceutical company produced capsules. Carrier Air Conditioning Company of America, a wholly-owned subsidiary of the Buffalo Forge Company, was established in November, 1908. Many of Carrier's installations at this time were in tobacco factories.

In 1914, although air conditioning sales were prospering, Buffalo Forge decided to get out of the business. They were reacting to the beginning of World War I in Europe. In taking stock of their business situation, they decided to concentrate on their original core business. As a result, seven young engineers left the Buffalo Forge Company to form the

Carrier Engineering Corporation on June 26, 1915. Carrier was elected president and Lyle became the general manager and treasurer. One of their early projects was to design refrigeration equipment that was more suitable to the cooling needs of air conditioning systems.

As the company grew, they needed more factory space. They purchased a plant in Newark, New Jersey. They began to fill orders for department stores and theaters. Carrier also won the contract to supply refrigerating equipment for Madison Square Garden in July, 1925. Next came installations in the House of Representatives in 1928 and in the U. S. Senate in 1929. A second manufacturing plant was purchased in Newark, and a third plant was built in Allentown, Pennsylvania.

In 1930, the Carrier Corporation was formed by merging the Carrier Engineering Corporation with two manufacturing companies, Brunswick-Kroeschell Company and York Heating & Ventilating Corporation. In 1937, Carrier Corporation centralized five plants in four New Jersey and Pennsylvania cities into one location, the closed factories and offices of the H. H. Franklin Manufacturing Company in Syracuse. Centralization allowed the company to become much more efficient. One of the first products to be developed at the Syracuse facility was the popular Weathermaster System in 1937, which grew from crude experiments begun in 1928. The Weathermaster design was completed in 1939.

During World War II, Carrier continued to produce air conditioning equipment, but it also manufactured airplane engine mounts, gun sight hoods, tank adapters, and the "Hedgehog," an anti-submarine depth charge device. In the mid-1940s, Carrier reduced his activities with the company because of a heart ailment. He was made Chairman Emeritus of the Carrier Corporation in February, 1948. He died in New York City on October 7, 1950.

WILLIAM TOLLEY

Dr. William Pearson Tolley, Chancellor of Syracuse University from 1942 to 1969, served the university during the time that it became a national university. Dr. Tolley's early years were spent in Honesdale and Carbondale, Pennsylvania, where his father, Adolphus Tolley, owned shoe stores. Adolphus Tolley moved his family to Binghamton in 1903, where he opened the Willey and Tolley shoe store.

Upon his graduation from Binghamton Central High School, Tolley enrolled in Syracuse University. His parents' goal was for the university to prepare their son for the ministry; his goal was to prepare himself for the law. However, upon his graduation from

Syracuse University in 1922, he enrolled in Drew Theological Seminary in Madison, New Jersey.

When Tolley received his bachelor of arts degree from Syracuse University, he was six credits short of a master of arts degree. He completed the six credits of coursework and his master's thesis while at Drew. He received his M.A. from Syracuse in 1924 and his bachelor of divinity degree from Drew in 1925. He continued his academic work at Columbia University, and earned a M.A. in 1927 and a Ph.D. in 1930.

Upon his graduation from Drew University in 1925, Tolley stayed on there as alumni secretary and assistant to the president while he studied at Columbia University. Now that he was earning a salary, he could make long term plans. He married his high school sweetheart, Ruth Canfield, after his graduation from Drew. In 1930, he had every intention of staying at Drew to implement the plans he helped to formulate.

The acting president of Allegheny College of Meadville, Pennsylvania, Dr. Clarence Ross, asked to speak with Dr. Tolley about becoming the next president of the college. The Allegheny College Board of Trustees had some strongwilled members, including Andrew Robertson, Chairman of the Board of Westinghouse Electric Corporation; Andrew Culbertson, a utility president; and Ida Tarbell, the journalist who so effectively chronicled the evils of John D. Rockefeller and the Standard Oil Company.

Robertson called Dr. Tolley to his office and asked him, "Why do you want to be president of Allegheny College?" Dr. Tolley replied, "I don't want to be president of Allegheny College. I'm not a candidate. Dr. Ross came to Madison to meet me, and then I received a summons to your office. I'm here. What do you have to say to me?"

Dr. Tolley's meeting with the Allegheny Board of Trustees seemed even less successful. One of the board members commented, "Dr. Tolley, I have no doubt you're a promising scholar and teacher. But we don't need another teacher at Allegheny. What we need is a fundraiser ... Under the direction of a scholar, this college could go broke. What do you say to that?" Dr. Tolley responded, "Of course a college president has to raise money. But where does the money come from? It comes first from the trustees. Second, it comes from the alumni. Leadership and fundraising have to start with the trustees, not the president ... If I should come to Allegheny, how much would you give?" Dr.Tolley thought that his responses had ruined his chances for the presidency of Allegheny College. However, they were impressed with his forthrightness; he was offered, and accepted the position.

His first unpopular decision was to de-emphasize football. Allegheny played nationally ranked teams such as the University of Pittsburgh. In order to compete, Allegheny had to provide football scholarships that they could not afford. Many alumni reacted negatively to de-emphasizing football, but, in the long run, it was viewed as the correct decision. The experience that he gained at Allegheny College matured him as a leader in academia. He developed a reputation as an efficient administrator.

When William Pratt Graham, Chancellor of Syracuse University, retired in 1942, Dr. Tolley was invited to become the seventh Chancellor of the University. He accepted, and began his new duties on September 19, 1942. When Dr. Tolley returned to Syracuse, the annual budget was $3.7 million, endowment was under $5 million, and the total assets of the campus and buildings amounted to less that $15 million.

Dr. Tolley was responsive to government requests to accommodate large numbers of G. I. Bill students. The enrollment doubled in the fall of 1946 to 11,937, and increased to 15,000 in 1948. Graduate enrollment grew from 400 in 1942, to 1,250 in 1946, and to 8,000 by 1964. Some university presidents refused to respond to the academic needs of the veterans, but Syracuse University supported the G. I. Bill students beyond reasonable expectations.

Dr. Tolley was not above ignoring protocol if he thought it was for the good of the university. Dr. Tolley and Ruth spent a week as houseguests of Thomas Watson, Sr., President of IBM, and his wife, Jeanette, and were shown a sculpture by a friend of theirs, Malvina Hoffman. They visited Malvina, who told the Tolleys that she was upset by conditions being faced by one of her teachers, the Yugoslavian sculptor Ivan Mestrovic.

During World War II, Mestrovic was imprisoned by the Germans. Through the Pope's intervention, he was released and allowed to travel to Italy. However, he was ill, unable to sell any of his work, and therefore was in financial trouble. Columbia University had just turned down Malvina's request to hire him. Dr. Tolley told Malvina to send him the following cable: You have appointment as professor of sculpture at Syracuse University, effective September this year. Will pay expenses for you and family to come to States. Don't worry. Love. Malvina."

Dr. Tolley returned to Syracuse and asked Norman Rice, Director of the School of Art, and Bill Hekking, professor of painting, whether they knew of Mestrovic's work. They both spoke highly of him. Then Dr. Tolley talked with L. C. Dillenback, Dean of the College of Fine Arts, and mentioned he had heard that the sculptor Ivan Mestrovic could be brought to this country. He asked Dillenback to check with Rice and Hekking to see what they thought about adding Mestrovic to the faculty. Dillenback found Rice and Hekking to be very enthuastic about the Yugoslav sculptor. Dr. Tolley then asked Dillenback what he thought about bringing Mestrovic to Syracuse. Dillenback was incredulous, "Do you know how to do it?" Dr. Tolley said, "I think I do." He didn't tell Dillenback that he had broken all the rules, but it had worked.

In the first twenty years of Dr. Tolley's administration, total enrollment grew from 5,000 to 20,000, including 5,200 at off-campus centers. Also, graduate enrollment grew from 500 to 5,500, and 600 evening school students grew to 5,500 evening and part-time students. Also, from 1942 to 1962, the size of the faculty tripled, while increasing in quality. Thirty new buildings were built on the campus from 1946 to 1962, with a total capital outlay of over $42 million dollars.

In 1942, the operating budget was under $5 million; in 1962, it was $38.5 million. The book value of the endowment increased from $4.5 million to $23 million over the twenty-year period. The university retained its passion for excellence during a time of considerable expansion. The university continued to grow, in all ways, during the last five years of Dr. Tolley's administration.

In a sense, Dr. Tolley placed Syracuse University on the map. Today, it is truly a national university. The University was fortunate to have had an individual like Dr. Tolley at the helm during its critical growth years. He began his career as an educator, never wavered from his path, and finished his career as an educator. Dr. Tolley was clearly a man who liked doing what he did. It is reflected in his July, 1988, quotation in the preface of his book, *At the Fountain of Youth: Memories of a College President:* "Ponce de Leon came to America looking for the fountain of youth. He did not find it. He should have looked for it on the campuses of our schools and colleges. It is on the campuses of our colleges that our outlook is full of promise and hope."

1890 House Museum, Cortland

TABLE OF CONTENTS

CHAPTER 5

EAST OF THE LAKES

CHAPTER 5

EAST OF THE LAKES

Out of childhood into manhood
Now had grown my Hiawatha,
Skilled in all the craft of hunters,
Learned in the lore of old men,
In all youthful sports and pastimes,
In all manly arts and labors.
Swift of foot was Hiawatha;
He could shoot an arrow from him,
And run forward with such fleetness,
That the arrow fell behind him!
Strong of arm was Hiawatha;
He could shoot ten arrows upward
Shoot them with such strength and swiftness
That the tenth had left the bowstring
Ere the first had fallen!

....

From *Song of Hiawatha* by Henry Wadsworth Longfellow

EAST OF THE LAKES--INTRODUCTION

EAST OF THE LAKES--DESCRIPTION

The region east of the lakes is a beautiful area of farm country, hills, and valleys. It is known as the home of the State University of New York--College at Cortland, and as ski country. There are three ski centers in the immediate area. Song Mountain is located in the Town of Preble, east of Routes 13 and 81; Labrador Mountain is located in the Town of Truxton, west of Route 91; and Greek Peek is located in the Town of Virgil, west of Routes 11 and 81.

A conspicious feature of the terrain in the area is the Valley Heads moraine, a ridge formed 12,000 to 14,000 years ago during a pause in the northward movement of the Wisconsin ice-age glacier. This moraine dammed the southern ends of the Finger Lakes. One section of the moraine stretches across the Otisco valley. Another part of the moraine, the Tully moraine, rises over 500 feet from the valley floor. The Tully moraine can be viewed from the Route 81 Expressway, about twelve miles south of Syracuse. The Tully Lakes, a group of kettle lakes, can be seen on top of the moraine near the Tully exit from the Route 81 Expresssway. Song Mountain, just to the south of them, provides a good view of the lakes. The Little York Lakes, south of Preble, are also kettle lakes.

Route 20 between Skaneateles and LaFayette is a section of the scenic Cherry Valley Turnpike. Route 20 borders the northern edge of the Allegheny Plateau, and crosses a number of troughs formed by the glaciers. The troughs run north-south, and drain southward toward the Susquehanna River. The Butternut trough just east of LaFayette is one of the most scenic of the crossings. Steep-sided Jones hill, 700 feet above Labrador Pond, is a popular jump-off spot for hang-gliders.

The Otisco valley joins the main valley, the Tioughnioga River valley, at Preble; Factory Brook valley, the extension of the Skaneateles Lake trough, joins the main valley at Cortland. Cortland is built on a plain at the juncture of several valleys, which contain the east and west branches of the Tioughnioga River, Trout Brook, Otter Creek, and the main branch of the Tioughnioga River.

EAST OF THE LAKES--BRIEF HISTORY

The Tioughnioga Valley in Cortland County was a popular hunting ground for the Onondaga Indians, keepers of the Iroquois Council fire in the Syracuse area. Cortland County and several neighboring counties were part of the Military Tract laid out after the Revolutionary War. Cortland County was formed from Onondaga County in 1808. Cortland was selected as the county seat even though Homer was larger at the time.

Cortland--Elkanah Watson was one of the first settlers of Cortland, and William Randall was another of the area's early pioneers. The first railroad through the area began operation between Syracuse and Binghamton in 1854. The Lehigh Valley Railroad was built between Ithaca and Cortland in 1872. The Cortland Normal School, predecessor of SUNY--College at Cortland, opened its doors in 1869. Cortland is known as the home of Alton B. Parker, who ran for President against Theodore Roosevelt; Elmer Sperry, inventor of the gyroscope and founder of Sperry Gyroscope Company; and the Gillette family, upon whom the Theodore Dreiser novel, *An American Tragedy*, is based.

Homer--Joseph and Rhoda Beebe and Rhoda's brother, Amos Todd, traveled up the Tioughnioga Valley from Binghamton, and became the first settlers in 1791. Andrew D. White, the first president of Cornell University and a U. S. Ambassador to Germany, was born in a home at the corner of Albany and South Main Streets in Homer.

Amelia Jenks Bloomer, for whom bloomers were named, was born in the village in 1818. The artist Francis Carpenter was born in Homer in 1830. He lived at the White House for six months during President Lincoln's term, and painted a portrait of Lincoln and an historical painting commemorating the signing of the Emancipation Proclamation. His painting of the signing of the Alabama Treaty hangs in Windsor Castle in England.

EAST OF THE LAKES--THINGS

ITEMS OF INTEREST

CORTLAND REPERTORY THEATRE

The professional actors of the Cortland Repertory Theatre perform in the Pavillion Theatre in Dwyer Memorial Park, which is located between Routes 81 and 281, north of Little York. During the summer, the theatre offers classical music, comedy, drama, musical theatre, and mystery. The main ticket office is located at 15 Main Street, Cortland.

GREEK PEAK SKI RESORT

Greek Peak Ski Resort is located west of Route 81, seven miles south of Cortland. It has a 900-foot drop with twenty-four trails. Greek Peak has a triple and four double chairlifts, two T-bars, and a rope tow. The resort has a cafeteria, a restaurant, a lounge, and lodging. It offers lessons, rentals, night skiing, and a nursery.

LABRADOR MOUNTAIN SKI AREA

Labrador Mountain Ski Area is located west of Route 91 in the Town of Truxton. It has twenty slopes, one triple and two double chair lifts, and two T-bars. The ski area has a 700-foot drop, 95% snowmaking capability, and night skiing. Labrador Mountain has three lodges with two cafeterias, a restaurant, and a lounge. The ski area offers a PSIA school, babysitting, and a rental shop.

SONG MOUNTAIN SKI AREA

Song Mountain Ski Area is west of Routes 11 and 81, fifteen miles south of Syracuse. The ski area has a 700-foot drop and twenty-five trails ranging from beginner to expert. Song Mountain has a triple and a double chair lift, two T-bars, and a tow. It also has a cafeteria, a restaurant, and a lounge. The ski area offers lessons, rentals, night skiing, and a nursery. Song Mountain's Alpine Slide and Water Slide are popular seasonal activities.

LAKES

OTISCO LAKE

> Tell us the story of your pristine morn,
> When did your breaker first assail the shore;
> --
> Tell us about the glaciers, drear and cold,

That spread their icy mantles on your breast.
Enshrouding you in gloom for time untold;
Quiescent and congealed from floor to crest.
Tell of the creatures that have passed away,
That never more shall tread your rambling shore.
Their ichnolites and fossil bones decay,
But you remain and billow as of yore.

From *Tell us Your Tale, Blue Lake!* by Edwin Becker

The Indian word Otisco means "waters dried away." The origin of the word is thought to be a sudden lowering of the water level in the distant past. Otisco Lake is 5.4 miles long and three quarters of a mile wide at its widest point; it has an average width of just over a half mile. It is sixty-six feet deep, has a volume of 21.1 billion gallons, and serves a watershed of thirty-four square miles.

Syracuse suburbs and the New York State Fairgrounds in Geddes use the lake as a public water supply. No water treatment plants discharge into the lake. The hamlets of Amber, Bay Shores, Rice Grove, and Williams Grove dot the periphery of the lake. The watershed includes many dairy farms. The southern end of the lake is affected by soil erosion, and the lake bottom at that end is silt.

LEGENDS AND STORIES

AN AMERICAN TRAGEDY

Theodore Dreiser's novel, *An American Tragedy,* was based on incidents in the life of Chester Gillette of Cortland. Chester Gillette was the oldest child of Frank and Louisa Gillette, who moved from place to place trying to eke out a living by running various religious shelters. Chester ran away at the age of fourteen, and worked at odd jobs to support himself. In 1902, Chester was invited by his uncle, Noah Gillette, the wealthiest man in Cortland, to work in his petticoat and skirt factory. At the factory, Chester met Grace Brown, who had moved to Cortland to escape her family's farm in South Otselic.

Through his relatives in Cortland, Chester met many attractive young women from wealthy families, and began to lose interest in Grace. When Grace informed him that she was pregnant, Chester invited her to a weekend at Big Moose Lake in the Adirondack Mountains. He took Grace out on the lake in a canoe, struck her on the head, knocked her out of the canoe, and rowed back to shore without her. The police found Grace's body, and tracked Chester to the Arrowhead Hotel on Eagle Bay. He claimed to be innocent from the beginning of the investigation.

The trial in Herkimer was the top news story of its time. Chester was found guilty, sentenced, and sent to the Auburn prison. He was electrocuted on March 29, 1908, and was the last person to be electrocuted at Auburn; Sing Sing Prison in Ossining took over the function for the State of New York.

In Dreiser's 1925 novel, Chester Gillette was Clyde Griffiths, Grace Brown was Roberta Alden, Cortland was Lycurgus, and Big Moose Lake was Big Bittern Lake. In the first half of *An American Tragedy,* Drieser discussed the social system that shaped Chester. He prepared the reader to believe that Chester could commit the crime. *An American Tragedy* was a best seller for the author, who was already known for *Sister Carrie, Jennie Gerhardt,* and *The Financier.* The novel was made into a movie, *A Place in the Sun,* starring Montgomery Clift and Elizabeth Taylor.

CANDIDATE ALTON B. PARKER

Alton B. Parker, the Democratic party's candidate for President of the United States in 1904, was born in Cortland on May 14, 1852. He graduated from Albany Law School in 1873, and practiced law in Kingston. He was a delgate to the Democratic National Convention in 1884. Parker was appointed chairman of the State Democratic Committee, and successfully managed the campaign of David Hill for governor. He was appointed to a vacant seat on the state supreme court, selected for the court of appeals in 1889, and appointed to the appellate division of the supreme court in 1896. In 1897, he was elected Chief Justice of the court of appeals by a surprising plurality of over 60,000 votes.

Beginning in 1895, he turned down several opportunities to be his party's candidate for governor. In court, he tended to be a liberal judge. For example, he upheld the right of labor unions to obtain a closed shop by threatening to strike, and he upheld the constitutionality of an act limiting the hours of work in bakeries. After the second defeat of Presidential candidate William Jennings Bryan in 1900, the democrats looked for a new candidate from the eastern wing of the party. Parker was popular in New York, and he had not been involved in factional differences within the party.

In order not to compromise his position as a judge or to appear to be seeking the nomination for President, he declined making any statements on public issues before the national convention. He was told that his reticence might cost him the nomination. Parker was nominated on the first ballot. During the campaign, his liberal record was downplayed, and he was presented as reliable and conservative.

The Republican candidate for President was Theodore Roosevelt. He was elected Vice-President in 1900, and became President when President McKinley was assassinated. Teddy Roosevelt was young, dynamic, and was known as the hero of the Rough Riders at

San Juan Hill in Cuba during the Spanish-American War. Parker received 140 electoral votes to President Roosevelt's 336. Parker was no match for Teddy, who is considered by historians to be one of the five near-great Presidents of the United States.

THE CARDIFF GIANT

The Cardiff Giant was discovered on Stub Newell's farm off Route 20 in the hamlet of Cardiff on October 16, 1869. Newell had asked his friends Gid Emmons and Hank Nichols to help him dig a well behind his barn. At about the three-foot level, they struck something hard. It appeared to be a fossilized Indian over ten feet tall. They cleaned the dirt off of him, and raised him to ground level. Soon crowds began to form, and Newell began to charge admission. Four-horse stagecoaches made the round trip from Syracuse at $1.00 a head.

An Onondaga Indian concluded that the giant must be real; he remembered his father talking about the Onondagas fighting stone giants. Visiting professors made pronouncements on the giant's authenticity. The State Geologist, Professor James Hall, said, "It is the most remarkable object yet brought to light in this country, and although not dating back to the Stone Age is nevertheless deserving of the attention of archaeologists." Alexander McWhorter, a graduate student, declared the figure to be the Phoenician God Baal. Dr. John Boynton, a local lecturer, thought that portions of the facial features reminded him of Governor DeWitt Clinton.

Mr. P. T. Barnum offered Newell $150,000 for the giant, or $60,000 for a three-month rental. Newell turned him down, but took on partners from the area, including David Hannum from Homer. Not to be outdone, Barnum had a copy of the giant made by C. C. Otto of Syracuse; he displayed it at the Wood Museum in New York, and billed it as "the only original giant." By the time Hannum reached Apollo Hall at 28th Street and Broadway in New York with the Cardiff Giant, he had to compete with Barnum's entry.

Hannum and the giant moved on to Boston in January, 1870, where there was less competition. They also toured Connecticut, New Hampshire, and Pennsylvania. An article in a Claremont, New Hampsire, paper in August, 1871, included the comment that: "The Cardiff Giant is giving a series of entertainments in Claremont. He is said to resemble General Grant inasmuch that he don't talk and his head is made of stone. So look out for another "mum" candidate for the Presidency ..."

Professor O. C. March uncovered the fact that George Hull, a relative of Newell's, purchased a block of gypsum twelve foot by four foot by two foot in Fort Dodge, Iowa, in 1868, and transported it to the shop of stonecutter Edward Burkhardt in Chicago. Burkhardt and two assistants simulated skin pores by using a metal hammer with needle points. They treated the giant with sulphuric acid to give it the dingy brown appearance of age. It was rubbed with water and sand to smooth the surfaces. Then, it was transported to Newell's farm and buried.

Except for a brief visit to the Pan-American Exposition in Buffalo in 1901, the Cardiff was stored in Fitchburg, Massachusetts for forty years. It was shown at the New York Fair in 1934 and the Iowa State Fair in 1935. The New York State Historical Association acquired the Cardiff Giant, and placed it in the Farmer's Museum in Cooperstown on May 19, 1948.

DAVID HARUM

Edward Noyes Westcott wrote *David Harum, A Story of American Life* in 1898. The fictionialized biography of David Hannum of Homer became the bestseller of its day. A half-million copies were sold in less than two years. Homeville in the book is Homer, Syrchester is a composite of Syracuse and Rochester, Peeble is Preble, the town north of Homer, and Buxton Hill is Truxton, the town east of Homer.

David Hannum, the model for David Harum in the novel, was a farmer, property owner, and storyteller, but was known primarily as a horse trader. Hannum's friend John Rankin, John Lenox in the book, said that on occasion Hannum would swap horses fifteen to twenty times a day with farmers who came to Homer. Hannum, with one notable exception, always came out ahead in horse trades.

Hannum had a horse known as a kicker. It looked like a horse worth $500, but due to its reputation as a kicker was worth only twenty-five dollars. Hannum sold the horse to a neighbor, who sold him to Dwight Miller, the postmaster of Homer. Miller clipped the horse's breast and trimmed his mane and tail so that he looked like a different horse. He then sold the horse back to Hannum for several hundred dollars more than Hannum had received from his neighbor.

Hannum was a great storyteller, and was popular with the children of the village. Many of his folksy, down-to-earth sayings were captured in the novel, including:

 o A reasonable amount of fleas is good for a dog. They keep him from broodin' on
  bein' a dog.

 o Some folks are like cider. They're sweet until it's time to work.

 o I'm as busy as a hummin' bird with two tails.

 o He's enough to give a buzzard a bilious attack.

Hannum's golden rule was: "Do unto the other fellow what the other fellow 'ud like to do to you, and do it fust."

Harrum was part owner and, later, sole owner of the Cardiff Giant. He lost money promoting this hoax to the public. At one point, Harrum owned most of the land around Skaneateles Lake. However, he was forced to sell during a downturn in the economy; he was not financially well off late in his life. His home in Homer, called the David Harum House, is presently operated as a bed and breakfast.

THE LEGEND OF MONA-SHA-SHA

An Iroquois hunter, Joninedah, moved his teepee away from his village to a temporary location to see if he could improve his luck hunting in a new area. His wife, Mona-sha-sha, and their young child liked their home in the serene glen next to a waterfall. However, Joninedah's luck didn't improve, and day after day he came home empty-handed. Mona-sha-sha fished and picked berries while her husband was away hunting during the day.

Every day Joninedah came home feeling that the evil eye was upon him. Mona-sha-sha tried to console him, but he did not respond to her smiles. In his despair, he was not kind to her, and Mona-sha-sha felt that he no longer loved her. She waited until he was asleep one night, strapped her child in a papoose on her back, and went out into the dark night. High above the waterfall, she climbed into her canoe, paddled downstream and was dashed over the falls.

Joninedah was surprised to find her gone in the morning. He went to the edge of the stream, and noticed that her canoe was gone. As he found his wife and child in the pool at the bottom of the falls, an albino doe and fawn ran by. It appeared that the Great Spirit had used this symbolism to speak of the dead. Overcome with grief, he plunged his knife into his chest, and joined Mona-sha-sha and their child in death.

THE NAMING OF TOWNS AND VILLAGES

New York State has about 500 place-names that originated from Indian names, including twelve of the state's sixty cities and twenty of sixty-two counties. The Hudson River valley has many place-names based on Dutch names from the time when New York City was New Amsterdam. However, visitors to the state are surprised to find over 200 classical place-names derived from Greek and Roman origins. Many of these 200 names are in the Finger Lakes Region, particularly in the eastern part of the region.

Simon DeWitt, the Surveyor-General of the State of New York from 1789 to 1790, is usually credited with assigning the classical names. He supervised the survey of a military tract encompassing four counties and parts of another four counties that were planned in townships six miles square. Parcels were offered to Revolutionary War veterans. New York City newspaper editors criticized him for his "classical spree." He responded that he "knew nothing of these obnoxious names, until they were officially communicated to him" by a land commissioner who had already given his approval to them. The names were added to maps by the Deputy Secretary of State, Robert Harpur, as directed by the Land Commission.

The classical names are most numerous in the Military Tract; however, over 100 are in counties outside the tract. Twenty-four of them are in Onondaga County. Christopher Morley, on a visit to the Finger Lakes Region, noted that: "Some Hellinist surveyor must have once swept over the land with a Greek theodolite, sprinkling lovely place-names from the classics." Classical city names include Ithaca, Syracuse, Rome, and Utica. Some of the thirty villages with classical names are Camillus, Fabius, Homer, Ilion, Marcellus, Mycenae, and Ovid. There are fifty-seven towns with classical names such as Brutus, Cato, Cicero, Cincinnatus, Manlius, Pompey, Sempronius, and Ulysses.

Although Greek and Roman place names predominate in central New York State, there are also names such as Carthage, Egypt, Phoenicia, and Tyre. Biblical names are also found in the state: Bethany, Bethel, Ephratah, Jerusalem, Nineveh, and Sodom. Neither Mr. DeWitt nor Mr. Harpur can be credited, or blamed, for the large number of classical place-names in the region. Professor Alexander Drummond of Ithaca speculated that early New York settlers felt an empathy with those who dwelled in the ancient democracies. New York pioneers considered that they were repeating the earlier democratic experiments, but with more favorable conditions.

THE STORY OF HANNAH'S STUMP

Hannah's Stump is off East Virgil Road between Virgil and Messengerville. It is just slightly more well known than other place-names in southern Cortland County such as Daisy Hollow, Frank's Corners and Frog Huddle. Hannah's Stump is a high rock named for Hannah Trowbridge from Gridley Hollow. She was courted by Isaac Bloomer. Isaac wanted to marry her, but hadn't gotten up enough nerve to pop the question. Hannah was a high-spirited type who liked to tease. In particular, she liked to tease Isaac, who was in love and vulnerable.

One day Hannah climbed to the top of a rocky cliff and stood, on her tiptoes on the top of an old stump that overlooked the road and the river in the valley below. She called out to Isaac, "I'll jump, Isaac Bloomer, unless you promise to marry me." The children and grandchildren of Hannah and Isaac Bloomer are happy that the old stump did not crumble into the valley, and that Isaac said, "Yes," in a loud, clear voice.

THE STORY OF THE WEDDING THAT WAS CALLED OFF

Dr. John Miller was born in Dutchess County on the Hudson River in 1774, and began the practice of medicine in the Town of Truxton in 1801. He had met a beautiful girl in Troy who accepted his proposal of marriage. They exchanged letters frequently while he was getting settled in Truxton, and establishing his medical practice. Her letters stopped coming, and Dr. Miller was perplexed at not hearing from his fiance for over a year.

He received a letter from a friend in Troy who told him that his fiance was to be married in Troy very soon. Dr. Miller had only twenty-four hours to travel over the poor roads between Truxton and Troy. However, he was an accomplished horseman who was used to riding sixty miles a day. The winter roads in late March made riding difficult, but Dr. Miller's reliable horse, Gershom, carried him the entire 130 miles. They barely made it across the Hudson River at Albany on the the last evening ferry. Dr. Miller's horse jumped onto the ferry just as it was leaving the shore.

The wedding party was already in the church when Dr. Miller pulled up outside. He ran into the church, and arrived just in time to hear the minister ask, "Does anyone forbid these banns?" Dr. Miller stuttered, "I--I--I do." The wedding ceremony was halted while Dr. Miller explained himself. The bridegroom-to-be had destroyed Dr. Miller's letters to his fiance, giving her the impression that he was no longer interested in her. They courted for another year, and were then married. The story ends well, since Dr. Miller and his wife built a beautiful manor house, and raised eight children.

PARKS, FORESTS, AND TRAILS

LABRADOR HOLLOW STATE NATURE PRESERVE

Labrador Hollow State Nature Preserve, located fifteen miles northeast of Cortland and five miles east of Route 81, is accessible from Route 91, Labrador Road, and Markham Hollow Crossroad. The main parking area is north of the pond off Markham Hollow Crossroad. The State Nature Preserve, which is part of 1,483 acres of state land, is located in a north-south valley with a floor that is only one-half mile wide and with steep walls that rise for several hundred feet. It is principally a northern hardwood forest with plant life normally found in high mountain bogs, such as those found in the Adirondack Mountains.

The 120-acre pond, although only an average depth of four feet, is a good warm water fishery. Largemouth bass are the primary gamefish. Most of the pond borders wooded wetlands, and there are bogs on the east and south sides. Drainage from the pond is to the south via Labrador Creek. Waterfowl hunting is permitted on the pond in season; Canada geese are the main waterfowl species in the nature preserve.

Tinker Falls, which is set in an eighty-foot high, natural rock amphitheatre, is located on Tinker Falls Creek in the southeast part of the nature preserve. The falls, which are spectacular during the spring runoff, can be reached by a foot trail from Route 91. Labrador Hollow State Nature Center is an excellent site for birdwatching; over 107 species of birds have been identified in the area, including twelve types of warblers.

One of the most popular locations for hang gliding in central New York is near the northern end of the east side of the valley, where westerly winds generate thermals along the walls of the valley. The launch site is at the top of a 700-foot hill. A State permit is required for hang-gliding at the Labrador Hollow Nature Center.

Hiking trails, through the cooperation of the Finger Lakes Trail Conference, are available in the nature center, the adjacent Morgan Hill State Forest, and on private land east of Labrador Hollow. Since some of the trails pass through private lands; hikers are asked to respect the rights of the owners.

The handicapped-accessible Labrador Hollow Wetland Boardwalk traverses a diverse wetland of mucky soil over a moraine of gravel and sand formed by the Wisconsin glacier. Many of the shrubs and trees grow on small hills, or "hummocks," which began as fallen trees or tree stumps covered with fungi, lichens, liverworts, and mosses. The boardwalk has seven stations:

o Station One--Mixed emergent / wooded swamp with Atlantic white cedars, cattails, and foam flowers

o Station Two--Hummocky mixed emergent / wooded swamp with Clinton's lilies and painted trilliums

o Station Three--Hemlock swamp with goldthreads, marsh marigolds, and starflowers

o Station Four--Shallow, floating marsh / aquatic bed with skunkgrass. Listen for green frogs, spring peepers, veeries, and wood thrushes.

o Station Five--Western inlet to Labrador Pond, fed by springs and surface water with swamp roses. Listen for cedar waxwings, red-winged blackbirds, and swamp sparrows. Look for shining turtles on fallen logs.

o Station Six--Labrador Pond with spatterdock and winterberry

o Station Seven--Shrub swamp highbush blueberry, miterwort, and purple great lobelia. Listen for bullfrogs. Look for beavers, green herons, hawks, and kingfishers.

Rules for Public Use for the Labrador Hollow Nature Center:

o Bathing, camping, fires, and swimming are prohibited.

o Boating is restricted to non-motorized boats, which must be carried into the pond at the designated access site.

o Off-road vehicular traffic is prohibited.

o Fishing is permitted only from a boat on the creek or pond; no fishing is allowed from the shoreline.

o Hunting and trapping is permitted only in selected zones of the nature center.

o Hang-gliding is allowed only by special permit.

LIME HOLLOW NATURE CENTER

The Lime Hollow Nature Center, located between Route 13 and McLean Road at 3091 Gracie Road, contains nature trails and an interpretive building. It can be viewed from Gracie and Lime Hollow Roads. The nature center is made up of several components:

o The Nature Conservancy owns a parcel of land adjacent to the Chicago Bog.

o Cortland County owns a walking trail along the old Lehigh Valley Railroad right-of-way from the Cortland-Tompkins County line to beyond the Lime Hollow Nature Center.

o The Tunnison Laboratory of Fish Nutrition is located on 106 acres owned by the U. S. Fish and Wildlife Service. The laboratory serves as the national hatchery manager's training school.

The hiking trails are used by cross-country skiers during the winter. The evolution of the Lime Hollow Nature Center is ongoing. Additional nature trails are under development; an interpretive building to provide visitors with year-round environmental education and recreational opportunities is planned.

MORGAN HILL STATE FOREST

Morgan Hill State Forest is located fifteen miles northeast of Cortland and five miles east of Route 81. It is east of the Labrador Hollow Nature Center. The state forest is accessible via Shackham Road off Route 91, and via Morgan Hill Road off Route 13. The state forest is a 5,560-acre upland forest ranging from 1,200 to 2,000 feet in elevation. It is a scenic area with several creeks and small valleys intersecting a forested landscape. Vehicle access via 13.7 miles of roads is good during the spring, summer, and fall; winter access is by foot, snowmobile, or cross-country skis.

Beginning in the late 1700s, farmers cleared forests to develop farms on Morgan Hill. Many of the farms were abandoned during the Great Depression due to worn out soil. The Civilian Conservation Corps planted millions of conifer seedlings on unused farm land throughout the Finger Lakes Region during the 1930s. This created wildlife habitat, stopped soil erosion, and made the land productive. These sixty-year old conifer forests represent forty-five percent of the Morgan Hill State Forest; hardwood and hemlock trees populate most of the rest of the state forest.

The Morgan Hill State Forest provides many opportunities for recreation:

o It is easy to drive and picnic throughout the state forest, because of a good road system and many small parking areas.

o Five miles of marked trails connect the western section of the state forest with the Labrador Hollow Nature Preserve, and continue east as part of the Finger Lakes Trail System.

o Special off-road motor vehicle trails traverse a seventeen-mile section of the forest.

o The state forest has sixteen and a half miles of snowmobile trails and many separate ski touring trails.

o Hunting is good throughout the state forest, particularly deer-hunting.

o Fishing in Spruce Pond, which is stocked with trout, is a popular activity.

o Camping is permitted throughout the forest.

SHOWS AND FESTIVALS

APPLE FESTIVAL

The Annual Apple Festival at LaFayette, located at the intersection of Route 20 and Routes 11 and I-81, has been held since 1972. The two-day festival in early October attracts approximately 100,000 people. In addition to pecks and bushels of apples, the festival has apple candy, apple cider, apple fritters, apple pies, and apple sundaes. For sale are apple pencils, pins, souvenirs, and stationery. Johnny Appleseed and Jenny Appleseed appear each year. The festival has amusement rides and about 350 craft booths.

The Annual Apple Festival is held on a hillside along Route 20, just east of the village. The festival grounds are adjacent to St. Joseph's parish center, on the south side of the street. Admission is free, but there is a small parking fee.

CENTRAL NEW YORK MAPLE FESTIVAL

The Central New York Maple Festival has been held on an April weekend in the Village of Marathon since 1971. Marathon is located at the intersection of Routes 11 and 221, and is an exit on the Route 81 Expressway about halfway between Syracuse and Binghamton. Over 50,000 people attend the maple festival each year.

An all-you-can-eat pancake breakfast is provided all day, each day, and other food is available as well. There is continuous entertainment both days. Examples of festival activities are: bake sales, book sales, quilt shows, and a juried craft show. Maple syrup is made in the Sugar Shack, which is located next door to the Maple Museum. The second floor of the Maple Museum contains antique farm tools and equipment that were used for making maple products. Items such as jack wax (hot, thick maple syrup poured over fresh snow) and maple lollipops are made on the first floor of the museum.

WATERFALLS

Many of these waterfalls are located on private property; owner's rights should be respected, particularly if the property is posted.

BRICKYARD FALLS

Brickyard Falls is an 80-foot cataract in Limestone Creek. It is located off Watervale Road in the Town of Pompey.

BROADFIELD FALLS

Broadfield Falls is on West Limestone Creek. It is located off Broadfield Road in the Town of Pompey.

BUCKTAIL FALLS

Bucktail Falls is a 35-foot cascade on Buckland Creek. It is located at the intersection of Moon Hill and Saw Mill Roads.

THE CASCADES

The Cascades are a 200-foot series of 20-foot falls located off Berry Road in the Town of LaFayette.

DELPHI FALLS

Delphi Falls is a 35-foot cascade on East Limestone Creek. It is located off Gardner Road in the Town of Pompey.

FELLOWS FALLS

Fellows Falls is a 175-foot waterfall off Route 80 in the Town of Tully. It is located near the hamlet of Vesper, three miles west of Route 81.

PEPPERMILL GULF

Peppermill Gulf is a 90-foot cascade located off Hogback Road in the Town of Onondaga.

RATTLESNAKE GULF

Rattlesnake Gulf is a series of fourteen vertical drops and cascades on Fall Creek. It is parallel to Otisco Road in the Towns of LaFayette and Otisco.

TINKER FALLS

Tinker Falls is an 80-foot falls set in a rocky chasm. It is located off Route 91, south of the Cortland-Onondaga County line in the Town of Truxton.

EAST OF THE LAKES--PLACES

COLLEGES AND UNIVERSITIES

STATE UNIVERSITY OF NEW YORK--COLLEGE AT CORTLAND

The State University of New York--College at Cortland, a traditional, residential liberal arts and sciences college, has 5,600 undergraduate students and 600 graduate students. The college, which is located on a hillside with a commanding view of the rolling hills and farmland nearby, was founded in 1868. The beautiful SUNY--Cortland campus, a blend of Greek revival, neo-Georgian, and modern buildings on 191 acres, is a short walk from the shops and restaurants of downtown Cortland.

The college is divided into two academic units: The School of Arts and Sciences and the School of Professional Studies. The faculty is professionally active, and engaged in research. However, their main commitment is to instruction of the forty-eight majors offered by the College. Campus facilities are outstanding, including a large, modern fine arts center, a natural science museum, a planetarium, state of the art communications facilities, and a showcase physical education center.

Hoxie Gorge, near Cortland, is the College's 170-acre natural preserve, which is used for field work in the natural sciences and outdoor recreation. Cortland's Brauer Memorial Field Research Station, located near Albany, is a classic region of fossiliferous limestone and shale formations of the Devonial age. It is the only major geological field station in the State University of New York system. The 446-acre Outdoor Education Center at Racquette Lake in the Adirondacks contains a camp and conference center along a five-mile shoreline. Cortland's study abroad program, the most comprehensive in the State University of New York system, has agreements with twelve institutions of higher learning in England, France, Germany, Ireland, Mexico, Spain, Switzerland, and the People's Repubic of China.

TOMPKINS-CORTLAND COMMUNITY COLLEGE

Tompkins-Cortland Community College, located off Route 13, north of Dryden, is one of thirty two-year community colleges of the State University of New York system. The community colleges provide local business and industry with highly skilled employees in a wide variety of occupational curriculums, and offer many transfer options to students who wish to pursue advanced degrees. Tompkins-Cortland Community College offers one Associate in Arts Degree, thirteen Associate in Science degrees, eighteen Associate in Applied Science degrees, and nine certificate programs.

The State University of New York approved the establishment of Tompkins-Cortland Community College on November 10, 1966. The college opened in September, 1968, in Groton; it moved to the new facility in Dryden in September, 1974. The mission of the college is to provide high quality post-secondary education and training, continuing studies, and community service.

The College's Business and Industry Center offers a wide variety of training programs, seminars, and services tailored to the area business community. The center works with area business and non-profit organizations to plan, develop, and implement a range of management training activities. It also offers courses, credit and non-credit seminars, and workshops for area businesses.

MUNICIPALITIES

CORTLAND

Cortland is located at the intersection of Routes 13 and 41. It is also on the I-81 Expressway between Syracuse and Binghamton. At an elevation of 1,129 feet, Cortland is one of the highest cities in the state. Cortland County has a scenic agricultural landscape with many dairy farms. It has a reputation as good fishing, hunting, and skiing country. The City of Cortland is the home of the State University of New York--College at Cortland, known for its international studies, teacher education, and athletic programs. The 1890 House Museum in Cortland is a historic house on the National Register.

Cortland was named for Pierre Van Cortlant, the first Lieutenant Governor of New York State. One of the early settlers of the Cortland area was Elkanah Watson (1758-1842). He fought in the Revolutionary War, and transported gold from Boston to North Carolina to pay for the French contraband smuggled through the British blockade. He worked with the Ambassador to France, Benjamin Franklin, and consulted for DeWitt Clinton on the construction of the Erie Canal. Cortland County was formed from Onondaga County in 1808, and Cortland became the county seat. SUNY--College at Cortland opened its doors in 1869 as the Cortland Normal School.

One of Cortland's favorite sons is Judge Alton B. Parker, who was born in on May 14, 1852. Successively, he was elected to the state supreme court, appointed to the court of appeals, and elected chief justice of the court of appeals. He was the Democratic candidate for President of the United States in 1904, but had the misfortune to run against Theodore Roosevelt. Another of Cortland's favorite sons is Elmer Sperry, inventor of the gyroscope, ship stabilizers, and bombsights, and founder of the Sperry Gyroscope Company.

HOMER

Homer is located north of Cortland at the intersection of Routes 41 and 90. It is also on the I-81 Expressway. Homer has stately homes on its main street, and a village green that is reminiscent of New England. It was settled in 1791, when Joseph Beebe, Rhoda Beebe, and Amos Todd entered the area via the Tioughnioga Valley. Many of Homer's early settlers came from New England, particularly Connecticut.

One of Homer's favorite sons is Andrew D. White, the first President of Cornell University. A favorite daughter is Amelia Bloomer, who made popular the bloomer costume that was worn by early members of the Women's Rights Movement. The artist Francis Carpenter was born in Homer in 1830. Dwyer Memorial Park, the summer home of the Cortland Reperatory Theatre, is located north of Homer in Little York. The historic pavillion in the park overlooks Little York Lake.

MUSEUMS

1890 HOUSE MUSEUM

The 1890 House Museum and Center for Victorian Arts, located one block west of Main Street at 37 Tompkins Street in Cortland, was built as the residence of nineteenth-century industrialist Chester Wickwire. Mr. Wickwire, a manufacturer of window screening, wire fencing, and other wire products, commissioned architect Samuel Reed to design his home based on the design of the James Bailey (of the Barnum and Bailey Circus) home in New York City. J. B. Tiffany consulted on the interior decoration of the thirty-room limestone mansion, and blended Chateauesque and Romanesque styles.

The interior features cherry and oak woodwork, parquet floors, ornate decorative stenciling, and stained glass windows. The opulent gold and white formal parlor has an ornamented ceiling, silk wall coverings, and wall-to-wall Wilton carpeting. All interior hardware is solid brass embossed with wire mesh, which symbolize the Wickwire products. The 1890 House, listed in the National Register of Historic Places, is operated as a historic house museum, and features restored period room settings, changing exhibitions, programs, and special events that focus on the architecture, history, culture, and decorative arts of the Victorian era.

The 1890 House Museum is operated by a non-profit organization chartered by the State of New York to preserve, protect, and interpret the 1890 House, and to promote public awareness of the architecture, culture, decorative arts, and history of the Victorian era. The museum has a four-room orientation center; the grounds feature landscaped lawns and a two-story carriage barn. The 1890 House Museum is open afternoons, except Mondays and major holidays. A nominal admission is charged. Special group tours are available. Portions of the house are handicapped accessible.

HOMEVILLE MUSEUM

The Homeville Museum, which is located at 49 Clinton Street (Route 41) in Homer, has seven rooms of military displays, and a three-room model railroad museum with five gauges of trains. Some of the specialities of the museum are the Civil War period, World War II, German and Japanese artifacts, and Lackawanna Railroad memorabilia.

Military relics include equipment, firearms, and uniforms from:

o The Indian War
o World War I
o The Korean War

o The Civil War
o World War II
o The Vietnam War

The Model Railroad Museum has model trains by:

o American Flyer
o Life Like
o Marx
o Cox

o Athearn
o Lionel
o Model Power

o Bachman
o Mantua
o Tyco

The museum displays items collected by Ken Eaton over a forty year period. The museum is open Thursday evenings and the second and fourth Sunday afternoons each month from May through October. Admission is free; donations are appreciated. Appointments may be made for group tours. Parking is available at the rear of the museum.

PLACES OF INTEREST

COUNTRY MUSIC PARK

The Country Music Park, located one mile north of Cortland, bills itself as the Nashville of the Northeast. It is comprised of the Hall of Fame Museum, the Joan West Memorial Outdoor Stage, and the Opry Barn. The Country Music Park also has campgrounds, a fishing and swimming pond, Koryland playground, and the Memorial Garden with a "Walkway to the Stars." Eckel's Trolley provides free train rides around the park.

The Hall of Fame Museum displays country music memorabilia and items from performers from Nashville, New York State, and the Northeast, including:

o Roy Acuff
o Loretta Lynn
o Ernest Tubb

o Roy Clark
o "Boots" Randolph
o Justin Tubb

o Wilma Lee Cooper
o Jerry Reed
o Conway Twitty

- o John Conlee
- o Dick Curless
- o Little Jimmy Dickens
- o Jack Greene
- o Grandpa Jones
- o Marty Robbins
- o Kenny Rogers
- o Jean Shepard
- o Ronnie Smith
- o Mel Tillis
- o Porter Wagoner
- o Dottie West
- o "Boxcar" Willie
- o B. J. Wright
- o Tammy Wynette

The Country Music Park has hosted country music stars such as Loretta Lynn, Jeanie C. Riley, Dottie West, and Tammy Wynette. The park, which opened in 1984, is operated by the Statewide Country Music Association, a non-profit organization. It is open all year. The Opry Barn offers live country music on Saturday evenings and Sunday afternoons.

TUNISON LABORATORY OF FISH NUTRITION

The Tunison Laboratory of Fish Nutrition, which is located three miles southwest of Cortland off Route 13, is operated by the U. S. Fish and Wildlife Service of the Department of the Interior. It is the world's oldest and the United States' only laboratory devoted to fish nutrition. The mission of the Laboratory is twofold:

1. To support the restoration of nationally important fish populations, such as the Atlantic salmon.
2. To support the growing U. S. aquaculture (fish farming) industry.

The Tunison Laboratory of Fish Nutrition began operations in 1932 as a joint effort of Cornell University, the New York State Department of Environmental Conservation, and the U. S. Fish and Wildlife Service. It was originally developed on 105 acres surrounding two natural springs; later, four wells were added to provide disease-free water for the twenty-four indoor raceways, laboratories, and outdoor raceways. During its history, the facility served as a National Fish Hatchery, and as the training school for National Hatchery managers. The laboratory was named for its founder, Abe Tunison, in 1971.

The primary focus of the Laboratory is the dietary requirements of anadromous fish (fish that migrate up rivers from the sea to spawn), including the development of optimum fish feeds and of maximizing fish growth. Feed manufacturers utilize the results of Tunison research to develop fish feeds with the least environmental impact. These feeds are used by federal, state, and private production hatcheries worldwide.

RESTAURANTS--HISTORIC

BENN CONGER INN

The Benn Conger Inn, a beautiful Greek Revival house built by a local industrialist just after World War I, is located at 206 West Cortland Street in Groton. The large, white mansion has an elegant decor that provides a pleasant atmosphere for dining. The dining area is decorated with Oriental pictures; the front dining room has a working fireplace.

The food served at the Benn Conger is advertised as American and Continental, but is quite varied and similar to the cuisine served in a European inn. The chef calls his food conservative but creative; all of the sauces are prepared in the classic French manner. He concentrates on preparing a few dishes, usually about six entrees (excluding specials), and the menu is changed quarterly.

A good selection of chicken, red meat, and seafood dishes are offered, and all of the desserts are homemade. The wine list is extensive.

THE ROSE INN

The Rose Inn, a striking example of classical Italianate architecture, is located at 813 Auburn Road in Groton. The centerpiece of the mansion, which was built in the early 1800s, is a stairwell made from Honduran mahogany that spirals up to a cupola in the center of the house. The walls of the foyer are framed with mahogany and American chestnut. The dining rooms adjacent to the foyer have been restored to their Victorian decor; the small dining rooms each accommodate ten people. A tasteful collection of antiques is displayed throughout the house, and the tables are decorated with antique glass, silver candleholders, and china on silver "rose" placemats.

The Rose Inn requires reservations, and offers a single *prix fixe* meal. Guests select one of four entree choices: beef, lamb, veal, or shrimp. The chef then decides how to prepare the dish based on one of these four choices. Since the cooking is made to order, a guest's request to eliminate a heavy cream sauce or mushrooms, for example, is accommodated. The service is personalized, and dining at the Rose Inn is a memorable experience. According to guests, the Rose Inn "is like having your own private caterers."

EAST OF THE LAKES-PERSONS

AMELIA BLOOMER

Amelia Jenks Bloomer, for whom bloomers were named, was born on May 27, 1818, in the Village of Homer, New York, the youngest of four daughters of Ananias Jenks, clothier, and Lucy Webb Jenks. Bloomer noted in her journal, "My earliest recollections are of a pleasant home in Homer, Cortland County, New York...." She attended Homer schools, and graduated from Homer Academy when she was seventeen years old. Following graduation, she accepted a teaching position in the Village of Clyde in Wayne County.

In 1836, Amelia and her family moved to Waterloo, which was the home of her sister, Elvira. In 1837, she became the governess and tutor for the three children of Mr. and Mrs. Oren Chamberlain in Waterloo. She met Dexter Bloomer, a law student, in nearby Seneca Falls, fell in love, and was married on April 15, 1840. She was pleased that her husband left out the word "obey" in their wedding vows. Her husband was an owner and editor of the *Seneca County Courier,* which was printed weekly in Seneca Falls.

The temperance movement was very active in the first half of the nineteenth century, and speaking out against "demon drink" was a popular pastime. Bloomer helped to establish the local temperance society, and contributed to its newsletter, *The Water Bucket.* She became an officer of the Ladies Temperance Society, and published the society's newsletter, *The Lily.* Later in life, Bloomer commented: "*The Lily* was the first paper published and devoted to the interests of women, and, as far as I know, the first one owned, edited, and published by a woman."

Her temperance society activities satisfied her need to contribute to society until 1847, when Elizabeth Cady Stanton moved to Seneca Falls. Elizabeth Cady Stanton and four other women called the first Women's Rights Convention in Seneca Falls on July 19-20, 1848. The announcement of the convention appeared in the *Seneca County Courier* on July 14, 1848:

> The first Women's Rights Convention to discuss the social, civil, and religious conditions and rights of women will be held in the Wesleyan Chapel at Seneca Falls on Wednesday and Thursday current, commencing at ten a.m. During the first day, the meeting will be exclusively for women, who are earnestly invited to attend. The public generally are invited to be present on the second day when Lucretia Mott of Philadelphia will address the convention.

Bloomer attended the convention and was impressed with the speakers, particularly with Elizabeth Cady Stanton.

In the spring of 1849, Dexter was appointed Postmaster of Seneca Falls, and his wife accepted the position of Assistant Postmaster. The new Assistant Postmaster provided an example "of a woman's right to fill any place for which she had the capacity." She performed well in the position for the next four years. She continued to edit and publish *The Lily,* and Elizabeth Cady Stanton began to write articles for *The Lily* using the pseudonym "Sun Flower." The newspaper became more militant, and the words "The Emancipation of Woman from Intemperance, Injustice, Prejudice, and Bigotry" appeared in the letterhead.

In 1850, Bloomer introduced two people to each other who were to have a significant impact on life in the United States. Bloomer wrote in her journal:

> It was in the spring of 1850 that I introduced Susan B. Anthony to Mrs. Stanton. Miss Anthony had come to attend an anti-slavery meeting in Seneca Falls, held by George Thompson and William Lloyd Garrison, and was my guest. Returning from the meeting we stopped at the street corner and waited for Mrs. Stanton, and I gave the introduction which resulted in a life-long friendship. Afterwards, we called together at Mrs. Stanton's house and the way opened for future intercourse between them.
>
> It was, as Mrs. Stanton says in her history, an eventful meeting that henceforth in a measure shaped their lives. Neither would have done what she did without the other. Mrs. Stanton had the intellectual, and Susan the executive, ability to carry forward the movement then recently inaugurated. Without the push of Miss Anthony, Mrs. Stanton would probably never have gone abroad into active life, or achieved half she has done; and without the brains of Mrs. Stanton, Miss Anthony would never have been so largely known to the world by name and deeds. They helped and strengthened each other, and together they have accomplished great things for woman and humanity. The writer is glad for the part she had in bringing two such characters together.

One of the many conditions that women had to tolerate in the mid-1800s was a lack of freedom in the style of dress. A woman's dress was complicated in the 1850s. Under her long skirts she wore a cambric petticoat, a plain longcloth petticoat, two flannel petticoats with scalloped hems, a lined petticoat with a hem that stood out, and lace-trimmed drawers. Three starched muslin petticoats usually replaced the flannel petticoats in hot weather.

In January, 1851, Dexter's successor as editor of the *Seneca County Courier*, wrote an article about women's clothing in London in which he mentioned that "improvement in the attire of females was being agitated." He suggested that women's dress should be less cumbersome and suggested that women wear Turkish pantaloons with a skirt that reached below the knee.

Bloomer responded in *The Lily*: "...now that our cautious editor of *The Courier* recommends it [wearing pantaloons], we suppose that there will be no harm in our doing so. Small waists and whalebones can be dispensed with, and we will be allowed breathing room; and our forms shall be what nature made them. We are so thankful that men are beginning to undo some of the mischief they have done to us."

In February, 1851, the issue of women's clothing was raised when Elizabeth Cady Stanton's cousin, Libby Smith Miller, visited her in Seneca Falls. Miller had just returned from a honeymoon grand tour of Europe. In Switzerland, she had seen women in sanatoriums wearing long, full Turkish trousers made of broadcloth with a short skirt that reached just below the knee. She made a traveling costume for herself in this style. Her cousin Elizabeth immediately adopted the style of dress. The two cousins visited Bloomer at the Post Office, and within a few days she donned the new costume.

Bloomer wrote an article about the new style of dress along with a sketch of it in the next issue of *The Lily*. Bloomer had no thoughts of completely adopting the style, of establishing fashion, or of attracting national attention. The *New York Tribune* was the first national newspaper to refer to Bloomer's article; that article was followed by many others. Some praised the costume, but many ridiculed it. Finally, one of the journalists referred to the new style of dress as the "Bloomer Costume" and the word entered the English lexicon. Bloomer tried to give credit to Libby Smith Miller for introducing the style to the United States, but newspaper publicity had established the word "bloomer" for all time.

Soon, half of the mail handled by the Seneca Falls Post Office was addressed to Bloomer. Women from all over the country wrote for more information on how to make the costume. The dress became popular with the Women's Rights Movement, and Bloomer was invited to England to speak about the costume.

Bloomer was elected corresponding secretary of the Women's Temperance Society for the State of New York in the spring of 1852. She lectured at Metropolitan Hall in New York City in February, 1853. Three thousand people bought tickets, and many were turned away; she had become a national figure.

In 1855, Dexter Bloomer purchased *The Western Home Visitor*, and the Bloomer family moved to Council Bluffs, Iowa. Amelia edited the newspaper; when she found the typesetters drinking, she replaced them with female typesetters. She crusaded for the temperance movement and the Women's Rights Movement for her entire lifetime. She died on December 30, 1894.

JOHN D. ROCKEFELLER

John Davison Rockefeller, founder of the Standard Oil Company, was born on July 8, 1839, in the Tioga County town of Richford, the second child of William Avery Rockefeller and Eliza Davison Rockefeller. William Rockefeller was a businessman, a trader, and a salesman for herbal remedies and patent medicines. He was adventuresome, impulsive, outgoing, and intolerant of opposing viewpoints. Eliza was intelligent, frugal, religious, and serene, with a strong belief in common sense and hard work.

In 1843, the Rockefellers moved to the Town of Moravia at the southern end of Owasco Lake. Most of William Rockefeller's income came from horse trading and selling patent medicines. He sold the Moravia property, and moved to Owego, where the family lived on River Road opposite Hiawatha Island in the Susquehanna River. John D. Rockefeller attended the River District School and the Owego Academy.

In the summer of 1853, the Rockefeller family moved to Cleveland, Ohio, where they lived in Strongsville, Parma, and in the city. Young Rockefeller attended Cleveland High School, received his high school diploma in 1855, and then attended Folsom's Commercial College. At Folsom's, he learned banking, bookkeeping, business computation, exchange, and mercantile practice. William Rockefeller stressed concentration, dependability, honesty, industriousness, and self-reliance with his sons. He once told a Strongsville neighbor: "I trade with the boys and skin 'em and I just beat 'em every time I can. I want to make 'em sharp."

Upon graduating from Folsom's, Rockefeller spent several weeks looking for a job, but not just for any job. " I did not go to any small establishments ... I was after something big." On September 26, 1855, he accepted a position as bookkeeper and clerk with Hewitt & Tuttle, commission merchants and produce shippers. He didn't even discuss salary: "I cared very little about that." The company "was delightful to me--all the method and system of the office."

Rockefeller learned about jobbers, merchants, railroads, and lake steamships, but particularly about transportation. Fast-growing Cleveland had five railroads serving it in the 1850s. In 1858, Rockefeller was ready for the next level of challenge, and that was to go into business for himself. He found a partner with similar interests, Maurice B. Clark, and they formed a partnership as commission merchants dealing in grain, hay, meat, and miscellaneous items. They each contributed $2,000 to the business, and opened Clark & Rockefeller on March 18, 1859.

His partner said of him: "He was methodical to an extreme, careful as to details and exacting to a fraction. If there was a cent due us, he wanted it. If there was a cent due a customer he wanted the customer to have it." Rockefeller gave generously to his church.

He engaged in considerable self-counseling: "I was afraid I could not stand up to prosperity, and I tried to teach myself not to get puffed up with any foolish notions."

On August 27, 1859, Colonel Edwin Drake opened the first commercial oil well in the United States in Titusville, Pennsylvania. Petroleum was shipped to Cleveland in large quantities, and a number of refineries were built along the Cuyahoga River. Clark & Rockefeller handled consignments of crude oil and kerosene. They knew that there was money to be made in the oil business. Rockefeller observed that drilling for oil was highly speculative, but once you had the oil, it had to be refined. Oil refining was much more of a sure thing than oil exploration and production, and refining costs were low.

Samuel Andrews, an English friend of Clark, and two of Clark's brothers joined them in an oil refining business called Andrews, Clark, & Company. At this time, the Atlantic & Great Western Railroad opened between the Pennsylvania oil fields and Cleveland, which was already connected to New York City by the Erie Railroad. Later, the New York Central-Lake Shore system opened across northern Ohio, and made Cleveland even more of a rail center.

Andrews, Clark & Company built their first refinery in the best location in the Cleveland area, on Kingsbury Run, a tributary of the Cuyahoga River. The three-acre site was on the Atlantic and Great Western Railroad, and had barge access to Lake Erie. The site was soon expanded to sixty acres, and then to one hundred acres.

Rockefeller became engaged to Laura Spelman, daughter of a wealthy Cleveland businessman, in March, 1864; they were married on September 8, 1864. Initially, they lived with his parents, and then moved next door at 29 Cheshire Street.

Inevitably, strains developed in the fast-growing refinery partnership. Rockefeller did not get along with Clark's two brothers, who were concerned about expanding too fast. Andrews sided with Rockefeller, but Clark voted with his two brothers, and Rockefeller came out on the short end of most votes. During the winter of 1865, Rockefeller bought out the Clarks, and continued the oil business under the name Rockefeller & Andrews. In 1866, Rockefeller brought his brother William into the partnership, and opened a second refinery, the Standard Works, at the head of Kingsbury run.

Henry Flagler joined the partnership in 1867 to deal with the railroad men; he was very effective at his job. Cleveland beat out Pittsburgh as a refining center for several reasons: it had more abundant capital and labor, it was a larger and more rapidly growing city, it was closer to western markets, and it had multiple railroads whereas Pittsburgh was locked into the Pennsylvania Railroad. Flagler was an expert at playing the Cleveland railroads against one another to hold down transportation costs. This was especially critical when the bottom fell out of the oil market in 1866 and 1867. Many small refineries went out of business.

In the early 1870s, Rockefeller met with his major competitors in the refining business. He told them to join with Standard Oil to take advantage of economies of scale, or to be forced out of business. When he proposed this, there were many refineries in the Pennsylvania oil region and in New York State, as well as twelve in Philadelphia and twenty-two in Pittsburgh. In the end, oil refining was a monopoly; in April, 1878, Rockefeller refined 33 million barrels a year out of a total of 36 million barrels in the United States. By 1880, Standard Oil refined 95% of the total oil output of the United States.

Allan Nevins analyzed the man in his biography, *John D. Rockefeller:*

> ... to a singular degree it was a career dominated by logic and plan.
> Some of the most famous of American lives are full of the unpredictable, the
> fortuitous, and the illogical. Not so with Rockefeller. His nature, for all its
> strength was simple; his intellect, never clouded by emotion, was direct and
> analytical; his will, fixed on a few large purposes, was unwavering. With
> no great personal magnetism or versatility or breadth, he accomplished two
> epochal tasks: he set an original pattern in the efficient organization of
> industry, and an equally original pattern in the efficient superintendence of
> benefactions. He was not a mere rearranger or manipulator of existing
> forces; he was a creator of new ideas and new systems. By his clarity of
> thought, keenness of foresight, and strength of purpose, he made his life an
> important part of the nation's history.

ELMER SPERRY

Elmer Ambrose Sperry, inventor of the gyroscope, was born at his maternal grandparent's home in Cincinnatus, Cortland County, on January 1, 1860. He was the only child of Stephen Sperry and Mary Burst Sperry. Sperry's mother died in childbirth, and his aunt Helen Sperry raised him for his first seven years. In 1867, Helen married and moved to Virgil, which was five miles from the Sperry farm. Young Sperry lived with his grandparents. Stephen Sperry had a traveling job, so his parents and his sister were important in the early shaping of his son's values. Before Sperry was ten, his grandparents moved from the farm to the Village of Cortland, and he moved with them.

The arrival of the Syracuse, Binghamton, & New York Railroad in Cortland in the 1850s, and the Utica, Ithaca, & Elmira Railroad in the early 1870s, did much to make Cortland more of a manufacturing center and less of an agricultural center. The opening of the Cortland Normal School in 1869, which provided teacher-training and tuition-free education through two years of college for local students, played a significant role in the preparation of Sperry for his life's work. He completed two years of a three-year course;

he indicated strengths in technology and weaknesses in liberal arts courses. He developed an interest in the emerging electrical technology.

His first invention was an automatically regulated electric generator that could supply constant current despite load variation. He talked one of Cortland's largest companies, the Cortland Wagon Company, into providing him with a lab, and into funding his development efforts. The company also helped him obtain the necessary patents for his inventions.

In addition to his work on the generator, he also developed a complete arc-light system between 1880 and 1882. The company chose Chicago as the location for their first electric arc-light system installation. The Sperry Electric Light, Motor, and Car Brake Company was incorporated in Chicago in February, 1883, and capitalized for $1,000,000. The new company's most visible display in Chicago was the brilliantly lit 300-foot tower of the Board of Trade building. However, competition was keen, and the company went out of business in August, 1887.

Sperry met Zula Goodman in Chicago. They dated, and they corresponded when he was away on frequent trips. They were married on June 28, 1887, and initially moved in with her parents at 3343 Vernon Avenue.

Sperry founded the Elmer A. Sperry Company in October, 1888. The breadth of his work was impressive. Two of his early inventions for the new company were an electric mining machine and an electric locomotive for mine haulage. His next project was the design of a streetcar for a syndicate of Cleveland businessmen. From 1880 to 1910, his inventing activity included electric light and power, mining machinery, streetcars, electric automobiles, batteries, and electrochemistry.

The Sperrys moved to Brooklyn, New York in 1905, where his chemical work was being conducted. While living in Brooklyn, Sperry began the work for which he is best known--the development of the gyroscope. In early 1907, he undertook a search of all the available technical literature on gyroscopes. He had a general interest in applying gyroscopes to useful purposes, but his initial interest was the stabilizing effects of the gyroscope.

His first gyroscopic invention was the Sperry marine stabilizer. This was the first project on which he received government support; the U. S. Navy was very interested in gyrostabilizers for their ships. He filed his first patent for a ship's gyroscope on May 21, 1908. The Navy was interested in ship stabilizers to provide a more stable gun platform for their warships; the entire complex system of modern naval gunnery is based on Sperry's inventions. Early in 1911, the navy chose the *USS Worden*, a 433-ton destroyer, for the first trials of a gyrostabilizer on an active warship. Sperry employed Carl Lukas

Norden (known later for the World War II Norden bombsight) to assist him. The first gyrostabilizer was fifty inches in diameter and weighed 4,000 pounds.

His next project was the gyrocompass. Again, the navy had a vested interest in gyrocompass development, particularly for submarines. The ship chosen for the trials of the first Sperry gyrocompass was the 800-ton destroyer *USS Drayton*. Sperry and his associates established the Sperry Gyroscope Company on April 14, 1910. The new company's sales grew 50% per year from 1911 through 1914, when World War I caused a significant increase in foreign sales. On one day in December, 1914, the Sperry Gyroscope Company, with assets of $1 million, received orders worth $832,000.

Sperry first began to think about developing a gyrostabilizer for airplanes in 1909, but he was diverted by ship stabilizer and gyrocompass development. He returned to the development of airplane stabilizers in 1912, and became the leading pioneer in the new field.

He began to talk with Glenn H. Curtiss as early as June, 1910, about stabilizers for navy aircraft. During World War I, Sperry designed and manufactured electrical gyroscopes for torpedoes and aerial torpedoes with automatic gyrocontrol. In 1915, Secretary of the Navy Josephus Daniels appointed him to the Navy Consulting Board.

Sperry resigned as president of the Sperry Gyroscope Company on July 28, 1926, at the age of sixty-six. He suffered a stroke on April 7, 1930, and died after a gallstone operation at St. John's Hospital, Brooklyn, on June 16, 1930.

Gliders at Harris Hill, near Elmira Heights

TABLE OF CONTENTS

CHAPTER 6

SOUTH OF THE LAKES

CHAPTER 6

SOUTH OF THE LAKES

Up and down the valley great planes roar overhead
Great trains crawl back and forth along the valley floor.
Eroding winds rush to and fro across the hills.
But as I write these words a music quickens
In the reeds along the river; a black bird calls and rises
and the river waters meander unheedingly away.

From *Home in these Hills* by Carleton Burke

SOUTH OF THE LAKES--INTRODUCTION

SOUTH OF THE LAKES--DESCRIPTION

The principal river valley south of the lakes is the Chemung River Valley. The Cohocton River flows from Cohocton through Bath and joins the Tioga River to form the Chemung River at Painted Post. The Chemung River flows through Corning, Elmira, and Waverly. At Waverly, the Chemung River joins the Susquehanna River, which then turns southward through Pennsylvania.

The main highway through the area is the Southern Tier Expressway, Route 17. Route 17 traverses the entire southern tier of New York State from Jamestown in the west to Orange County, north of New York City, in the east, passing through the Catskill Mountains along the way. The Southern Tier Expressway, bounded by scenic hills along its entire route, traverses beautiful farm country.

Corning and Elmira are the main population centers south of the lakes. Corning, with the Corning Glass Center, is the third largest tourist attraction in New York State, after New York City and Niagara Falls.

SOUTH OF THE LAKES--BRIEF HISTORY

In 1712, the Tuscaroras from the Carolinas joined the Iroquois Confederation, which was originally comprised of the Cayuga, Mohawk, Oneida, Onondaga, and Seneca Nations. In 1745, the Delaware Indians, who were pushed from their lands by settlers, moved into the Chemung River Valley with the permission of the Iroquois Confederation. Chemung is the Delaware Indian word for "big horn."

The Indian path along the sides of the Chemung River was known as the Great Warrior Path. The Andaste Trail, named after the Andaste Indian tribe, was established along the sides of the Cohocton and Canisteo Rivers west of Painted Post. One branch of the trail

223

terminated at the falls on the Genesee River at Rochester, a second branch headed west to Niagara Falls and into Canada, and a third branch led to the Allegheny River in western New York.

In 1781, U. S. spokesman Timothy Pickering, representatives of the Continental Congress, and the Iroquois met in Newtown, near Elmira, to address the issue of the settlement of American colonists in western New York. After three weeks of meetings with Chief Cornplanter, Chief Red Jacket, and the 1,400 Indians attending, the Treaty of Painted Post was signed. It granted the whites permission to settle in the Lands of the Painted Post and the Genesee Region.

In July, 1788, the Iroquois signed a treaty at Buffalo Creek conveying 2,600,000 acres of land to the Phelps and Gorham Company. The land extended from Pennsylvania to Lake Ontario and from a north-south line near Geneva to the Genesee River. Much of the land of the Phelps-Gorham Purchase was sold to Robert Morris, "financier of the Revolutionary War," and subsequently to a group of English capitalists headed by Lord Pulteney.

Lord Pulteney's land agent, Charles Williamson, developed the Village of Bath for its access to Philadelphia and Baltimore via the Cohocton, Chemung, and Susquehanna Rivers. Willamson's lieutenants, Charles Cameron and Benjamin Patterson, cleared Pulteney Square in Bath, and built the land agency house, log cabins, and a tavern. Construction of a theatre and a newspaper office for the *Bath Gazette* followed shortly afterwards. Williamson was one of the heaviest contributors to the development of the region into the early 1800s. He established many roads in the area, including a road between Williamsport, Pennsylvania and Painted Post, and from Painted post westward along the Cohocton River.

Two of the earliest settlers in the "Land of the Painted Post," were Samuel Harris and his son, William, who moved to the area from Pennsylvania in 1786. Their log cabin was the headquarters for the surveyors of the Phelps-Gorham Purchase in the area. In 1798, Benjamin Patterson piloted a raft to Baltimore from the area with a load of lumber; lumbering became one of the major industries in the region. Patterson is also known for building the first distillery in Painted Post, which later became the first tannery in Steuben County.

The completion of the Chemung Canal in 1833 provided a boost to the area's economy. It joined Seneca Lake at Watkins Glen with the Chemung River at Elmira, and it had a feeder canal from Horseheads to Corning. The Corning & Blossburg Railroad opened in 1840 to move coal and lumber from Blossburg to the feeder canal of the Chemung Canal at Corning. The New York & Erie Railroad extended its line to Elmira in 1849, the same year that the Chemung Railroad opened between Elmira and Seneca Lake. New markets to the east and west were opened when the New York & Erie Railroad joined with the Corning & Blossburg Line.

The Elmira and Williamsport Railroad opened in 1854 to transport New York State grain, plaster, and salt to Pennsylvania, and to return with coal and iron. The Corning & Blossburg Railroad was combined with other short-line railroads to become the Fall Brook Railway, which projected northward to Geneva in 1877. The Fall Brook Railway became part of the New York Central Railroad in 1899. The peak of railroad traffic in the region was reached in the 1920s. The first section of railroad to be abandoned was the track between Horseheads and Ithaca in the 1930s.

SOUTH OF THE LAKES--THINGS

ITEMS OF INTEREST

BATH FISH HATCHERY

The Bath Fish Hatchery, located on Fish Hatchery Road off Route 54 between Bath and Hammondsport, is run by the New York State Department of Environmental Conservation. The hatchery specializes in trout, and begins each year with about 900,000 brown trout eggs, 1,000,000 lake trout eggs, and 400,000 rainbow trout eggs. The facility, which was established in 1894, distributes stock to nine New York State counties: Broome, Cayuga, Chemung, Schuyler, Seneca, Steuben, Tioga, Tompkins, and Yates. Surpluses are shipped to other parts of the state, including Lake Champlain, Lake Erie, Lake Ontario, and Long Island.

Some of the fish that hatch in November and December are stocked the following fall when they are four to five inches in length. The remainder, called yearlings, are about fourteen months old and eight to ten inches in length when they are stocked in March, April, and May. The average lake trout produces from 3,000 to 5,000 eggs. The harvested eggs are placed in an incubator with fresh water running over them continuously until they hatch. The hatchery uses 900 to 950 gallons of spring water a minute year-round.

Lake trout grow as large as thirty pounds in the natural lake habitat, and live for thirty to forty years. The life span of brown trout is eight to ten years. The trout are fed at the nursery with a commercially formulated diet that includes amino acids, fats, fish meal, oils, proteins, and vitamins. The hatching rate is about ninety-seven to ninety-eight percent, and the survival rate from eggs until they are stocked in lakes or streams is from seventy-five to eighty percent. The survival rate of natural spawn is only four to five percent.

The Bath Fish Hatchery is working with the U. S. Fish and Wildlife Service to return the Great Lakes to their original condition. The U. S. Fish and Wildlife Service in Warren, Pennsylvania, provides fish to be stocked in Lake Erie and Lake Ontario each year.

The hatchery ensures that the fishing is good in all of the Finger Lakes. Some of the regional streams considered good for fishing are Cayuga Creek in Schuyler County, the Cohocton River in Steuben County, and the east and west branches of Owego Creek in Tioga County. The hatchery provides, on request, information on the quantities, sizes, and types of fish stocked in streams in the region.

The hatchery welcomes visitors. New concrete fish holding tanks were constructed in 1992-93. Fish food is available for a nominal fee to feed the trout in the tanks.

CORNING LPGA CLASSIC

The Corning Ladies Professional Golf Association Classic has been held at the 6,006-yard Corning Country Club course since 1979. The proceeds of the Classic, $1.4 million over the first twelve years, were donated to twelve area hospitals. The Corning LPGA Classic attracts the top women professional golfers. In the opinion of one of the event's organizers, it is one of the most popular stops on the tour "because Corning is one of the smallest cities on the tour; the golfers are treated like royalty."

The $500,000 Classic attracts about 150 golfers and a gallery of over 50,000. The Corning LPGA Classic is considered to be the first event in Corning's summer tourist season. Merchants on Market Street, Corning's classy street of shops, decorate their shop windows for the event to welcome the golfers and fans of world-class golf.

ELMIRA PIONEERS BASEBALL TEAM

The Elmira Pioneers are a Short Season (June 17 through September 4) Class A farm team for the Boston Red Sox. The Pioneers, a member of the New York-Penn League (NYP League), play at Dunn Field Stadium. Dunn Field can be reached by taking the Church Street exit of Route 17, and crossing the Madison Avenue bridge to Maple Avenue. The players are on rung two of the ladder to the major leagues. They have to advance through Long Season A, Advanced A, AA, and AAA ball before they arrive in the big leagues. Johnny Mize and Pee-Wee Reese began their baseball careers at Elmira. Also, Wade Boggs and Lou Pinella played at Elmira before they moved up to the major leagues.

The Elmira Pioneers feature buyout nights and baseball card nights. Baseball entertainers such as baseball clown Max Patkin, the Phillie Phanatic, and the San Diego Chicken all have performed at Dunn Field. The ticket prices are reasonable, and an afternoon or an evening at the ballpark provides good family entertainment.

MARK TWAIN OCTAGONAL STUDY

Samuel Clemens wrote many of his books in an octagonal-shaped study overlooking the Chemung River outside of Elmira. The author married Olivia Langdon of Elmira and, although they lived in Hartford, Connecticut, they spent their summers at the Langdon's home at Quarry Farm. The octagonal study was a gift from his sister-in-law, Susan Crane, in 1874. He thought it to be "... the loveliest study you ever saw." In 1952, the study was moved from East Hill at Quarry Farm to the campus of Elmira College.

The author wrote many of his books in the octagonal study, including *The Adventures of Huckleberry Finn, The Adventures of Tom Sawyer,* and *A Connecticut Yankee in King*

Arthur's Court. It is listed in the National Register of Historic Places. The study is open to visitors daily during the summer.

NEWFIELD COVERED BRIDGE

The Newfield Covered Bridge, located six miles southwest of Ithaca off Route 13, is the only public-use covered bridge in the Finger Lakes Region, and is the oldest one in New York State. Less than twenty-five covered bridges remain of the 250 that were once in use in the state. The bridge, the most westerly of the state's "original" covered bridges, is located over the west branch of the Cayuga inlet, in the Village of Newfield.

The banks of the Cayuga inlet were once lined with saw mills, tanneries, and woolen mills. The original bridge, which was built of logs by mill owner Eliakim Dean in 1809, was uncovered. It was replaced in 1851.

A lattice truss was used to support the bridge. It was a pattern of diagonally criss-crossing beams constructed into a lattice that extended the 115-foot length of the bridge. The lattice beams were attached to one another with wooden pins called treenails (later called trunnels). The sixteen-foot wide bridge cost $800, and took two years to complete.

By the early 1970s, the bridge had deteriorated to the point where the Tompkins County Highway Department declared the bridge to be unsafe, and considered tearing it down. Grant and Marie Musser, members of the New York State Bridge Society from the nearby Town of Lansing, convinced the county highway department of the historical significance of the bridge.

Milton S. Grafton, author of the book, *The Last of the Covered Bridge Builders,* and an authority on covered bridge construction, was commissioned to inspect the bridge. His inspection revealed that some of the trusses had lost their camber; the bridge was buckling, even though four buttresses had been placed on each side of the bridge for exterior support in the mid-1940s. When the bridge was restored, the laminated arches were made from twenty-two 2x12x20-foot pine timbers.

SCHWEIZER SOARING SCHOOL

The Schweizer Soaring School is located adjacent to the Schweizer Aircraft Corporation factory at the Elmira-Corning Regional Airport. The soaring school trains sailplane pilots and offers sailplane rides, which can be scheduled in advance.

The Schweizer brothers' interest in aircraft was inspired by Charles Lindbergh's first solo trans-Atlantic flight in 1927. They built a primary glider on their parents' farm in Peekskill, and entered the Second Annual Soaring contest at Elmira in 1931.

Ernest, William, and Paul Schweizer established the Schweizer Aircraft Corporation and Soaring School at the Elmira-Corning Regional Airport (then called the Chemung County Airport) in 1943. The Schweizer 1-26 sailplane, which was manufactured in the 1950s, introduced "class" soaring in the United States. Pilots compete with one another in identical sailplanes, by class. Annual class soaring competitions began in the 1950s.

TIOGA SCENIC RAILROAD

The Tioga Scenic Railroad, 25 Delphine Street, Owego, operates on tracks owned by the Tioga County Industrial Development Agency. Three-hour round trip excursions between Owego and Newark Valley originate at the Owego Depot, which was built in 1869. The depot can be reached by taking Route 17 Exit 64, and proceeding north on Route 96. Passengers are provided with a free shuttle from the Newark Valley Depot to the Farmstead Museum for demonstrations of farm life and cooking.

The Tioga Scenic Railroad offers deluxe meals in their dining car on the regular dinner excursion, for private parties, and for special events. Special excursions, which are offered throughout the year, include: the Bunny Express, Father's Day Breakfast, a Fall Foliage Tour, a Halloween Train, Santa's Winter Express, a Musical Odyssey, and an excursion with a magician performing illusions at your table.

The railroad's monthly "Get Away With Murder" excursion uses a troupe of professional actors to set the stage for passengers who attempt to solve a crime. This three-hour excursion includes dinner. The Tioga Scenic Railroad welcomes charters.

VITRIX HOT GLASS STUDIO

The Vitrix Hot Glass Studio, located in the Hawkes Building at 77 West Market Street in Corning, was opened in 1979 by Tom and Barbara Buechner. The work at the Studio is part of the American studio glass movement; the ancient skills and techniques of glassblowing are combined with contemporary designs to make distinctive gifts and collectibles. The studio glass movement was started in 1962 by Harvey Littleton, whose father was the inventor of Pyrex.

Over twenty galleries around the United States carry Vitrix glass products; many sales of Vitrix glass occur at craft show booths, where buyers from galleries and stores place their orders. Vitrix pieces have been exhibited in many countries, including the Czech Republic, Germany, Iceland, and Japan.

The ingredients of glass, other than sand, include arsenic, lead, lime, and potash, depending on the type of glass the glassblower chooses to use. The main source material used by Vitrix is cullet, which is already melted when it is shipped from West Virginia. In addition to the furnace and workbench, the main tools are the blowpipe and punty rod (or "punty iron") to which the glass is attached.

The glassblower collects a "gather" of molten glass on the end of a blowpipe from a pot in the furnace or from the end of a punty iron. The glassmaker blows strongly into the open end of the blowpipe to balloon the glass. The punty iron is used to add bits of glass to the main piece on the end of the blowpipe for decoration. The glassmaker rolls the gathered glass on the blowpipe back and forth on the extended arms of the workbench to keep the molten glass from sagging, and to shape it. Pressure is applied to the glass, and openings widened, using a tong-like device called the "jacks." Flat surfaces are shaped using wet wooden paddles, straight edges are cut with shears, and dividers and calipers are used to measure the length and circumference of the piece.

Glass is blown into a wooden mold to assume a predetermined shape, or the piece is symmetrically shaped by being rolled against a metal slab called the "marver." The final steps are reheating the glass in the "glory hole" of the furnace, attaching the glass to the punty rod, and filing the neck of the glass to remove it from the blowpipe. Visitors can watch glass being blown in the Vitrix Hot Glass Studio Monday through Friday. Glass items are for sale in the Vitrix gallery, which is open Monday through Saturday.

LEGENDS AND STORIES

THE BIG HOUSE WITH THE AISLE OF PINES

The site of "the big house," located near the Schuyler-Steuben County line in the Town of Wayne, is just off the roller coaster road between Hammondsport and Watkins Glen. Railroad-builder Samuel Hallett built the three-story, southern plantation-style mansion in the 1850s, so that his wife could be near her family. He called the mansion, which had twenty-four massive pillars along the front, "Lake Home."

He furnished it luxuriously with imported furniture, floor-to-ceiling mirrors from France, and a well-stocked library. The property included a sunken garden and a private race track behind a double row of Norway Spuce trees that served as a windbreak. Water was supplied by gravity from a large spring a half mile up the hill behind the house. The water was used both for drinking and to supply the large fountains of Aphrodite and Neptune. The roof walk provided a spectacular view of Keuka Lake and the nearby Lamoka and Waneta Lakes.

Hallett was a banker at Hornell, and then became associated with the Hocking Valley Railroad Company. He founded the Samuel Hallett and Company bank in New York City.

Visitors to the Hallett home were the Countess de Pompon of France, Governor Barrows of Tennessee, and James Gordon Bennett, publisher of the *New York Herald.*

In 1863, Hallett and his partner, General John C. Fremont, purchased a controlling interest in the Leavenworth, Pawnee, and Western Railroad, which was the first section of the Union Pacific Railroad. Fremont dropped out of the partnership when financial difficulties threatened, but Hallett continued on alone. When his Eastern Division of the Union Pacific was connected with the Western Division, the combination became the first intercontinental railroad in the country.

Hallet, who managed the Eastern Division from Kansas, was killed in the streets of Wyandotte, Kansas, on July 27, 1864, at the age of thirty-seven. His assassin was never brought to justice. It was speculated that he was shot by a discharged employee or a land speculator whose property was not favored with a right-of-way from the railroad.

Ann McDowell Hallett, a society figure who had entertained frequently, became a recluse and a spiritualist who attempted to communicate with her dead husband. She lived the next thirty years as a bedridden invalid. The neighbors claimed that occasionally she rode a white horse in the middle of the night to the family cemetery on the property. She died in 1893, and was buried next to her husband in the Hallett burial plot. On her deathbed, this eccentric woman gave one earring of an expensive pair of earrings to each of two daughters-in-law. The Hallett children did not stay in the area; the vacant house became known as "the haunted house on the hill."

The second life of the big house began in the first decade of the twentieth century when it was leased to George Birge, a millionaire businessman from Buffalo. Birge, whose father was the founder of the wallpaper firm, M. H. Birge and Sons, reorganized the Birge Bicycle Company into the Pierce Arrow Motor Car Company in 1896. Birge attempted to buy the big house, but Hallett's son wouldn't sell it. After being rejected for a ninety-nine year lease, Birge signed a twelve-year lease with an agreement from Hallett to renew it.

He moved the mansion back from the road, and located it in the center section of the double row of Norway spruces. He renamed the house, "Aisle of Pines," and reoriented it so that it faced Keuka Lake. Birge made substantial improvements to the mansion, including the addition of a large wing at the rear for the kitchen, pantries, and servants' rooms. The interior was completely redecorated with ample use of Birge wallpaper. Extensive landscaping was done on the grounds, and a drainage system, a new water system, a swimming pool, and a superintendent's cottage were added.

Birge and his family used the home until his death in February, 1918. Mrs. Birge didn't live in the house after the death of her husband, but she authorized the maintenance of the house and grounds until the lease expired in October, 1923. The Birge family again attempted to buy the estate, but were turned down by Julia Hallett, the widow of Samuel L. Hallett. She also refused to allow the Birge family to renew the lease.

Julia Hallett intended to bequeath the estate as a home for elderly women. That wasn't done, but the State of New York did receive the deed at one point. The house was vacant for many years, and experienced several fires and considerable vandalism. This all occurred before the public's interest in the restoration of historic houses was elevated. Memories of the Hallett and Birge families remain at the site of "the big house."

THE LEGEND OF THE RIVER

Tonadahwa, a beautiful Seneca maiden, was rowing her canoe down the river far from her village one afternoon when she thought she heard her intended husband call to her. He had once risked his life to save her from danger, and she had eyes only for him. She steered for the bank to join him when another brave, one of her spurned suitors, jumped into her canoe with a look of triumph on his face. He grabbed her paddle, and tried to take control of the canoe when he was struck in the chest by an arrow. He jumped out of the canoe with the paddle in his hands, and pushed the canoe out into the rapids.

Her canoe was transported through the rapids at great speed; Tonadahwa chanted her death-song, and waved goodbye to her lover on the shore. Her husband-to-be raced along the bank to the waterfall downstream. He jumped into the waterfall from a high bank when he could no longer see the canoe in the rapids. The Spirit of the River caught the young brave, saved him from death, and placed him on a ledge at the bottom of the falls where Tonadahwa was placed in his arms.

He walked carefully through the raging waterfall carrying his prospective bride to safety. When the unconscious maiden awakened, both she and her brave thanked the Great Spirit for their safety. The Senecas claimed that if you walked by that waterfall, you could hear, with a background of rushing water and murmuring pines, the painful cry of the brave as he jumped over the waterfall.

ROBERT'S RULES OF ORDER

General Henry Martin Robert wrote the book, *Robert's Rules of Order,* in 1876, while living in a house on Front Street in Owego. His rules were based on parliamentary procedure used by the British Parliament. These procedures were also used by the colonists in town meetings in New England. Until 1876, Thomas Jefferson's book on parliamentary procedure, which was published in 1801, was used for town meetings. Jefferson's book was also used by the United States Congress until Cushing's *Manual* was published in 1844.

Henry Robert, an engineer and a U. S. Army general, adapted the earlier parliamentary rules to meet the needs of "ordinary societies." His *Robert's Rules of Order* became the guide for clubs, organizations, and schools in the United States. It established procedures to deal with meetings that started late or lasted too long, and reduced the disruptiveness of autocratic chairmen and selfish cliques. It enlightened attendees of meetings, and reduced the probablility of minority resolutions being forced through the approval process.

Subsequently, Robert published three additional books: *Robert's Rules of Order Revised,* in 1915; *Parliamentary Practice, An Introduction to Parliamentary Law,* in 1921; and *Parliamentary Law,* in 1923. He died in 1923 at the age of eighty-six.

THE SLEUTH OF SOUTH CORNING

Herbert McDonell, the sleuth of South Corning, is a forensic science expert who is better known outside the area than within it. McDonell, considered to be "a modern Sherlock Holmes," invented the current method of detecting latent fingerprints. He is the author of the book, *Bloodstain Pattern Interpretation,* and has a world-wide reputation for pioneering the court's acceptance of bloodstain evidence. He is also known for his testimony in difficult cases. Cases for which McDonell provided testimony include:

Robert Kennedy Assassination--McDonell subscribes to the disputed theory that a security guard, not Sirhan Sirhan, was the actual killer of Senator Kennedy in 1968. He bases his belief on the fact that the fatal shot was fired from within one to two inches of the back of the Senator's head, and Sirhan was not closer than three feet in front of him.

Martin Luther King, Jr., Assassination--McDonell does not dispute the charge that James Earl Ray killed the African-American leader in 1968; however, he is unable to support the physical evidence of the FBI's scenario of how the shooting occurred.

The 1969 Black Panther / Chicago Police Shoot-Out--McDonell proved that the attack on the Black Panthers in Chicago was one-sided. He presented evidence that proved that the police fired first, and that the sleeping Panthers fired only one shot in response to the police's 100 rounds. The police killed two Panthers and wounded four others. McDonell's testimony was pivotal in dismissing the charges against the Panthers in a federal court.

Jean Harris / Scarsdale Diet Doctor Murder--McDonell testified that the evidence supported Jean Harris' statement that Dr. Herman Tarnower's death in 1981 was a "tragic accident" that resulted from her own failed suicide attempt. McDonell is referenced in the acknowedgements in Jean Harris' book, *Stranger in Two Worlds.*

Benigno Aquino, Jr., Murder--McDonell examined the Aquino autopsy, laboratory, and toxicology reports, and determined that the assassin accused by the

Philippine government was not in a position to fire the shot. McDonell testified that the fatal wound behind Aquino's left ear must have been caused by a shot from a government security guard.

McDonell graduated from Alfred University, worked on a graduate degree in chemistry, and was employed by Corning, Inc., until 1972. That year he established his own laboratory of forensic science, and became a full-time criminologist. He also began to consult, and teach in the field. McDonnell was mentioned in the 1966 Perry Mason mystery, *The Case of the Worried Waitress*. For his work in criminology, he was presented with the 1974 John A. Dondero Memorial Award. The first winner of the award was J. Edgar Hoover. In 1984, McDonell coauthored a book with Alfred Allen Lewis entitled *The Evidence Never Lies--The Case Book of a Modern Sherlock Holmes*.

THE STORY OF STEUBEN GLASS

The nucleus of the Steuben Factory was formed in 1903, when the English glassmaker Frederick Carder moved to Corning to design and make "blanks" for the T. G. Hawkes' cut glass company. Carder founded the Steuben Glass Works to produce "art glass" in a variety of colors and shapes. The Corning Glass Works, in order to expand its capacity to meet orders generated by World War I, purchased the Steuben Glass Works in 1918. Corning formed the Steuben Division of the Corning Glass Works, and resumed the manufacture of art glass after the war.

The Steuben Division produced a wide variety of glass objects without any distinctive style, and it was not financially successful. After a series of reorganizations in the 1920s, the board of directors of the Corning Glass Works considered discontinuing Steuben products, and shutting down the division. Arthur Houghton, Jr., great-grandson of the founder of Corning, asked if he could study the company's potential in manufacturing fine glass. In the fall of 1933, Arthur Houghton was given the assignment of turning the division around, and was appointed chief executive officer of Steuben Glass, Inc.

He made two changes that not only revived the business, but also made it a unit that contributed significantly to Corning's earnings. His first directive was that creative, distinctive design of glass objects must dominate the new Steuben Glass. This was accomplished by departing from the policy of letting the experienced glassblowers create their own designs. Combining glass designing and glassblowing tasks at the apex of a top craftsman's career had been practiced almost universally down through the decades of European and American glassmaking. The talented glassmaker was motivated to make items that were fancier and more complex than his fellow craftsmen, but not necessarily more aesthetic. It had not occurred to the glassmaking industry that a consistent, planned approach to design from outside the glassblowing room might generate works of art on a higher level.

The second crucial change was to make glass products out of transparent, untinted crystal. Lead, lime, and potash were added to silica, a component of sand, to aid in dissolving the silica when exposed to high heat. Iron-bearing elements in the added elements, or "flux," gave the glass a green tint. A decolorizer, manganese, was then required to neutralize the green cast. Adding the manganese was tricky; too much gave the glass a pink tint, and, even with precisely the recommended quantity, the glass might be gray or lacking in clarity.

The problem was solved in 1932 at Corning by 200 chemists working through 50,000 glass formulations; pure, transparent crystal could be produced consistently without discoloration. The stage was set for the turnaround of Steuben Glass. Arthur Houghton selected John Gates to oversee the design activity; Gates, in turn, brought in Sidney Waugh, a noted sculptor. The three men, all in their twenties, met to "discuss the possibility of attempting truly great and creative work in the art of glassmaking."

Arthur Houghton went to the board of directors with a bold request: "We have a small group of skillful and experienced workmen and an extraordinarily pure crystal glass. Let us have a small amount of capital and a reasonable amount of time, give us a completely free rein, and we will attempt to make the finest glass the world has ever seen." Approval was given to proceed with their proposal. Robert Leavy, an experienced glassmaker among a talented group of glassmaking veterans, was named production manager.

Headquarters for Steuben Glass were in New York City, and the two principal sales locations were in Corning and Manhattan. One of the major differences between the marketing strategies of the old Steuben Glass Works and the ones the new Steuben Glass incorporated was selling price. The new prices were much higher, but the works of art took experienced craftsmen a long time to make. The world-class designs in clear, untinted crystal suggested quality to the buying public.

Sidney Waugh created his Gazelle Bowl in 1935. A series of exhibitions began at the Knoedler Gallery in New York that year; Steuben Glass won the gold medal at the Paris Exposition in 1937, and comparable recognition was received at the World Fairs at New York and San Francisco in 1939 and 1940. The 1950s were the take-off years for the popularity of Steuben Glass. Presidents Truman and Eisenhower presented Steuben glass to the Heads of State of other countries, which is a tradition that continues to this day.

Ceremonial pieces produced by Steuben Glass during the 1950s include:

o The United Nation's Bowl, made for Trygve Lie of the United Nations in 1950

o The Norway Cup, given to King Haakon VII in 1955

235

o The Papal Cup, which Francis Cardinal Spellman gave to Pope Pius XII in 1956

o The La Fayette Medallion, which President Eisenhower presented to President Coty of France in 1957

o The Queen's Cup, given to Queen Elizabeth II on a visit to the United States in 1957

o An engraved vase with the presidential seal given to Chairman Krushchev in 1957

In the 1960s and 1970s, Steuben Glass began to combine crystal with precious metals, such as gold and silver, in creating elegant works of art. Examples of crystal and gold pieces from this era are: "The Myth of Adonis" in 1966, "The Four Seasons" in 1969, "The Carousel of the Sea" in 1970, and "The Unicorn and the Maiden" in 1971. The story of Steuben Glass is a noteworthy success story; it helps to verify the quality of American workmanship.

PARKS, FORESTS, AND TRAILS

BIRDSEYE HOLLOW STATE FOREST

The Birdseye Hollow State Forest is located in the Towns of Bradford, Urbana, and Wayne. It can be accessed via Route 226, Savona, from the south; via Route 16, Telegraph Road, from the west; via Route 96, Birdseye Hollow Road, and North Urbana Road from the north; and via Route 226 and Dumak Road from the east. Parker Pond, Round Lake, Sanford Lake, and the Sanford Lake Day-Use Area are located in the southern part of the state forest. Birdseye Hollow Park is located off Birdseye Hollow Road just north of the point where Telegraph Road intersects the state forest.

The Birdseye Hollow State Forest has a self-guided Forest Stewardship Demonstration Tour with six stops to show the various stages of forest growth from seedling / sapling stands to mature forests almost 100 years old. The demonstration tour is designed to indicate how forests change over time, and how forest management helps to maintain forest diversity. The six stops are:

1. BLACK WALNUT--a valuable hardwood used for furniture and paneling. This stand was thinned in 1978, and will be harvested in 2040.

2. PROTECTION FOREST--upland oaks on steep slopes that preclude intensive management. This stand is not included in the harvesting plan.

3. CONIFER PLANTATION--red pine planted in 1964 on an abandoned agricultural fields, and thinned in 1985. Conifer stands provide a habitat for red squirrels, small birds such as the pine siskin, and are winter cover for white-tailed deer.

4. FOREST REGENERATION--mainly aspen and red oak, which require full sunlight. The life cycle began with a forest cut in 1985. This stand and similar

stands provide habitat for "early stage" species of wildlife, such as cottontail rabbits, ruffed grouse, and scarlet tanagers.

5. MATURE FOREST--has reached the end of its life cycle, and will soon be regenerated. Mature stands provide a habitat for wildlife species that live in older forests, such as cavity nesting birds, gray squirrels, and pileated woodpeckers.

6. THINNING--a sugar maple stand that originated from a heavy cutting in the 1930s, and was thinned for fuelwood in 1985. Half of the stand has been thinned, and half left uncut. The growth per tree is greater in the thinned part.

CONNECTICUT HILL WILDLIFE MANAGEMENT AREA

The 11,610-acre Connecticut Hill Wildlife Area, located sixteen miles southwest of Ithaca off Route 13, is the largest Wildlife Management Area in New York State. Access from Route 13 is from Corn Hill Road and Summerton Road. Connecticut Hill, part of the Appalachian Highlands, lies within a belt of high, rough land. It is one of the highest points in the area, and the top of the hill offers scenic vistas of the region. The management area has many streams and man-made ponds that were built from 1948 to 1950 to attract waterfowl. They have attracted other wildlife, including beavers.

The Wildlife Management Area has a variety of flora and fauna, including mature forests of American beech, birch, hemlock, and maple as well as young oak and pine forests. Scattered throughout the Wildlife Management Area are fields, open meadows, and stands of evergreen trees. The diverse habitat attracts ruffed grouse, songbirds, waterfowl, and wild turkeys as well as beavers, rabbits, grey squirrels, muskrats, red foxes, and snowshoe hares.

Farming began in the area in the late 1700s, but poor soil conditions forced area farmers to abandon their farms by the early 1900s. Initially, New York State acquired 10,000 acres of Connecticut Hill for use as a game refuge.

The Wildlife Management Area, which is open all year, offers a variety of educational and recreational activities, including birdwatching, cross-county skiing, fishing, hunting, nature study, picnicking, and primitive camping. The New York State Archers Association maintains public archery courses on Connecticut Hill. The Finger Lakes Hiking Trail traverses the Wildlife Management Area, and a Department of Environmental Conservation trail passes through hemlock and white pine forests.

Rules for Public Use:

o Vehicle travel off of any maintained public road is prohibited.

o Snowmobiles must be confined to town roads designated for snowmobile use.

o All-terrain vehicles are prohibited anywhere in the area.

o Swimming is prohibited.

o Camping is limited and requires a permit from the Regional Wildlife Manager.

o Horseback riding is permitted only on maintained roads.

ERWIN WILDLIFE MANAGEMENT AREA

The Erwin Wildlife Management Area, located five miles west of the City of Corning, is a 2,490-acre upland tract. It can be reached by taking Smith Hill Road west from the Coopers Plains exit of Routes 15 and 17, or by taking Bearton Road west from the Gang Mills exit of Route 15. The Wildlife Management Area offers bird watching, cross-country skiing, hiking, fishing, hunting, and picnicking. Fishing is permitted in a nine-acre trout pond in a scenic forest setting. Rabbits, deer, squirrels, raccoons, and ruffed grouse are hunted in season, and marsh ponds provide limited hunting for waterfowl.

The Erwin Wildlife Management Area was purchased by the Department of Environmental Conservation in 1928. Extensive logging had been done in the area prior to that time. Vegetation is principally second growth hardwoods, which are interspersed with softwoods and other species. Marsh ponds, small water impoundments, and wildlife feeding areas have restored a more productive wildlife habitat. Extensive plantings of shrubs attract many varieties of songbirds, which can be heard from the nature trails. The Raymond L. Murray Park, a day-use picnic area, has a 100-foot fire tower that provides a beautiful view of the region.

Camping is allowed by permit only, during the hunting season. The use of all-terrain vehicles, four-wheel drive vehicles, and motorcycles is prohibited in the Wildlife Management Area except on truck trails.

FINGER LAKES TRAIL

The Finger Lakes Trail is a 400-mile-long trail that extends from the Catskill Mountains to Niagara Falls, where it connects with the Bruce Trail. It also links to the Appalachian trail, which extends from Maine to Georgia. The Finger Lakes Trail was built for backpacking, cross-country skiing, hiking, and snowshoeing. Motorized vehicles are prohibited. With some gaps, the trail extends west-east across the Finger Lakes Region through Bath, Watkins Glen, south of Ithaca, to near Cortland. Among the parks and forests it traverses are:

o Sugar Hill State Forest

o Finger Lakes National Forest

o Robert Treman State Park

o Watkins Glen State Park

o Connecticut Hill State Wildlife Refuge

o Buttermilk Falls State Park

In addition to the main west-east trail, the Finger Lakes Trail has branches, including a branch through Letchworth State Park at Portagevile, the Bristol Hills Branch to Naples, the Interloken Trail to Finger Lakes National Forest, and the Cortland branch.

PINNACLE STATE PARK

Pinnacle State Park is located on the north slope of Orr Hill, which is part of the Allegheny Plateau of the twin tiers of southern New York State and northern Pennsylvania. The 680-acre park, located two miles south of the Village of Addison off Ackerman Road, offers cross-country skiing, golf, hiking, hunting, and picnicking. Pinnacle State Park has spectacular vistas of the Canisteo River Valley, Harris Hill, the area's rolling hills, and the Village of Addison.

The park has a sixteen-kilometer cross-county ski trail. There is fishing for bass, bluegills, and bullheads, and hunting for deer, small game, and turkeys. Pinnacle State Park has a lodge and picnic facilities, including a picnic shelter and restrooms. Through an agreement with the New York State Department of Environmental Conservation, visitors can cross-country ski and hike through the 794-acre McCarthy Hill State Forest adjacent to the park. The woodlands provide a habitat for ruffed grouse, turkeys, and deer.

The park has a nine-hole golf course with white and blue markers on the tees to provide an eighteen hole challenge. The "front nine" covers 3,234 yards, and the "back nine" is 3,259 yards long. There are four elevated greens, twenty-eight sand bunkers, and water hazards on five holes. Hemlock trees populate the slope behind the lodge, and oaks and pines cover the hills around the golf course. Golf services include: a driving range, golf cart rentals, golf pro, pro shop, putting green, and restaurant. The golf season is from April 14th through October 31st.

Pinnacle State Park once was the Ackerman Farm, a private recreational golf and ski facility, and a recreational area owned by Corning, Inc. The company donated the property to the people of the State of New York in 1978. Pinnacle State Park was opened in April, 1979, and the 115-acre "Levi Pond" area was added in 1986. The park is open all year.

MARK TWAIN STATE PARK

Mark Twain State Park, located at 4229 Middle Road in Horseheads, is home to the 18-hole Soaring Eagles Golf Course and the three geodesic domes of the J. Ralph Murray Athletic Education Center of Elmira College. The geodesic domes contain a field house, gymnasium, ice rink, and an Olympic-sized swimming pool for college use. The par 72 golf course, one of the most scenic and challenging in the state, is 6,625 yards long in a rolling valley landscape. It offers club rentals, driving range, a PGA pro, pro shop, practice area, putting green, and a restaurant / clubhouse.

Soaring Eagles Golf Course, originally called Francourt Farms Golf Course, was designed by Archibald "Pete" Craig in 1963. Elmira College bought it in 1970; the college renamed it Soaring Eagles, which is the college's team name. In 1990, 464 acres, including the golf course and athletic facility, were purchased by New York State.

Mark Twain State Park is a combination of fields, ponds, and woodlots; it has a marsh on the western boundary. The varied habitat attracts deer, foxes, rabbits, and raccoons, as well as herons, song birds, and waterfowl. Under the Soaring Eagles Golf Course are hundreds of feet of gravel, sand, and silt, all deposited by the retreating glacier 14,000 years ago. The rolling, hummocky landforms on the golf course are "kames," which are piles of sand and gravel left by the Wisconsin-age glacier. The water hazards on the golf course are "kettle ponds," water-filled depressions also left by the glacier.

The golf season at Soaring Eagles Golf Course is from April 1st until Election Day. Nearby Pinnacle State Park at Addison has a nine-hole golf course.

TANGLEWOOD COMMUNITY NATURE CENTER

The Tanglewood Community Nature Center, located on West Hill Road near Elmira, was established to help people appreciate, enjoy, and understand the natural environment. The Nature Center provides an environment for learning about the relationship between animals, man, and plants, and air, soil, sun, and water. Tanglewood Forest has over forty species of shrubs and trees, and more than 150 kinds of wildflowers. It provides a habitat for about 100 kinds of birds and 20 species of mammals. Additional nature trails are provided beyond Tanglewood Forest in Personius Woods, which is another part of the nature center off West Hill Road.

The Runey Education Building has interpretive displays and a nature library with a hands-on room in which young people can handle the exhibits. The Runey Education Building overlooks a bird santuary with bird feeders and a small pool; outdoor microphones pick up the sounds of wildlife, which are transmitted to speakers inside the building. The Tanglewood Gift Shop has a wide variety of nature gifts and field guides.

The Tanglewood Community Nature Center is supported by contributions, memberships, and memorial gifts. The Runey Education Building and the Tanglewood Gift Shop are open Monday through Saturday and Sunday afternoons. The nature trails are open during daylight hours.

SHOWS AND FESTIVALS

MARK TWAIN MUSICAL DRAMA

The Mark Twain Musical Drama is performed in an air conditioned 1,500-seat geodesic dome of the J. Ralph Murray Athletic Education Center of Elmira College. It is located three miles north of Route 17, off Route 14. It is a musical dramatization of the life and works of Mark Twain, including *The Adventures of Huckleberry Finn, The Adventures of Tom Sawyer, A Connecticut Yankee in King Arthur's Court,* and *Life on the Mississippi.* The cast of over sixty are professional actors supported by local talent.

Lavish sets on a stage the size of a football field include replicas of Jim and Huck's raft floating down the Mississippi River, Twain's Quarry Farm home, and a real horse and carriage. The *New York Times* reviewer called it "an extravaganza of singing, acting and dancing." The NBC *Today Show* commented: "This is big-time show business. A spectacular performance." *USA Today* observed: "A stage the size of a football field. It would have cost $4 million to produce this in New York City."

The two-hour production is performed Tuesday through Saturday evenings, with matinees on Wednesday, Thursday, and Sunday. Performances are given from late June until mid-September. Group rates are available.

THOMAS HOMESTEAD MUSIC FESTIVAL

The Thomas Homestead, an 1830s farmhouse located five miles north of Route 17 Exit 40 at Savona, has provided, since 1983, a late July weekend of bluegrass, blues, folk, and country music. Evening concerts are held in a wooded amphitheatre. In previous years, the festival has included children's concerts, a clogging demonstration, contra and square dancing, horse-drawn wagon rides, mimes, and puppets.

There are craft demonstrations and sales booths of items such as albums, baskets, handmade jewelry, performer tapes, pottery, quilts, T-shirts, and wood crafts. Food vendors offer a choice of items, including barbecued chicken, hamburgers, hot dogs, sausages, and vegetarian fare. Camping is free with the price of a weekend ticket. Facilities and services for the handicapped are provided.

SOUTH OF THE LAKES--PLACES

COLLEGES AND UNIVERSITIES

CORNING COMMUNITY COLLEGE

Corning Community College, located on a 275-acre campus on Spencer Hill south of Corning, was founded in 1956. The college receives its authority from the State University of New York and is governed by fourteen trustees. Seven trustees are appointed by its supporting counties: Chemung, Schuyler, and Steuben; six are appointed by the Governor of New York State; and one is selected by the students.

Six academic divisions offer over thirty programs and over 800 credit and non-credit courses on the campus and at ten off-campus locations in Chemung, Schuyler, Steuben, and Tioga counties. Associate degrees in Arts, Applied Science, Occupational Studies, and Science are offered by the college. In addition, many one-year certificate programs are offered.

Additions to the present campus, which was occupied by the college in 1963, are a Nursing-Technology building erected in 1969, a state-of-the-art Learning Center built in 1982, and a $2.75 million addition to the Science Building completed in 1989.

ELMIRA COLLEGE

Elmira College is a private, coeducational, liberal arts college emphasing both general and professional education. The College's academic programs are based upon a strong general education in the liberal arts and sciences; particular attention is given to the development of communication skills and the exploration of world cultures. Elmira College offers a Field Experience Program, work study in cooperative education, study tours, and other special academic opportunities.

The planning for Elmira College began in 1851 by sponsors of higher education for women. Elmira College was founded in 1855; it was the first college for women with a course of study and degree requirements comparable to the men's colleges. Elmira College is considered to be the "mother of women's colleges." However, Oberlin College in Ohio was the first institution of higher learning in the United States to offer women a collegiate education. The first "coed" graduated from Oberlin in 1841.

From the time of its founding, Elmira College has placed a strong emphasis on international education, which is reflected in its academic offerings and its opportunities for study and travel abroad. The college became coeducational in all of its academic programs in 1969. One of the college's publications, *The Sybil*, established in 1876, is one of the oldest student-run magazines in the United States.

Mark Twain's Study was moved from East Hill at Quarry Farm to the Elmira College campus in 1952. Also, Hamilton Hall houses a Mark Twain exhibit on the campus. The college's Center for Mark Twain Studies at Quarry Farm sponsors public lectures by internationally-known Mark Twain scholars. The college's close association with the author began when Jervis Langdon, Twain's father-in-law, became one of the founding trustees. Mark Twain's wife, Olivia Langdon Clemens, was an Elmira native who studied at the college.

Quarry Farm, where Twain wrote for twenty-two summers, was presented to Elmira College by the Langdon family in 1983. The Center for Mark Twain studies at Quarry Farm includes the main house, a barn, and servants' quarters on seven acres overlooking the Chemung River valley and the City of Elmira. It is listed in the National Register of Historic Places.

MUNICIPALITIES

BATH

Bath, located at Exits 38 and 39 of the Southern Tier Expressway (Route 17), is the county seat of Steuben County. Bath is the home of a large Veteran's Administration Medical Center, which has a museum of military artifacts. The Bath National Cemetery is adjacent to the medical center.

Two districts in the center of Bath, as well as thirty private homes throughout the village, are listed in the National Register of Historical Places. The County Office row along the eastern boundary of Pulteney Square is an architectural point of interest, as are residential buildings in Greek Revival, Italianate, Queen Anne, and Tuscan styles.

The Bath Fish Hatchery is north of the village, off Route 54. Bath, which is surrounded by dairy farms, hosts the Steuben Dairy Festival in early June. The village sponsors a "Christmas in July" festival with sidewalk sales, crafts, food, and bathtub races down Liberty Street. Elm Cottage Museum is a local history museum with a mid-nineteenth century setting.

Bath was founded in 1793 by Charles Williamson, land agent for Lord Pulteney's estates. Williamson and his men cleared Pulteney Square in Bath, and built the agency house, log cabins, and a tavern. The first newspaper in the region was printed at Bath, the *Bath Gazette*. The first theatre in western New York was also located at Bath; it offered plays by the French playwright Moliere. In 1795, Williamson laid out a racetrack in the village, and announced a fair, with horse races, wrestling matches, and a barbecue. Two thousand people from the eastern seaboard attended the fair. This was the first in an unbroken string of fairs that allows Bath to claim that its Steuben County Fair, held in August every year, is the oldest continuous county fair in the United States.

CORNING

Corning, which is the home of Corning, Incorporated, and the Corning Glass Center, is the third largest tourist attraction in New York State, after New York City and Niagara Falls. It is located on the Southern Tier Expressway, Route 17, and the Chemung River. Each year over a half-million tourists visit the Corning Glass Center, and tour the Museum of Glass, the Hall of Science and Industry, and the Steuben Factory. English double-decker buses transport tourists from parking areas to the glass center and other attractions.

The Rockwell Museum of Western American Art has the largest collection of Western American Art in the East and a notable collection of Carder Steuben glass. The restored Benjamin Patterson Inn is the oldest residential structure in the valley. The Corning Ladies Professional Golf Association Tournament, which is held each May, officially opens the tourist season. Market Street, restored after the flood of Hurricane Agnes in May, 1972, and placed on the National Register of Historic Places in 1974, is a street of shops, factory outlets, and restaurants.

The City of Corning is on the site of the Indian village of Assinisink, which was destroyed by the British in 1764. The first permanent settler, Frederick Calkins from Vermont, built a log cabin along the Chemung River in 1789. Many of the early settlers were from New England, New Jersey, eastern New York, and Pennsylvania. Most of them were farmers who participated in the early lumbering industry in the region. An early settlement on the north bank of the Chemung River was called Knoxville. Knoxville's economy received a boost in 1833, when the Feeder Canal to the Chemung Canal at Horseheads was completed.

In 1835, Erastus Corning and eight other Albany capitalists formed a land company, and purchased 340 acres of land on the south side of the Chemung River. Corning's name was given both to the land company and to the village that evolved on the site. Erastus Corning, who never lived in Corning, went on to become the first president of the New York Central Railroad and a very wealthy man.

In 1864, Amory Houghton moved the Brooklyn Flint Glass Works to Corning. Not only were coal, sand, and canal and railroad shipping facilities readily available, but the citizens of Corning were willing to invest in the venture. They invested $50,000 of the initial $125,000 required to start the Corning Flint Glass Works. Amory Houghton was elected the first president.

Intense competition forced Houghton to sell out to Nathan Cushing of Boston. Amory Houghton, Jr., was appointed plant manager, and brought the company around by concentrating on specialized glass products. Amory, Jr., was installed as president of Corning Glass Works when it was formed in 1875. Bulbs for Thomas Edison's incandescent lamps became one of the company's major products. The invention of Pyrex in 1915 was another major advance. The Steuben Glass plant, founded by Frederick Carder in 1903, was purchased by the Corning Glass Works in 1918.

The opening of the Corning Glass Center in May, 1951, spurred tourists' interest in the area. Hurricane Agnes caused the Chemung River to overflow its banks in 1972, causing severe flooding in the Corning area. Afterward, the city was determined to not only clean up, but also to make improvements. Market Street was restored, and made into a street of shops, restaurants, and factory stores to assist in attracting tourists to the City.

ELMIRA

Elmira, the largest city south of the lakes, is located on the Southern Tier Expressway (Route 17), and the Chemung River. Elmira is known as "Mark Twain Country" because the author married an Elmira girl, and spent over twenty summers writing in the area. He wrote at Quarry Farm, which is now the Elmira College Center for Mark Twain Studies. His octagonal studio, which once overlooked the Chemung River Valley, is now located on the campus of Elmira College. Mark Twain and his wife, Olivia Langdon Clemens, and their family are buried in Elmira's Woodlawn Cemetery.

The restored Clemens Performing Arts Center is one of the cultural centers of the southern tier. It is the home of the Elmira Symphony and Choral Society. The Arnot Art Museum houses a collection of old masters, nineteenth-century American and European paintings, and sculpture.

The charming Near Westside Historic District, listed on the National Register of Historic Places in 1983, has a variety of architectural styles including: Colonial Revival (1890-1920), Eastlake (1870-1890), Greek Revival (1820-1860), and Italian Villa (1850-1880). It also has Italianate (1850-1880), Queen Anne (1880-1900), Second Empire (1860-1880), and Tudor Revival (1920-1940). The Historic District, which covers an area of twenty square blocks, contains the largest number of homes of Victorian style architecture in New York State. Many of the most notable homes are on Church, Gray, and Water Streets, and have broad, beautifully-landscaped lawns.

Mathias Hollenbeck, of Wilkes-Barre, Pennsylvania, established a trading post in 1783 at Newtown Point, where Newtown Creek joins the Chemung River. The first permanent settler was John Hendy, who was also from Pennsylvania. He planted crops at Newtown Point in 1788, and built a log cabin near Rorick's Glen. Pioneers built a new village, DeWittsburg, northwest of Newtown Point, and Henry Wisner established another village, Wisnerburg, in what is now the heart of Elmira. The three villages merged into one village called Newtown in 1815.

The name was changed to Elmira in 1825. The roots of the word "Elmira" are Moorish; it was originally written El Mira, meaning "fair outlook." The name was chosen by Judge Coryell, who stayed at Teall's Tavern while visiting Newtown. Nathan Teall's six-year-old daughter Elmira was a favorite of the judge, and he suggested that the village be named for her.

One of the founders of Elmira, John Arnot, arrived in Newtown in 1819 from Albany. He began as a clerk in a store, and was soon co-owner of the store. He was a leader in building the early canals and railroads, and was one of the incorporators of the Erie Railroad. He developed coal mines in Pennsylvania, and became a major figure in the business, civic, and financial activities in the southern tier. The Arnot Art Museum and the Arnot-Ogden Hospital bear his name today.

The Chemung Canal, which ran from the Chemung River at Elmira to Seneca Lake at Watkins Glen, was begun in 1830, and completed in 1833. The canal provided a boost to the Elmira economy, and many boatyards and sawmills were built at this time. The twenty-mile-long Junction Canal linked the Erie Railroad with the coal mines of Pennsylvania in 1855. However, the canals began to take second place to the railroads in the last half of the 1800s.

Motion picture pioneer Hal Roach is one of Elmira's favorite sons. He was the producer for Harold Lloyd, Laurel & Hardy, and the Little Rascals.

HORSEHEADS

The Village of Horseheads is located at the intersection of the Southern Tier Expressway (Exits 52N and 52S), and Route 14. Route 13 angles northeast from Horseheads to Ithaca. The origin of the name "Horseheads" is explained in an inscription on a boulder in Hanover Square: "In 1779 near this spot, General John Sullivan mercifully disposed of his pack horses worn out by faithful service in the campaign against the six nations of the Iroquois. The first white settlers entering the valley in 1789 found the bleached skulls and named the place 'Horseheads.'" Horseheads is a sister city of Bato-Machi, Japan; Bato translated literally is "horse heads."

Hanover Square, at the intersection of five streets in the center of the village, is listed in the State and National Register of Historic Places. The Horseheads Historical Society, located in the Zim Center at Grand Central Avenue and West Broad Street, exhibits a collection of cartoons and paintings by "Zim." "Zim," is Eugene Zimmerman, a nationally published cartoonist and caricaturist. Zim designed both his home at Pine and West Mill Streets, and the bandstand in Teal Park; they are listed on the State and National Register of Historic Places, along with a nearby residential district.

Upon his arrival from New Jersey in 1789, John Brees, the first permanent settler, built a log cabin on what is now South Main Street. Another early settler was Nathan Teal, who deeded 144 acres to James Sayre in 1807 for a burial ground, and another section "for use of inhabitants." The latter section became Teal Park at South Main and Steuben Streets. Horseheads became a minor boomtown in the early 1830s when the Chemung Canal linked Elmira with Watkins Glen. Horseheads was the junction of the Feeder Canal from the Chemung Canal to Corning. The first two boats on the canal, the *General Sullivan* and *Lady Sullivan*, were built in Horseheads.

OWEGO

Owego, the county seat of Tioga County, is on the Susquehanna River at the intersection of the Southern Tier Expressway and Route 38. It is the home of the Tioga Gardens and Conservatory and the Tioga Scenic Railroad. The restored Tioga County Courthouse, built in 1872, is on the Historic Register. The Tioga County Historical Society Museum is located on Front Street in a section of beautiful old homes. Historic Riverow is a row of restored buildings; it contains the Cellar Restaurant, the Riverow Cafe, and specialty shops offering antiques, books, clothes, crafts, gifts, and miniatures. One of Owego's festivals, the Annual Strawberry Festival, is held in mid-June.

The Indian name for Owego was Ahwagah, or "where the valley widens." The first home in Owego was a log house built along the river in 1787 by Amos Draper, who started trading with the Indians in 1783. James McMaster, a veteran of the Revolutionary War, settled in Owego with his family in 1788, which was the year that the village was laid out.

In 1884, Belva Lockwood, the headmistress of a girls' school in Owego, became the first woman to run for the presidency of the United States. General Henry Robert wrote his book, *Roberts Rules of Order* while living in his home on Front Street. Another favorite son is John D. Rockefeller. He attended Owego Academy, and lived along the Susquehanna River (opposite Hiawatha Island, three miles east of Owego) prior to moving to Cleveland to make his fortune with the Standard Oil Company. Hiawatha Island, which was a resort in the late 1800s and early 1900s, is now a nature study park.

PAINTED POST

Painted Post is located on the Southern Tier Expressway, at the point where the Cohocton River joins the Tioga River to form the Chemung River. Route 15, which is combined with Route 17 west of Bath, turns south to Pennsylvania at Painted Post.

Painted Post received its name from a carved oak post erected at the junction of the Cohocton, Tioga, and Chemung Rivers by the Iroquois. The figures of twenty-eight men were cut into the post and painted red. The crudely carved post also had thirty headless figures carved into it. The early settlers did not understand the symbolism of the post, but they named the area "The Lands of the Painted Post." It is thought that the Indians erected the post to commemorate a victorious battle.

Painted Post is known for the monument of Iroquois Chief Montour and for a replica of the carved post that stands in the town square. The Town of Erwin Museum in the Town Hall on West Water Street displays a collection of Civil War items, colonial artifacts, and Indian relics. It is open daily in July and August, on Tuesday and Thursday afternoons in the months of November and March through June. It is also open by appointment in December through February.

Two of the first settlers in the area were Samuel Harris and his son, William, from Pennsylvania. They built a log cabin near the confluence of the Cohocton and Tioga Rivers that was used as headquarters by the surveyors of the Phelps and Gorham Purchase in 1789. Colonel Eleaser of Morristown, New Jersey, brought thirty-seven people to the area on flatboats via the Chemung River in 1790. They settled south of Painted Post on land overlooking the Tioga River. Arthur Erwin of Erwin, Pennsylvania, also established a settlement in the area in 1790.

MUSEUMS

ARNOT ART MUSEUM

The Arnot Art Museum, located at 235 Lake Street in Elmira, contains a collection of nineteenth- and twentieth-century American paintings and sculpture; seventeenth-, eighteenth-, and nineteenth-century European paintings; and small collections of Egyptian, Oriental, and Pre-Colombian art. The nineteenth-century American collection includes landscapes by Bierstadt, Cole, Cropsey, James and William Hart, Hope, and George Waters, and portraits by Street, Stuart, Sully, and Susan Waters. Paintings by twentieth-century artists include those by Burchfield, Clarence Carter, Davies, Henri, Jones, and Metcalf.

The Arnot Art Museum opened in 1913 in an 1833 mansion built by John Arnot, Sr. His son, Mattias H. Arnot, added a residential picture gallery in the 1890s for his own collection. That collection includes works by sevententh-century artists: Brueghel, Claude, de Lorme, Murillo, Teniers, and van de Velde; and nineteenth-century masters: Breton, Courbet, Daubigny, Diaz de la Pena, Jacque, Millet, Rousseau, and Troyon. A three-story addition to the Museum was opened in 1986.

Major temporary exhibitions are displayed in the Falk and Tripp-Rose Galleries. The West Gallery on the second floor is used for exhibitions of work by contemporary regional artists. The Falck Overlook Gallery is used to display selections from the permanent collection. The Terrace Overlook Gallery showcases works from the Egyptian, Oriental, and Pre-Columbian collections.

The Museum Shop offers exhibition publications, museum reproductions, original works by regional artists and craftspeople, and other special gift items. The museum is open Tuesday through Saturday, except on holidays, and is handicapped accessible. A nominal admission fee is charged. The museum welcomes group tours, which must be scheduled two weeks in advance.

BEMENT-BILLINGS FARMSTEAD

The Bement-Billings Farmstead, located off Route 38 one mile north of the Village of Newark Valley, is a living history museum listed on the New York State and National Registers of Historic Places. The farmhouse was the home of Asa Bement, Jr., who was one of the sixty shareholders of the Boston Purchase Company. Bement, a middle-class farmer-tradesman, settled along the east branch of the Owego Creek with his wife, Abigail, in 1794. He built a barn, a blacksmith shop, a gristmill, a house, and a sawmill.

Their home is on its original site; it has been restored to its 1840s condition by the Newark Valley Historical Society. The society has furnished the home with the artifacts and furniture of the period. A replica of the blacksmith shop has been constructed on the property, and a barn, corn crib, sap house, and tool shed have been moved to the property from nearby farms.

There are demonstrations of blacksmithing, cooking, and spinning. Special events include:

o Plowing Day in May   o Harvest Day in August   o Depot Days in July

o Wool Market in June   o Apple Festival in October

Workshops are scheduled throughout the season.

The Bement-Billings Farmstead provides hands-on tours for school children, a junior interpreter project, summer workshops, and "Tour & Tea" hospitality visits for adults. The

Farmstead is open on weekends from May through October. A nominal admission fee is charged. Groups are accommodated on weekdays by appointment. A shuttle bus transports visitors between the farmstead and the Newark Valley Depot Museum, which is also operated by the Newark Valley Historical Society.

CORNING MUSEUM OF GLASS

The Corning Museum of Glass, along with the Hall of Science and Industry and the Steuben Factory, is one of the three components of the Corning Glass Center complex. The museum, which contains the world's greatest collection of glass, provides many displays of the 3,500 year-old glassmaking craft. Exhibits take visitors through the glassmaking history of ancient Egypt, the Roman Empire, the Islamic Empire, Medieval and Renaissance Europe, and the New World. Over 24,000 objects are on display; they range from prehistoric weapons chipped from volcanic obsidian to contemporary hand-formed glass. The museum has films that appeal to the entire family, games for children, and special exhibitions.

Exhibits range from a 2,000 year-old perfume bottle to a carved glass bottle made during the Ch'ien Lung dynasty in China during the eighteenth century and to the Corning Ewer made in Iran during the tenth century. Other modern displays include an eleven-foot-high leaded glass window designed by Louis Tiffany in 1905, and a contemporary chess-set with glass pieces. The museum has many special showings, including exhibits of china and glassware used by U. S. Presidents and "Russian Glass of the 17th-20th Centuries."

The admission fee to the Corning Museum of Glass is included in the ticket for the Corning Glass Center complex. The museum is open seven days a week, except for Thanksgiving Day, December 24th and 25th, and New Year's Day. The world's most comprehensive library on glass and glassmaking, the Rakow Library, is open Monday through Friday. The Corning Glass Center complex also includes extensive gift shops, and a shop for Corning products--the current line plus a selection of "closeouts" and discontinued items at reduced prices. Food service is provided in the Cafe and the Snack Shop. Arrangements for group tours of the complex may be made in advance.

NATIONAL SOARING MUSEUM

The National Soaring Museum, located adjacent to the Harris Hill Soaring Field, has 28,000 square feet of exhibits of classic and contemporary sailplanes as well as displays on aerodynamics, flight history, meteorology, and other flight-related subjects. The National Soaring Museum opened in July, 1969, on the site selected by the Soaring Society of America. The museum chronicles the development of sailplanes, which utilize the natural energy of the sun and the wind. Exhibits include a full-size replica of the Wright Brothers' 1911 glider #5. Soaring films are presented hourly in the museum's theater.

The museum includes a number of aircraft designed and built by the Schweizer Aircraft Corporation at their factory adjacent to the Elmira-Corning Regional Airport. These craft range from the SGP 1-1 primary glider to the high-performance SGS 1-35. Visitors to the museum can use the cockpit simulator to experience the feeling of being at the controls of a sailplane.

The museum has a gift shop stocked with mementos related to soaring. The National Soaring Museum is open seven days a week; an entrance fee is charged.

ROCKWELL MUSEUM OF AMERICAN WESTERN ART

The Rockwell Museum of American Western Art, located at Cedar Street and Dennison Parkway in Corning, is housed in a Romanesque-revival style building designed by A. J. Warner of Rochester. The restored brick building, which was built in 1893, housed Corning's City Hall, fire house, and jail until the early 1970s. Today it houses the works of the great masters of the American West, such as Frederic S. Remington and Charles M. Russell, as well as the Frederick Carter Steuben Glass collection and a collection of antique toys.

The collection of paintings from the 1830s to the 1920s includes works by Albert Bierstadt, the Rocky Mountain landscape painter; Oscar E. Berninghaus, E. Irving Crouse, and Joseph Henry Sharp, of the Taos Society of Artists; and George Catlin and Alfred Jacob Miller, explorer artists of the 1830s. One of the most eye-catching works is Olaf Seltzer's twenty-five by four and a half foot painting, "The Prowlers," which hung in the Mint Saloon in Great Falls, Montana, for fifty years. The Frederic Remington collection includes nine original bronze castings and twenty-two paintings. Antique firearms, Native American artifacts, and Navajo weavings are displayed on the third floor.

Over 2,000-pieces of Steuben glass produced under the direction of Frederick Carder from 1903 to 1933 are exhibited on the second floor. Also displayed are many examples of Carder's fine studio pieces produced during the 1940s and 1950s. The Rockwell collection includes glass in every color made by Carder. Gold purple and gold ruby are the rarest colors; the most well-known is blue and gold Aurene glass. The antique toy collection, also exhibited on the second floor, includes cast iron and tin toys, cast iron banks, dolls, domestic toys, large toys, model trains, and toy trains.

The founder of the museum, Robert F. Rockwell, grew up in Gunnison County, Colorado, where he developed his interest in western scenery and art. Rockwell began to collect western art in 1960. He became a close friend of Frederick Carder, and started to collect his work as well. His collection was displayed in the Rockwell Department Store in Corning, and was frequently loaned out. In June of 1982, it was moved to its permanent home in the Rockwell Museum.

The Museum Shop on the premises offers books, catalogues, gift items, jewelry, photographic slides, and postcards. The facility is fully accessible to the handicapped. The Rockwell Museum is open daily, except for Christmas Eve, Christmas Day, Thanksgiving Day, and New Year's Day. A nominal admission fee is charged for adults. Guided tours are available; reservations can be made for group tours.

ZIM HOUSE

Zim House, located at 601 Pine Street in Horseheads, was the home of the world-famous caricaturist and political cartoonist Eugene Zimmerman. Zim House is owned and maintained by the Horseheads Historical Society, which also operates the Horseheads Historical Museum in the Zim Center at Grand Central Avenue and Broad Street. Zimmerman produced cartoons for *Puck* and *Judge* magazines. His political cartoons were used in the campaigns of William Jennings Bryan, Grover Cleveland, and Elmiran David B. Hill. He also did projects for Thomas Edison at his New Jersey laboratory.

Zimmerman was president of the American Association of Cartoonists and Caricaturists. He wrote *Foolish History of Elmira, Foolish History of Horseheads,* and *Homespun Phoolosophy*, and illustrated Ring Lardner's *Regular Fellows I Have Known.* He revised the art course of the Correspondence Institute of America, and prepared twenty illustrated course textbooks on caricature, cartooning, and comic art.

Zimmerman was born in Basle, Switzerland, on May 25, 1862. He immigrated to the United States in 1869, and moved to Elmira in 1878. His first full-time job was as a sign painter for the Empire Sign Company in Horseheads. In 1883, he was hired by Joseph Keppler, the famous cartoonist and publisher of *Puck* magazine. He moved to the staff of *Judge* magazine in 1885. He married Mabel Beard of Horseheads on September 19, 1886. They had one child, Laura.

Zimmerman and his father-in-law, Alvah Beard, built Zim House in the Queen Anne style. Fine carpentry is in evidence throughout the house, including the ornate staircase and many examples of cherry and oak woodwork. The two-story studio includes bayonets, Indian artifacts, Japanese Samurai swords, and Zim memorabilia. Zim's sketches, including a caricature of Mark Twain, cover the living room walls. Also hanging on a living room wall is a caricature of Zim by Enrico Caruso, opera star and caricaturist. Zim designed the leaded glass window on the north wall. The dining room includes a collection of cut crystal, drinking mugs, and plates.

In January, 1980, Laura Zimmerman donated her home and its contents to the Horseheads Historical Society in memory of her father. She asked for the property to be preserved and exhibited to the public for education, enjoyment, and information. The contents included the cartoons, correspondence, personal papers, and sketches of her father. The Zim House is open Thursday afternoons June through September, by appointment, and on special weekends. Group tours are available. The Horseheads Historical Society Museum is open Monday through Friday and Saturday afternoons. The museum includes a "Zim" room that contains memorabilia and original art work of Eugene Zimmerman.

PLACES OF INTEREST

HALL OF SCIENCE AND INDUSTRY

The Hall of Science and Industry, along with the Corning Museum of Glass and the Steuben Factory, is one of the three components of the Corning Glass Center complex. It has exhibits that illustrate how glass is made and used in the home, in industry, and in science. It also has push-button exhibits, films, and live demonstrations that provide fun and learning opportunities for visitors of all ages.

Visitors can bend glass without breaking it, play with lasers, and watch glass reflect and transmit light. They can peer down a six-foot bar of glass that is so clear that they can see through it. The Hall of Science and Industry provides lampwork art demonstrations in which glass animals / figures are made by skilled lampwork artists; they heat glass rods to a high temperature and shape hot glass into works of art. Lampwork art demonstrations have been a part of the glass center's programs since 1951. A movie transports visitors on an imaginary trip through an optical fiber at the speed of light. One demonstration shows how people around the globe will be brought closer together through fiber optics.

One of the largest pieces of glass ever poured is displayed at the entrance to the Hall of Science and Industry--the first casting of the 200-inch mirrored disk for the telescope at the Hale Observatory on Mt. Palomar in California. The twenty-ton disk was poured on March 25, 1934. The Hall is open seven days a week, except for Thanksgiving Day, December 24th and 25th, and New Year's Day. The admission fee to the Hall of Science and Industry is included in the ticket to the Corning Class Center complex.

HARRIS HILL

The Harris Hill Soaring Corporation evolved from an Elmira regional enterprise to a national organization when it sponsored the first National Soaring Contest in 1930. The soaring field is one element of the Harris Hill complex owned and maintained by Chemung County. A picnic area part way up Harris Hill, several points on the road to the soaring field, and the field itself provide spectacular views of the Chemung River Valley. Harris Hill is located south of (and uphill from) Exit 51 of the Southern Tier Expressway.

The Soaring Society of America distinguishes between gliding and soaring: "Gliding is coasting downhill on an inclined plane of air; soaring is maintaining or gaining altitude in upcurrents of air. Upcurrents occur for a variety of reasons, the most common being uneven heating of the ground by the sun which results in rising columns of bubbles of hot air called thermals...." Sailplanes can gain 1,000 feet of altitude a minute by taking advantage of these rising warm air currents.

Captain LeBris of France made one of the first glider flights in 1855. Otto Lilienthal made many glider flights in Germany between 1891 and 1896. Glider pioneer Octave Chanute made 2,000 flights in the United States beginning in 1896. Gliders became popular in Germany after World War I because the Treaty of Versailles did not permit them to develop and fly powered aircraft.

The Harris Hill Soaring Corporation offers sailplane rides daily during the summer months and on weekends during the rest of the year, weather permitting. There is a fee for the ride. Reservations for rides cannot be made in advance; the policy is first come, first served.

STEUBEN FACTORY

The Steuben Factory, along with the Corning Museum of Glass and the Hall of Science and Industry, is one of the three components of the Corning Glass Center complex. Visitors have gallery seats from which they can watch skilled craftspeople manipulate a glob or "gather" of glass into a work of art made of Steuben glass. Steuben glass is made by the off-hand process used by glassmakers since the beginning of the craft; no production or quasi-production equipment or methods are used.

Craftspeople are organized into "shops" of a master glassblower (known as a "gaffer," from the old English for "grandfather") and two or three assistants. The gaffer's assistants include:

o The "gatherer," who takes the molten glass from the furnace and gathers, blows, and kneads it prior to passing it to the servitor

o The "servitor," or server, who does the initial glassblowing, and gives it to the gaffer

o The "bit gatherer," who takes from the pot in the furnace small gatherings that are used for bases, handles stems, and decorative additions to the main piece

The raw materials sand, lead, and potash are thoroughly mixed while dry, powdered glass is added for smoothness, and the total composition is melted at high temperature in a melting furnace. The molten glass is a bright red, heavy, viscous fluid when it is in a condition to be worked. The gatherer places his blowpipe, a four to six-foot long steel tube, into the furnace and removes his "gather." He shapes it by blowing and by rotating it on a flat metal slab at the mouth of the furnace. He may also use a wet applewood form for shaping at this point.

The glassmaker uses a pontil, a solid steel rod with a serrated tip, to add small gathers to the main piece, and to detach the molten glass from the blowing-rod. He also uses a "woodjack," a two-pronged fork with cherrywood tips, and a cherrywood paddle for shaping, metal shears for cutting, and dividers and calipers for measuring the length and circumference and for more precise shaping. The servitor rolls the blowing-rod back and forth on the arms of his workbench, evolving the shape of the piece.

The creation of the object is the responsibility of the gaffer. He inserts the piece into the reheating furnace, the "glory-hole," periodically to maintain the proper temperature. When the piece is completed, it is broken from the pontil by being hit with a metal tool at the end of the rod. Then, it is moved to the "lehr," or annealing oven, on a forked stick. The piece is transported on a belt through a series of reduced temperatures in the lehr, where it is annealed via a hardening and cooling process that lasts from five to eight hours.

The piece is then moved to the finishing room for removal of the pontil mark and cutting. Three types of cutting may be done to the piece: "hollow" cutting by a wheel, V-shaped "bevel" cutting, and flat "panel" cutting. Cutting is used to decorate the glass, and to remove imperfections. Engraving of a complex object may take several months. An example of a complex piece is the "Merry-Go-Round Bowl" presented to Queen Elizabeth II of England in 1947 as a wedding gift.

Corning is the only location where Steuben glass is made, and the two principal sales locations are at the Corning Glass Center and at their flagship store at Fifth Avenue and 56th Street in Manhattan. The design center is also located in New York City. Steuben glass is also available at selected department stores around the world, including Neiman Marcus and Takashimaya.

TIOGA GARDENS AND CONSERVATORY

The Tioga Gardens and Conservatory, located off Route 17C in Owego, is a garden and floral center with exotic flowers and shrubs. The gardens contains a complete selection of tropical plants and accessories, including cacti and orchids. The conservatory provides a controlled environment for exotic plant life, and has tropical birds and a waterfall. Tioga

Gardens has a beautifully landscaped two-acre water garden with fountains, pools, water lilies, and other water plants. The water garden can be reserved for parties, picnics, and weddings.

Tioga Gardens offers a professional design service for floral designs, exterior landscaping, interior landscaping, and seasonal decorations. Herb plants and herb-related products are available at Tioga Gardens. There is a gift shop on the grounds and also a stand that sells fruit and vegetables in season.

WATSON HOMESTEAD

Thomas Watson, Sr., founder and first Chairman of the Board of the IBM Corporation, established the Watson Memorial Homestead Foundation to preserve his homestead. Then he deeded the homestead to the Western New York Conference of the United Methodist Church. The Watson Homestead, located three miles north of Coopers Plains between Bath and Corning, is a year-round conference and retreat center serving all charitable, educational, religious, and social service organizations.

The Watson Homestead has a variety of accommodations and meeting rooms available for banquets, planning sessions, retreats, senior citizen activities, training courses, workshops, and youth activities. The homestead can provide easels, lecterns, and audio-visual equipment to support planned programs. Up to 280 people can be accommodated in sleeping facilities. The Main Lodge, which contains meeting and recreation facilities, houses ninety-six people. Home cooked meals are served either buffet or family style in a 400-seat dining hall. The dining facility, which has knotty cedar paneling and laminated western fir arches, is also open for luncheons, dinners, and banquets.

Small groups are accommodated in the Hillside Retreat House, which has lounges, a snack area, and sleeps sixteen. Three retreat centers, each equipped with a fireplace, large living area, ping pong table, and snack area (sink-stove-refrigerator), serve group meeting needs for up to thirty-two people. Four modern, winterized cabins, which sleep twenty each, contain a fireplace, a large meeting room, and recreational facilities.

The Jeanette K. Watson Chapel, dedicated to the memory of Thomas J. Watson's wife, has seating for 300, an organ, a piano, and a public address system. An olympic-sized swimming pool facility , which is open year-round, has locker rooms and showers. The 600-acre Watson Homestead provides a setting for many recreational activities, including basketball, softball, and volleyball. Hiking the backwood trails is also a popular activity.

HISTORIC SITES

BENJAMIN PATTERSON INN

The Benjamin Patterson Inn, located at 59 West Pulteney Street in Corning, is the centerpiece of the Corning-Painted Post Historical Society Museum Complex. Other units of the complex are the Blacksmith Shop, the Browntown Schoolhouse, the De Monstoy Cabin, and the Starr Barn.

The Benjamin Patterson Inn, the oldest frame structure in the valley (built in 1796), is an authentic example of a frontier inn. It has been restored and furnished as it was in the eighteenth century, with a kitchen, tap room, and a women's parlor on the first floor, and a ballroom and two bedrooms on the second floor. In several places, the interior of the walls has been left exposed to allow a view of construction details. There is an old-fashioned herb garden on the grounds. The inn is listed in the National Register of Historic Places.

The Blacksmith Shop displays the tools of the village "smithy," and features a replica of an 1800s bellows and forge. The Browntown Schoolhouse, which was built in 1878 and used until 1955, retains the atmosphere of a late nineteenth-century one-room schoolhouse. The De Monstoy Cabin, built in 1784, is furnished simply and sparsely, as it would have been by pioneer settlers. The Starr Barn, with structural beams salvaged from an 1860s barn, displays tools used for planting, cultivating, and harvesting.

The museum complex is open Monday through Saturday; a nominal admission fee is charged. A knowledgeable guide provides individualized tours. Special arrangements can be made for tours at other times.

NEWTOWN BATTLEFIELD RESERVATION

The Newtown Battlefield Reservation, located five miles southeast of Elmira, was established in 1912. It is the site of a major battle, the only staged battle, of the Sullivan Campaign of 1779. General Washington ordered Major General John Sullivan to destroy the homes and crops of the member nations of the Iroquois Confereracy to prevent them from joining the British and becoming a threat to the Continental Army from the west.

General James Clinton's army traveled from the Mohawk Valley to join with Sullivan's forces at Tioga Point (Athens, PA) on August 22, 1779. The combined army of over 3,000 marched along the Chemung River, and reached the site of the battlefield on August 29, 1779. Scouts had informed General Sullivan that a force of 1,000 to 1,500 men, made up of Canadian Rangers, Tories, and Indians, was ahead of them waiting in ambush. Some of Sullivan's Colonials slipped in behind the force commanded by the Mohawk Chief, Joseph Brant, and provided the decisive factor in the victory for Sullivan's Army.

The 330-acre Newtown Battlefield Park consists of hilly terrain with woodlands; it is 600 feet above the valley floor and 1,507 feet above sea level. The woodlands include hickories, maples, oaks, and four varieties of pine trees. The park is a habitat for ruffed grouse, white-tailed deer, and wild turkeys.

On August 29, 1879, the centennial of the Battle of Newtown, a stone momument was dedicated at the top of Sullivan Hill. It was replaced with a granite monument in 1912. The Newtown Battlefield Reservation was designated a historic landmark, and placed on the National Register of Historic Places in 1973. Several interpretive signs describing the Battle of Newtown are located at the overlook south of the monument.

The park has hiking trails, two reservable pavilions, picnic areas with tables and fireplaces, playing fields, and a playground. There are also flush toilets, hot showers, pay telephones, and a trailer dumping station.

RESTAURANTS-HISTORIC

PIERCE'S 1894 RESTAURANT

Pierce's 1894 Restaurant, located at Oakwood Avenue and West 14th Street in Elmira Heights, is considered by many people to be the finest restaurant in the Finger Lakes Region. Joseph Slocum Pierce has been quoted as saying that it is the best restaurant between New York and Chicago. The menu is Continental, American, and Chinese. The restaurant property has been in the Pierce family since 1894; however, it has not always been a restaurant.

Crawford Pierce opened a straw hat factory on the site, and then converted it into the Double Decker Cigar Factory. By the early 1900s, it was the Crawford Hotel, with a dining room and public bar. Crawford Pierce bought the building next door, and installed two bowling alleys. His son, Crawford Joseph Pierce, turned the business into a pool hall and a gas station with seven pumps. The salesroom for radios and tires eventually became the Pine Room of Pierce's 1894 Restaurant.

Crawford reopened the bar when Prohibition was repealed in 1934, and it became a popular lunch spot because of the culinary ability of Crawford Joseph's wife, Emma Slocum Pierce. The next generation of Pierce owner / proprietors was represented by Joseph Slocum Pierce, a 1942 graduate of the School of Hotel Administration of Cornell University. Joe Pierce, upon his return from service in the U. S. Air Force during World War II, expanded the lunch room and bar into a restaurant with a remodeled bar.

Joe Pierce and his wife, Lee, made many changes and expansions to the restaurant in its evolution to its current seating capacity of 375. The Pierces' made significant additions to the restaurant over the years, including Austria-trained Executive Chef Gottfried Troger in 1957, a Chinese-Cantonese section of the kitchen in 1955, and an on-premise bakery with a pastry chef in 1963.

Four first-floor dining rooms each seat approximately fifty. The mirrored "Pine Room" was built in 1948, and shares the bottle collection of over 3,000 bottles with the vintage 1933 bar. The "Parlor" is decorated with ivory, lavender, and rose in Victorian style, with antique dolls, loveseats, period lamps, velvet drapes, and tapestries. The "Crawford Room" has an oriental decor with a curved ceiling, pale ribbed oak, and rare 19th century mirrors. The "Village Room" has a German atmosphere with brick, dark-stained oak and solid, chunky chairs.

Most banquets and functions are held in the "1894 Room" on the second floor. The walls of the room are highly polished Brazilian rosewood planks decorated with tapestries. The Wine Cellar Dining Room is the pride of Pierce's 1894 Restaurant. It can seat eight to twenty-two guests, by reservation, at a single black walnut table. The room is decorated with mint coins, old silver, port bottles, and rare twenty dollar bills. The walls are wine racks, and wagon wheel chandeliers with glass grape bunches are hung from the wood beamed ceiling. The Wine Cellar Dining Room is surrounded by wine cellars housing part of the 300,000 bottle wine cellar containing 900 labels.

The restaurant is a perennial collector of Four Star Mobil and *Holiday* awards. Craig Goldwyn, in his article, "The Wines and Fortunes of Pierce's," in *Restaurant Hospitality* provided his version of Pierce's Law: ATMOSPHERE + QUALITY FOOD + SERVICE + INVOLVEMENT = CLASS = SUCCESS. Pierce's 1894 Restaurant is open Tuesday through Saturday evenings and Sunday from noon until 9:00 PM.

SOUTH OF THE LAKES--PERSONS

MARGARET SANGER

Margaret Higgins Sanger, birth control pioneer, was born in 1879 in Corning, New York. She was the sixth of eleven children of Michael Higgins and Anne Purcell Higgins. Michael Higgins was a mason and stone carver who was frequently out of work. He was a strong-willed individual who supported Henry George's single tax concept, and invited Robert Ingersoll, "the Great Infidel," to speak in Corning. His liberal beliefs caused him to lose customers, and the family was poor. Anne Higgins, who had seven miscarriages in addition to her eleven children, died of tuberculosis at the age of forty-eight.

Margaret's sister paid her tuition to Claverack College for one year. Then she completed nurse's training at the Manhattan Eye and Ear Institute in New York City. She met William Sanger, an architect, while she was in nurse's training; they were married on August 18, 1902. The Sangers moved to Hastings-on-Hudson, New York. While living in Westchester County, Sanger presented a short course on the subject of reproduction to a group of mothers and their children. This was the first step in her lifetime association with the subject of birth control and planned parenthood.

The Sangers moved back to New York City, and Margaret made speeches for the socialist newspaper, the *Call*, on the economic problems of the working class poor and the problems of family life. The *Call* asked her to write a series of articles on motherhood issues. In her articles, she addressed the functions of the reproductive organs, the physiology of a woman's body, and venereal disease. The twelve part series was called "What Every Woman Should Know." Although articles on these subjects are common today, they were not in 1913.

The main obstruction to publishing such articles was the Comstock Law of 1873. Anthony Comstock, an official of the U. S. Post Office, had the authority to open mail, and rule as to whether the contents of the mail were obscene. He notified the *Call* that if they published Sanger's article on veneral disease, he would revoke their mailing permit. The following week, the woman's page of the *Call* was blank except for the words: "WHAT EVERY GIRL SHOULD KNOW--NOTHING! BY ORDER OF THE POST OFFICE DEPARTMENT."

Sanger returned to work as a nurse. Many of the requests for care were from the lower east side, where many of Manhattan's poor lived. Frequently, she would be asked: "Tell me how to avoid having a baby for a while. We cannot afford another one yet." She could tell them preventative measures that the husband could take, but they wanted to know what they personally could do to prevent conception. They didn't believe that Sanger had nothing to tell them.

She collected as much information on the subject of contraception as she could find. She spent six months researching the subject, and was surprised how little information existed. One of the few references was a book written over fifty years previously by a Massachusetts physician, Charles Knowton. It was entitled *The Fruits of Philosophy, or the Private Companion of Young People*. Margaret went to Europe to find more information.

Upon her return to New York in 1914, Margaret edited and published a magazine called *The Woman Rebel* that had the slogan: "No Gods, No Masters." An early issue contained a statement of a woman's duty: "To look the whole world in the face with a go-to-hell look in the eyes, to have an ideal, to speak and act in defiance of convention." It didn't take Comstock long to react. He reviewed his complaints with the Postmaster General, and informed Sanger that *The Woman Rebel* couldn't be sent through the U. S. Mail.

In addition to her work with *The Woman Rebel,* Sanger wrote *Family Limitation,* which was a pamphlet that described various contraceptive techniques. Sanger discussed, in a very straightward style, the birth control devices available to women; she supplemented the text with diagrams. Twenty-two printers turned her down. One printer said: "That can never be printed. That's a Sing Sing job." Finally, she found a printer who printed 100,000 copies of the pamphlet in off hours, so his employees wouldn't know about it.

She was notified that she had been indicted by the U. S. Government on nine counts of violation of the Criminal Code. If she was convicted on all nine counts, she faced forty-five years in jail. She received no notice to appear in court, and then was asked why she had not appeared in court. The court gave her lawyer less than a day to prepare her case. She decided to run, and to fight another time. Using an assumed name, she traveled first to Canada and then to England.

In England, Sanger met Havelock Ellis, essayist, psychologist, and author of the seven volume work, *The Psychology of Sex.* Ellis had received medical training, specialized in obstetrics, and was known as a reformer. He had a profound influence on Sanger's thinking. In Holland, she met Dr. Aletta Jacobs, the first woman in Holland to be granted a medical degree. In 1878, Jacobs established the first birth control clinic in the world. Between 1878 and 1915, a series of birth control clinics were established across Holland.

Before she left for England, Sanger had established the National Birth Control League. Sanger attended a meeting of the league's executive committee upon her return to inquire about the level of support she could expect from them during her trial. The president of the league informed her that she could expect no support since they were an organization that obeyed the law. Sanger was told that the goal of the league was to get the laws changed, and that they would not support a person who had broken the law.

Both the District Attorney and the judge received many communications in support of Margaret. Nine distinguished Englishmen, including Arnold Bennett and H. G. Wells, sent a letter to President Wilson in her defense:

> We understand that Margaret Sanger is in danger of criminal prosecution for circulating a pamphlet on birth control problems. We therefore beg to draw your attention to the fact that such work as that of Mrs. Sanger received appreciation and circulation in every civilized country except the United States of America, where it is a criminal offense....
>
> Hence, not only for the benefit of Mrs. Sanger, but of humanity we respectfully beg you to exert your powerful influence in the interests of free speech and the betterment of the race.

The judge postponed the case three times; finally, Sanger was notified that the case had been dismissed.

Sanger opened her first birth control clinic in the Brownsville section of Brooklyn on October 16, 1916. It was visited by 140 women on its first day. On the tenth day of the clinic's operation, the police impounded her equipment, files, and birth control literature. Sanger, her sister Ethel, and one of her assistants were taken to jail, where they spent the night before being released on bail. Sanger and Ethel both received sentences of thirty days in the workhouse. Sanger, over the objections of the matron, gave birth control lectures in the workhouse.

Upon her release, Sanger made a movie called *The Hand That Rocks the Cradle,* which was not permitted to be shown to the public, because it contained the words "birth control." She published a magazine called the *Birth Control Review,* which contained articles by Havelock Ellis and H. G. Wells on economic and social topics that were population-related. It was the principal publication of the birth control movement for twenty-three years.

Sanger's appeal in the case involving her birth control clinic in Brooklyn was upheld by Judge Frederick Crane of the New York State of Appeals on January 18, 1918. His decision, which became known as the Crane decision, allowed clinics to be established in which physicians could inform women about birth control techniques.

In 1921, Sanger formed the American Birth Control League to provide direction, and to solicit financial support, for the birth control movement. The league is still in existence as Planned Parenthood of America. She established the Birth Control Clinical Research Bureau; the Birth Control League referred patients to the bureau. The research bureau was raided by the police department in April, 1929, and its records were impounded. In a hearing, it was decided that the police department had acted without authority.

In 1933, the Post Office seized a package containing birth control devices that was addressed to the director of the Birth Control Clinical Research Bureau. The director filed charges to force the case to go to court. On January 6, 1936, the judge ruled that the bureau should receive its package. The government appealed, but lost their appeal. The appeals judge ruled that the Comstock Law's "design, in our opinion, was not to prevent the importation, sale or carriage by mail of things which might intelligently be used by conscientious and competent physicians for the purpose of saving life or promoting the well-being of their patients." On June 10, 1937, the American Medical Association resolved that doctors should be informed of their rights in prescribing contraceptives, and in educating the public on the subject.

In 1952, Sanger helped found, and served as the first president of, the International Planned Parenthood Association. She retired in Tucson, Arizona, where she spent her last four years in a nursing home. She died in 1966 of congestive heart failure at the age of eighty-seven. Two of her statements typify her outlook on life:

> Some lives drift here and there like reeds in a stream, depending on the changing currents for their activity. Others are like swimmers knowing the depth of the water. Each stroke helps them onward to a definite objective.

> Life has taught me one supreme lesson; this is that we must--if we are to really *live* at all ... --put our convictions into action.

MARK TWAIN (SAMUEL CLEMENS)

Samuel Langhorne Clemens, the author of *Huckleberry Finn* and *Tom Sawyer*, was born on November 30, 1835, in Florida, Missouri. He was the sixth child and fourth son of John Clemens and Jane Lampton Clemens. Clemens was born in a two-room rented clapboard house in a frontier village with a population of 100. In his later life, he said that many important people in history couldn't claim to have increased the population of their community by one percent when they were born.

Clemens was born two months prematurely. His mother admitted: "When I first saw him, I could see no promise in him. But I felt it was my duty to do the best I could. He was a poor looking object to raise." When she was in her eighties, he asked her if she was concerned about him when he was a baby. She said, "Yes, the whole time." He asked, "Afraid I wouldn't live?" She paused, and said, "No, afraid you would."

When Clemens was four years old, the family moved to Hannibal, Missouri, where his father opened a general store on Main Street. Hannibal, which he called that "half-forgotten paradise," was his home for fourteen years. It provided much of the backdrop for his novels. Clemens and his friends all had the goal of working on a Mississippi River steamboat--as a clerk, engineer, firemen, or pilot--preferably as a pilot.

John Clemens died of pneunomia when Clemens was eleven years old. He contributed to the family finances by delivering papers after school. In 1848, Clemens worked as a "printer's devil" for the local newspaper, the *Courier*. In 1850, he worked for his brother, Orion, when he moved back to Hannibal from St. Louis and started a weekly newspaper.

Clemens left home in 1853, and worked for a St. Louis newspaper to earn money to go to America's first World's Fair in New York. He enjoyed the libraries and the theater, and then moved on to Philadelphia, where he worked as a typesetter on the *Inquirer*. He visited Washington, D. C., and returned to the Midwest by way of New York.

He read a article about the Amazon River and decided to go there, harvest the coca plant, and make his fortune. In Cincinnati, he met Horace Bixby, pilot of the riverboat *Paul Jones*. His early ambitions returned, and he persuaded Bixby to train him as a river pilot. He decided not to go to South America. His experiences with Bixby formed the basis for his book, *Life on the Mississippi,* which he wrote twenty-five years later. Clemens earned his license as a Mississippi River pilot in September, 1859, and at the age of twenty-three was earning as much as the Vice-President of the United States. However, the outbreak of the Civil War ended both navigation on the river and his job as a river pilot.

Clemens traveled to Carson City, Nevada with his brother, Orion, who had just been appointed secretary of the Nevada Territory. While in Nevada, he tried prospecting, without any luck, both in the Humboldt region and the Esmerelda Hills. Next, he hiked 130 miles to Virginia City to write for the *Enterprise,* where he first began to use the name Mark Twain. Artemus Ward, the best-known humorist of the time, visited Virginia City and encouraged Twain to submit a piece to the New York *Sunday Mercury*. It was published in early 1864.

The restless Twain moved to San Francisco in May, 1864, to work for the *Daily Morning Call*. While in San Francisco, the Sacramento *Union* paid him to do a series on the Hawaiian Islands. Upon his return from Hawaii, he went on the lecture circuit. He lectured at Cooper Union in New York City. While in New York, he published his first book, *The Celebrated Jumping Frog of Calaveras County and Other Sketches*.

The San Francisco *Alta California* financed a trip around the world in return for periodic reports. Clemens sailed from New York to Europe on the steamship *Quaker City*. Twain met Charles Langdon of Elmira, New York, on the ship, and they became friends. Charles showed his new friend a miniature portrait of his sister, Olivia Langdon, and forty years later, Twain said: "From that day to this, she has never been out of my mind." He met Olivia and her family in New York over the Christmas holidays of 1867.

Twain worked on his book, *The Innocents Abroad,* in early 1868, and didn't get to Elmira to visit Olivia until August. Olivia's father, a wealthy coal dealer, didn't know what to make of this humorist of the West and Midwest, but he was very comfortable with him. Twain proposed to Olivia and was rejected; Olivia thought that they should maintain a brother-sister relationship. She was ten years younger than he, and wasn't sure of herself. Twain made two more visits to Elmira. When Mr. Langdon was assured of Twain's character and his ability to support his daughter, Olivia accepted his proposal. They were engaged in February, 1869, and married in 1870.

Twain bought a one-third interest in the *Buffalo Express,* and he and his new wife moved to Buffalo. In the spring of 1871, Twain and Olivia stayed at Quarry Farm overlooking Elmira and the Chemung River Valley. This began a practice that lasted for over twenty years; Twain wrote many of his books while summering at Quarry Farm. He wrote *Roughing It* during the first summer.

The Twains moved to Hartford, Connecticut, from Buffalo. It was to be their "permanent home." They built a large, unusual home in the Nook Farm literary colony, a 100-acre tract on the western edge of Hartford. Other Nook Farm authors included Harriet Beecher Stowe, who wrote *Uncle Tom's Cabin,* and Charles Dudley Warner, editor of the *Hartford Courant* and of *Harper's* magazine. Twain's house had nineteen large rooms, a pilothouse balcony, Gothic turrets, and a porch like a riverboat deck. They lived in the house from 1874 until 1891; it is now a Mark Twain Museum.

Twain began writing *The Adventures of Tom Sawyer* in 1870, but the bulk of it was written during the summer of 1874 at Quarry Farm. He finished writing *The Adventures of Huckleberry Finn* in his octagonal study at Quarry Farm in 1875.

By 1884, Twain owned his own publishing company. He published the *Memoirs* of Ulysses S. Grant, which the ex-President wrote to pay off the debts of Grant and Ward, his unsuccessful Wall Street firm. Grant finished this *Memoirs* several days before dying of throat cancer. Within a year of his death, Julia Grant received royalties of $350,000, the largest sum earned by an author up to that time.

In 1889, Twain published *A Connecticut Yankee in King Arthur's Court* . In 1896, he undertook an around-the-world lecture tour to replenish his finances. In August, while sailing from South Africa to England, he and Olivia learned that their daughter, Suzy, who had stayed with an aunt in Elmira, had died of meningitis. Both Twain and Olivia were staggered by this blow. She had been their favorite.

Twain was lionized upon his return to New York. He was awarded honorary doctorates by Oxford University, Yale University, and the Universty of Missouri. He said, "If I am not called at least 'Doc' from now on, there will be a decided coolness."

Olivia died on June 5, 1904, in Florence, Italy, where they had gone for her health. Twain moved to Stormfield, Connecticut, near Redding, in 1908. His daughter, Jean, who lived with him, died on December 23, 1909. Upon her death, he said, "I shall never write any more." He died on April 21, 1910, and was buried in Elmira, New York. Twain's life spanned almost seventy-five years, and was bracketed by two Halley's comets. Halley's comet crossed the skies two weeks before he was born in 1835, and again near the time that he died in 1910.

THOMAS WATSON

Thomas John Watson, the founder of the IBM Corporation, was born on February 17, 1874, in East Campbell, between Bath and Corning. He was the first of five children of Thomas Watson and Jane White Watson. Watson's father, also named Thomas, was in the lumber business. The family lived in East Campbell until Watson was seven years old, when the house burned down. It was rebuilt, but the family moved to Cooper's Plains, then to the Town of Addison, and to Painted Post. The moves between these Steuben County villages were driven by diminishing stands of trees, and the fact that the lumber business was very competitive.

His father wanted him to read law, but Watson did not want to pursue that path. He chose to apply for a temporary teaching certificate for three years, and then enrolled at the Albany Teachers' College. However, one day of teaching changed his mind, "I can't go into a classroom with a bunch of children at nine o'clock in the morning and stay until four."

Watson enrolled at the Miller School of Commerce in Elmira. He completed the accounting and business courses there in May, 1892, and accepted a position as bookkeeper in Risley's butcher shop in Painted Post. He soon formed the opinion that "he couldn't sit on a high stool and keep books all my life." Willard Bronson, a neighbor of the Watsons, operated a hardware store and a consignment business. He acquired Estey organs, pianos, and sewing machines, and sold them on consignment around the country-side from a wagon. Watson went on the road selling for Bronson; it was the first of his many sales jobs.

He learned the importance of a good appearance, and the importance of making a good first impression. He sold for Bronson for two years without a raise in salary and without many kind words from his boss. Bronson was astounded when Watson quit the job after two years. Only then he proposed a raise; he even offered to sell Watson the business. His father suggested that he leave the area; he thought that Buffalo might be a good place to look for a job.

Watson looked for a job in Buffalo for several weeks. His selling experience was his main strength. Finally, he was offered a job selling sewing machines for the Wheeler and Wilcox Company. However, after a short time, he was let go. It wasn't because of any shortcoming on his part, but because they didn't need another salesman. A co-worker, C. B. Barron, was let go at the same time. Barron went to work selling stock shares in the Buffalo Building and Loan Association; he invited Watson to join him.

Watson wanted to go into business for himself, so with savings and a loan from his father, he opened a butcher shop. He hired a clerk to run it, while he sold shares for the Buffalo Building and Loan Association. He had to sell the butcher shop when Barron ran off with all of the building and loan funds, including Watson's commissions. Watson went to the office of the National Cash Register Company to make arrangements for the new owner of the butcher shop to take over payments on his cash register. While he was there, he applied for a job. He met the manager of the Buffalo office, John J. Range. Range wasn't interested in hiring him, but Watson persisted.

John Henry Patterson, chief executive officer of the National Cash Register Company, made the cash register virtually indispensable to businessmen. Then he monopolized its manufacture and distribution. Watson made no sales in his first two weeks, and Range made his disappointment clear. Watson absorbed Range's constructive criticism, and, within a year, was one of the most successful National Cash Register salesmen in the East. By the time he was twenty-five, Watson was the top salesman in the Buffalo office.

Patterson was a successful manager because he combined paternalism with an emphasis on training. He realized that his salesmen responded to a fear of punishment and the promise of reward. Patterson knew just how hard he could push Watson. He became the prime shaper of Watson's life over the next eleven years.

Patterson selected him to be the manager of the Rochester office in the summer of 1899. Watson moved the sales of the Rochester branch from near the bottom of all of the company's offices to sixth from the top within several months. He used some ruthless techniques to best his main competitor, the Hallwood Company; his performance was followed closely by Hugh Chalmers, the company's general manager, and by Patterson. The National Cash Register Company had between eighty and ninety-five percent of the sales of new cash registers. However, Patterson wanted to take aggressive action to reduce the impact of the sales of used cash registers.

Patterson gave Watson $1,000,000 to set up a company to front for the National Cash Register Company in driving out the used cash register competition in the United States. Watson established Watson's Cash Register and Second Hand Exchange on Fourteenth Street in Manhattan. He undercut the prices of one of his main competitors, and bought him out. Watson moved to Philadelphia, and then to Chicago, where he repeated his New York activities. He made the second hand machine business a profitable unit of the company, and was invited to work at the company headquarters in Dayton.

Eventually, Chalmers could no longer stand Patterson's dictatorial style, and, as the number two man in company, disagreed with some non-business decisions. Chalmers was fired, and Watson was appointed in his place. Patterson went to Europe for two years, and by the time he returned, Watson had doubled the company's sales volume to 100,000 cash registers a year in 1910. The increase in sales was partly due to a redesign of the cash register by Charles (Boss) Kettering; he replaced the manual operation of the cash register with an electric motor. Kettering moved on to General Motors, where he designed the self-starter for automobiles.

The company's monopolistic practices in the second-hand cash register business caught up with them. On February 22, 1912, John Patterson, Thomas Watson, and twenty-eight other company managers were indicted on three counts of criminal conspiracy. They were placed on trial in Cincinnati for restraint of trade and maintaining a monopoly.

While he was waiting trial, Watson met Jeanette Kittridge of Dayton. Her father was president of a railroad car manufacturing company. The Kittridges were neighbors and friends of Patterson, and Jeanette was Patterson's choice of a wife for Watson.

On February 13, 1913, Patterson, Watson and the other managers were found to be guilty as charged. Patterson was released on $10,000 bail; Watson was released on $5,000 bail. Watson wanted to postpone the wedding until the results of the appeal were known. Jeanette disagreed. She was as strong-willed as he was; together they were a powerful team. Shortly after their marriage, Watson, in a pattern reminiscent of the Chalmers experience, was fired. Watson began to look for another job.

Charles Flint assembled a company called the Computing-Tabulating-Recording Company (CTR) by combining a computing scales company, a time recorder company, and the Tabulating Machine Company. CTR was unprofitable, and Flint was looking for a new manager. He offered the position to Watson. However, Watson was not appointed to the board of directors because of the pending law suit. On March 13, 1915, the District Court verdict was set aside, and a new trial granted. There was no new trial, and Watson was cleared of any wrongdoing. CTR elected Watson president and general manager of the company.

Watson authorized the redesign of the Hollerith tabulating machine and the Tabulating Machine Company unit became the star unit of CTR. From 1914 until 1920, gross income of CTR increased from $4 million to $14 million. In 1924, Watson renamed the company International Business Machines. Watson was appointed chief executive officer, and, for the first time, was really in charge of the company.

IBM actually grew during the Great Depression. By 1940, IBM was still small, $50 million of sales per year, but it had become the largest company in the office equipment industry. World War II made IBM a large company. Gross income went from $40 million a year in 1939 to $140 million a year in 1945; by 1949, the company was five times larger than it had been in 1939.

Thomas Watson, Jr., became president in 1952, and his brother Arthur was appointed general manager of the IBM World Trade Corporation. From 1914 through 1953, assets of the corporation grew by a multiple of twenty-four, the data processing business by a multiple of 316, development expenditures by 500 times, and employees by thirty-four times.

Thomas Watson, Jr., became chief executive officer of the IBM Corporation on May 8, 1956. Just over a month later, on June 19, 1956, Thomas Watson, Sr., died of a heart attack.

Genesee Country Museum, near Mumford

EPILOGUE

The Finger Lakes Region recognizes the importance of tourism to its well-being; it also recognizes the importance of conservation to tourism. Considerable effort is underway to provide service to the tourism industry, and to conserve the abundant natural resources of the region. Both tourism and conservation are vital to the region as we move toward and into the twenty-first century.

Tourism, New York State's second largest industry, contributes almost a billion and a quarter dollars to the economy of the Finger Lakes Region each year. Tourism created 29,000 new jobs in the region over a recent thirteen-year period. It supported 5,400 businesses with a payroll of over $750 million. Over $70 million of tax revenue is generated by tourism in the fourteen-county Finger Lakes Region.

The Finger Lakes Association, based in Penn Yan, is one of the leaders in promoting the region. It was established in 1919 to address the region's economy, natural resources, and transportation needs. The Finger Lakes Association is a non-profit organization formed to preserve and promote the Finger Lakes Region.

The Finger Lakes Regional Tourism Development Corporation, a not-for-profit affiliate of the Finger Lakes Association, was formed in 1993 to provide financial and technical assistance for the Finger Lakes Region tourism industry. The corporation promotes the enhancement of tourism to keep the Finger Lakes Region competitive, and to keep the economy of the region growing into the twenty-first century--a century in which tourism is forecasted to be the largest industy in the region.

The executive summary of the October, 1991 publication, *Finger Lakes Region: Tourism Development Opportunities,* contains a section on existing tourism assets in the region:

> Natural resources are the foundation of the Region's tourist industry. Principal resources are the eleven Finger Lakes, spectacular waterfalls, streams, canals and Lake Ontario, with its varied shoreline. Scenic hills of forest and fields of valleys are a delight to many visitors. The region's abundant wildlife attracts hunters and fishermen from surrounding areas, while also providing a special dimension for those engaged in photography and natural appreciation.

> Natural assets frequently provide the basis for man-made attractions of various kinds such as ski areas and wineries. The Region's history and its culture are illustrated in museums, historic sites and related facilities. Local industries and educational institutions are special assets, drawing visitors into the economic life of the Region's communities.

Among the groups that have a regional lake protection and conservation focus are:

o Finger Lakes Initiative, sponsored by the U.S. Fish and Wildlife Service--

A forum of resource professionals and interested citizens that meets monthly to discuss issues pertinent to the protection / improvement of the Finger Lakes Region

o New York State Federation of Lake Associations--a federation of lake associations in New York State, not just in the Finger Lakes Region

o Water Resources Board of the Finger Lakes Association, Inc.--comprised of eighteen counties participating in the Finger Lakes Aquatic Vegetation Control and Lake Management Program

In addition, many lake associations place an emphasis on lake protection and conservation, including:

o Coalition for Hemlock and Canadice Lakes
o Canandaigua Lake Pure Waters, Ltd.
o Canandaigua Lake Watershed Task Force
o Cayuga Lake Conservation Association
o Keuka Watershed Improvement Cooperative
o Owasco Lake Watershed Association (OWL)
o Tri-County Lake Association (Skaneateles Lake)

o Conesus Lake Association, Inc.
o Honeoye Valley Association
o Keuka Lake Association, Inc.
o Keuka Lake Foundation
o Lamoka Waneta Lakes Association
o Citizens of Otisco Lake (COOL)
o Seneca Lake Pure Waters Assoc.

Water quality monitoring is an ongoing activity in the Finger Lakes Region. In recent years, this has included analysis of the following lakes: Canandaigua, Honeoye, Keuka, Otisco, Seneca, and Skaneateles. Much lake protection activity occurs upland in the effective management of natural areas. The Finger Lakes National Forest, the New York State Department of Environmental Conservation, the Finger Lakes Land Trust, and the Nature Conservancy take many actions that benefit lake quality.

The ongoing efforts of the U. S. Fish and Wildlife Service and the County Soil and Water Conservation Districts also have a positive effect on lake quality. In addition, public and private organizations cooperate on conservation projects. For example, a lake association's volunteers collect samples that are tested with Department of Environmental Conservation funding, and the results are reported in a County Soil and Water Conservation publication.

Considerable planning is underway to expand the utilization of the region's waterways, particularly the Erie Canal. Recreational use of the canal is increasing. Fishing and pleasure-boating are popular activities. Tourboats and Lockmaster hireboats provide leisurely cruises along the canal. Long-distance cruises from the Great Lakes via the Erie Canal to the Hudson River and the Atlantic Intra-Coastal Waterway, are becoming more frequent. The towpaths of the canal are active with bicyclists, hikers, joggers, roller-bladers, and cross-country skiers.

Epilogue

In 1991, a 24-member Canal Recreationway Commission was established to prepare a statewide canal plan. In 1993, the New York State Canal Corporation began work to preserve and revive this superb waterway. The Canal Corporation activities are based on three principles: the preservation of pristine canal wilderness areas, conservation of historic canal structures, and enhanced recreational opportunities for people in the communities near the canals. In addition, many local governments and interest groups are working with the State of New York to make the optimum use of this magnificent resource in their back yards.

Speaking of the Finger Lakes Region, Cayuga County Planner Robert N. Brower has observed: "The diversity of the product is what makes it relatively unique. The crux of our economic future will depend on our ability to protect these lakes." That diversity includes eleven beautiful lakes, scores of waterfalls and gorges, and scenic hills and valleys spread over 6,125 square miles that are steeped in history. All of this is within a day's drive from the major population centers of the Northeast.

Of all the spots on God's green earth
The one I'd choose for my own
Would be the wonderful finger lakes
With their beauty of great renown
Sparkling waters and verdant hills
Nestled beneath azure skies;
To one who'd make this spot his home,
He would live in a paradise
Indians say that God's own Hand
Planted His finger prints here
To bless the land for his children
To show them his garden rare
And as I gaze at its beauty
I cannot help but feel awed
To think that this marvel of nature
Was blessed by the Hand of God.

From *Inspiration* by A. Glenn Rogers

Mark Twain's Octagonal Study, Elmira College

BIBLIOGRAPHY

Ackerman, Carl W. *George Eastman.* Boston: Houghton Mifflin, 1930.

Allen, James E., Jr. *An Uncommon Man: The Story of Dr. William Pearson Tolley and Syracuse University.* New York: The Newcomen Society, 1963.

Anderson, Helen Travers. *The Diamonds are Dancing.* N. p.: n. p., 1976.

Anderson, Mildred Lee Hills. *Genesee Echoes.* Castile, NY: n. p., 1956.

Andrist, Ralph K. *The Erie Canal.* New York: American Heritage, 1964.

Baum, Frank Joslyn, and Russell P. McFall. *To Please a Child: A Biography of L. Frank Baum, Royal Historian of Oz.* Chicago: Reilly & Lee, 1961.

Beale, Irene A. *Genesee Country Senecas.* Geneseo, NY: Chestnut Hill Press, 1992.

Becker, Edwin. *Out of the Finger Lakes Country, Part II.* Dexter, MO: Candor Press, 1949.

Belden, Thomas Graham, and Marva Robbins Belden. *The Lengthening Shadow: The Life of Thomas J. Watson.* Boston: Little, Brown, 1962.

Bennett, Porter Kingsbury. *Cortland County Chronicles, Volume 3.* Cortland, NY: Cortland Press, 1983.

Blodgett, Bertha Evaleth. *Stories of Cortland County.* N. p.: n. p., 1932.

Bloomer, D. C. *Life and Writings of Amelia Bloomer.* Boston: Arena, 1895.

Bourne, Russell. *Floating West: The Erie and Other American Canals.* New York: Norton, 1992.

Boyd, William P. *History of the Town of Conesus.* Conesus, NY: Boyd's, 1887.

Brandon, Ruth. *A Capitalist Romance: Singer and the Sewing Machine.* Philadelphia: Lippincott, 1977.

Brodie, Fawn M. *No Man Knows My History: The Life of Joseph Smith, The Mormon Prophet.* New York: Knopf, 1971.

Cahn, William L. *Rochester's Orchestra: 1922 to 1989.* Rochester, NY: Citizens for a Quality Philharmonic, 1989.

Carmer, Carl. *Listen for a Lonesome Drum: A York State Chronicle.* New York: Farrar & Rinehart, 1936.

Chemung County Historical Society. *Chemung County: Its History.* Elmira: N. p., 1961.

College and University bulletins, various

Collier, Peter, and David Horowitz. *The Rockefellers: An American Dynasty.* New York: Holt, Rinehart and Winston, 1976.

Converse, Harriet Maxwell. *Myths and Legends of the New York State Iroquois.* Port Washington, NY: Ira J. Friedman, 1962.

Cooper, Ilene. *Susan B. Anthony.* New York: Franklin Watts, 1984.

Cornplanter, Jesse J. *Legends of the Longhouse.* Port Washington, NY: Ira J. Friedman, 1963.

Cross, Whitney R. *The Burned-over District: The Social and Intellectual History of Enthusiastic Religion in Western New York, 1800-1850.* New York: Harper, 1950.

D'Ambrosio, Mary. "Matilda Gage." *Syracuse Magazine* Mar. 1981: 33.

DeMotte, Charles, and Katherine W. Sundgren. *Restaurant Guide to the Finger Lakes Region.* Ithaca, NY: McBooks Press, 1988.

Dessauer, John H. *My Years With Xerox: The Billions Nobody Wanted.* Garden City: Doubleday, 1971.

Edmonds, I. G. *The Girls Who Talked to Ghosts: The Story of Katie and Margaretta Fox.* New York: Holt, 1979.

Fausold, Martin L. *James W. Wadsworth, Jr.* Syracuse: Syracuse UP, 1975.

Finger Lakes Magazine. Ithaca, NY: The Grapevine Press, selected issues--Summer, 1985 to July-August, 1992.

Fitzgerald, John R. *The New Erie Canal: A Recreational Guide.* N. p.: n. p., 1993.

Furman, C. E. *Valley of the Genesee: A Poem.* Rochester, NY: Daily Union and Advertiser, 1879.

Gattey, Charles Neilson. *The Bloomer Girls.* New York: Coward-McCann, 1967.

Green, Walter Henry. *History, Reminiscences, Anecdotes and Legends of Great Sodus Bay, Sodus, Sloop Landing, Sodus Village, Pultneyville, Maxwell and the Surrounding Regions.* Sodus, NY: Self-published, 1947.

Harlow, Alvin F. *The Road of the Century: The Story of the New York Central.* New York: Creative Age, 1947.

Hatch, Alden. *The Wadsworths of the Genesee.* New York: Coward-McCann, 1959.

Hawke, David Freeman. *John D.: The Founding Father of the Rockefellers.* New York: Harper, 1980.

Hill, Donna. *Joseph Smith: The First Mormon.* Garden City, NY: Doubleday, 1977.

Huggins, Nathan Irvin. *Slave and Citizen: The Life of Frederick Douglass.* Boston: Little, Brown, 1980.

Hughes, Thomas Parke. *Elmer Sperry: Inventor and Engineer.* Baltimore: John Hopkins UP, 1971.

Ingels, Margaret. *Willis Haviland Carrier: The Father of Air Conditioning.* Garden City: Country Life Press, 1952.

Jackson, Herbert G. *The Spirit Rappers.* Garden City: Doubleday, 1972.

Jennings, Walter Wilson. *A Dozen Captains of Industry.* New York: Vantage, 1954.

Lader, Lawrence. *The Margaret Sanger Story, and the Fight for Birth Control.* Garden City: Doubleday, 1955.

Lader, Lawrence, and Milton Meltzer. *Margaret Sanger: Pioneer of Birth Control.* New York: Crowell, 1969.

Larned, J. N. *The Life and Work of William Pryor Letchworth.* Boston: Houghton Mifflin, 1912.

Lauber, John. *The Making of Mark Twain: A Biography.* New York: American Heritage, 1985.

Leisure Hour Club of Homer. *A Look Over Our Shoulder.* N. p.: n. p., 1985.

Longfellow, Henry Wadsworth. *The Song of Hiawatha.* Chicago: Ferguson, 1968.

McKelvey, Blake. *Rochester: A Brief History.* New York: Edwin Mellen, 1984.

Martin, John H. and Phyllis G. *The Lands of the Painted Post.* Corning, NY: Bookmarks, 1993.

Melzer, Milton. *Mark Twain: A Writer's Life.* New York: Franklin Watts, 1985.

Merrill, Arch. *Bloomers and Bugles.* New York: American Book-Stratford, 1958.

---. *Fame in Our Time.* New York: American Book-Stratford, 1960.

---. *Pioneer Profiles.* New York: American Book-Stratford, 1957.

---. *The Ridge: Ontario's Blossom Country.* Rochester, NY: Gannett, 1944.

---. *Rochester Sketchbook.* Rochester, NY: Gannett, 1946.

---. *Shadows on the Wall.* Interlaken, NY: Empire State Books, 1952.

---. *Southern Tier, Volume One.* Interlaken, NY: Empire State Books, 1986.

---. *Southern Tier, Volume Two.* New York: American Book-Stratford, n. d.

---. *Stagecoach Towns.* Rochester, NY: Gannett, n. d.

---. *The Towpath.* Rochester, NY: Gannett, 1945.

Midlakes Navigation Company, Ltd. *New York State Canal Guide: Everything the Canaler Needs to Know & More.* Self-published. N. p.: n. d.

Miller, Douglas T. *Frederick Douglass and the Fight for Freedom.* New York: Facts On File, 1988.

Monroe County Parks Department. *A Guide to the Parks in Monroe County: Special Limited Edition 1888-1988.* Rochester: N. p., 1989.

Nevins, Allan. *John D. Rockefeller.* New York: Scribner's, 1959.

New York State Department of Environmental Conservation pamphlets, various

New York State Office of Parks, Recreation and Historic Preservation pamphlets, various

New Yorker, ed. *The New Yorker Book of Poems.* New York: Viking, 1969.

Bibliography

O'Connor, Lois. *A Finger Lakes Odyssey*. Lakemont, NY: North Country Books, 1975.

Onondaga Historical Association. "The Franklin: Syracuse's Automotive Heritage." 3 (1992)

Parker, Arthur C. *Seneca Myths and Tales*. Buffalo: Buffalo Historical society, 1923.

Plaut, James S. *Steuben Glass: A Monograph*. New York: Dover, 1972.

Pound, Arthur. *Lake Ontario*. Indianapolis: Bobbs-Merrill, 1945.

Pryor, Elizabeth Brown. *Clara Barton: Professional Angel*. Philadelphia: U of Pennsylvania P, 1987.

Rabbitt, Mary C. "John Wesley Powell: His Life & Times." *Geotimes* May-Jun 1969: 10-18.

Rapp, Marvin A. *NEW YORK STATE: A Student's Guide to Localized History*. New York: Columbia UP, 1968.

Rogers, A. Glenn. *Forgotten Stories of the Finger Lakes: Dramatic Tales of Fact and Legend*. Geneva, NY: Self-published, 1954.

Rodgers, William. *THINK; A Biography of the Watsons and IBM*. New York: Stein and Day, 1969.

Roseboom, William F., and Henry W. Schramm. *They Built a City: Stories and Legends of Syracuse and Onondaga County*. Syracuse: Manlius Publishing, 1976.

Shipps, Jan. *Mormonism: The Story of a New Religious Tradition*. Urbana: U. of Illinois P., 1985.

Sloate, Susan. *Clara Barton: Founder of the American Red Cross*. New York: Fawcett, 1990.

Smith, Erminne A. *Myths of the Iroquois*. Washington, D. C.: Smithsonian Institution, 1983.

Spencer, John D. *The Twelve Who Came Early*. Syracuse: Onondaga Valley Community League, 1975.

Stearns, Monroe. *Mark Twain*. New York: Franklin Watts, 1965.

Swanson, June. *I Pledge Allegiance*. Minneapolis: Carolrhoda, 1990.

Taylor, Eva. *A Short History of Elmira*. Elmira: Steele Memorial Library, 1937.

Thompson, Stith., ed. *Tales of the North American Indians*. Bloomington: Indiana UP, 1968.

Tolley, William Pearson. *At the Fountain of Youth: Memories of a College President*. Syracuse: Syracuse UP, 1989.

Topalian, Elyse. *Margaret Sanger*. New York: Franklin Watts, 1984.

Van Diver, Bradford B. *Roadside Geology of New York*. Missoula, MT: Mountain Press, 1985.

von Engeln, O. D. *The Finger Lakes Region: Its Origin and Nature*. Ithaca: Cornell U. P., 1961.

Wadsworth, William P. *Riding to Hounds in America: An Introduction for Foxhunters*. Berryville, VA: The Chronicle of the Horse, 1962.

Waite, D. B. *The History of the Town of Canadice*. N. p.: n. p., 1908.

Wampler, Cloud. *Dr. Willis Carrier: The Father of Air Conditioning*. New York: The Newcomen Society, 1949.

Weiner, Susan. *Finger Lakes Wineries*. Ithaca, NY: McBooks Press, 1990.

Weisberg, Barbara. *Susan B. Anthony*. New York: Chelsea House, 1988.

Tioga Gardens and Conservatory, Owego